Strategies for Electronic Commerce and the Internet

Strategies for Electronic Commerce and the Internet

Henry C. Lucas, Jr.

The MIT Press
Cambridge, Massachusetts
London, England

This book was set in Sabon by Binghamton Valley Composition and printed and bound in the United States of America.

Library of Congress Cataloging-in-Publication Data

Lucas, Henry C.
  Strategies for electronic commerce and the Internet / Henry C. Lucas, Jr.
     p. cm.
  Includes bibliographical references and index.
  ISBN 0-262-12242-1 (hc.: alk. paper)
  1. Electronic commerce—Planning. 2. Strategic planning. 3. Business enterprises—Computer networks—Planning. 4. Internet. I. Title.

HF5548.32 .L83   2002
658.8'4—dc21   2001032625

For Ellen

Contents

Preface

The last half of the twentieth century has witnessed a revolution in information technology. (IT) Popular and academic articles describe the "new economy" and new business models enabled by IT. Computers, databases, and communications networks are pervasive in postindustrial countries. The Internet provides standards for worldwide connectivity, and its impact on business and commerce has been dramatic. I believe that the Internet and electronic commerce are a "frame-breaking" change for the twenty-first century, just as was the Industrial Revolution two hundred years ago. A Brookings Institution study estimates that the Internet is contributing 0.2 to 0.4% to productivity growth, about 10% of total growth in productivity in the late 1990s (Litan and Rivlin 2001).

The initial Industrial Revolution began in England with late eighteenth-century technological breakthroughs in the production of textiles, coal, and iron, and the innovation of steam engines. Economic historians use these specific or "core" examples of innovative change to develop general principles underlying industrialization. Spinning and weaving breakthroughs in textiles represent the general principle of substituting power-driven machines for human labor. Technological developments in iron (and coal) processing illustrate the substitution of abundant mineral substances for scarcer animal and vegetable materials. Steam engines generalize to the substitution of inanimate converters of energy for traditional animate (human, plant, and animal) converters.

Each specific technological breakthrough represented a quantum leap forward in production and productivity. As the general principles involved were extended to other industries, economic growth, measured by production per person, increased and became self-sustaining. From textiles, machine production spread to other industries. Iron led directly to steel, and as the chemical technologies involved were increasingly understood, a host of new materials were developed and used across a range of modern industries. Steam engines were forerunners of internal combustion engines and nuclear reactors.

How does the Internet compare? Today, the Internet allows global market access for a vendor; over 150 million people can access the Web site of someone with a product or service to sell on the Net. Many organizations are developing electronic customer/supplier relationships, resulting in a dramatic increase in efficiency. There is a movement toward purchasing "hubs" in which a Web site joins together buyers and sellers, for example, shippers with trucking companies. Led by Detroit automakers, a number of industries are establishing purchasing sites to reduce the cost of dealing with suppliers. Companies are integrating their supply chains and providing suppliers with access to their production plans.

The Internet has given rise to new business models. Companies such as Dell Computer and Cisco Systems integrate technology into all of their operations. Cisco processes almost all of its orders on the Web, and handles 70 percent of its customer service on the Internet. Companies adopting the Internet are substituting technology for physical assets. The Internet enables auction markets in which buyers bid on items for sale at any time from any location with a Net connection. In addition to developing commerce, the Internet offers the potential for new forms of distance-education and learning, and for improving the quality of medical care.

The Internet and electronic commerce lead to a restructuring of organizations, new tasks and responsibilities for employees, and very different ways of operating a business. Many, if not most, of these changes are invisible compared to the Industrial Revolution, which changed the landscape with factories, railroads, highways, and migrations from rural to urban areas. Compared to the massive physical changes of the Industrial Revolution, information technology is more subtle. However, we should not be misled by the lack of change in the physical environment. Consider the following process:

1. A customer sitting in her office accesses a supplier's Web site to order a piece of computer equipment.

2. Using a browser on her computer, the customer configures the product.

3. Because the Web site knows the rules for product configuration, the customer and supplier are assured that the order is correctly specified.

4. The customer sends the order electronically to the supplier, who receives it instantly.

5. The supplier instantly routes the order to a contract manufacturer in Singapore who enters the order into its scheduling system, and returns an available-to-promise delivery date. The supplier does not manufacture products for stock, it manufacturers only in response to an order.

6. The supplier allows the customer to monitor the progress of her order by inquiring against its production tracking system, which is updated by the contract manufacturer's production systems.

7. The contract manufacturer ships the equipment directly to the customer; the "supplier" never touches the items in the order.

8. The associated financial transactions occur electronically as well.

This process for ordering a piece of computer equipment differs dramatically from pre-Internet days when all of the steps were manual and required a large number of documents. The electronic process has saved time and money; it has reduced errors and resulted in better customer service and higher satisfaction. Information technology has enabled companies to develop new structures and management techniques: the company in the example is a virtual manufacturer. It designs and markets products, but does not actually build them, even though its name is on the equipment the customer receives.

The technology revolution will have winners and losers, companies that succeed and flourish and those that fall by the wayside. Some new firms will become dramatic successes, and some will fail. Traditional companies that adapt have a bright future; those who stay with their traditional business models are at great risk. How do you predict which firms will be successful? How does a manager respond to competitors who adopt the Internet and electronic commerce? How does one obtain a competitive advantage in times of intense competition and proliferating information technology?

This book presents an approach for analyzing and developing business strategy for electronic commerce and the Internet. The first part of the book discusses strategy and new business models. Chapter 1 reviews different approaches to corporate strategy, and develops a dynamic model for strategy in a world in which the Internet and e-commerce have become dominant forces. The model draws heavily on a resource-based view of competitive advantage. In particular, it focuses on how one obtains an initial advantage and then adds resources to sustain that advantage in a dynamic, competitive economy. Notions of network externalities, critical mass, and assets to augment one's resources are key to the model. Also important is the idea that a firm's resources form a system that itself becomes an emergent resource for competitive advantage. We use this model throughout the rest of the book to examine the strategies of a number of firms, and to make recommendations to management for formulating a strategy for electronic commerce and the Internet.

Chapter 2 presents new business models enabled by technology. These new models are a part of the revolution prompted by the Internet. Chapter 3 discusses some of the new ways to organize within the firm to take advantage of technology; of particular interest is the kind of virtual organization where teams form and disband to work on specific projects and tasks.

The second part of the book looks at the Internet strategies of traditional firms. Despite the publicity about dot.com startups, by far the largest number of businesses in the United States and the world are traditional; they existed long before the Internet and electronic commerce. Most people work at these traditional companies. How does this type of firm change its business model to take advantage of the Net and e-commerce? Chapter 4 presents examples of companies that have added resources to create a system of resources resulting in a competitive advantage. Chapter 5 looks at two great examples of manufacturing companies that have adopted new business models and have thrived—Dell and Cisco. Chapter 6 is concerned with the services industry, particularly retail stock brokers. We examine the ways in which the Internet forced traditional brokers to unbundle trading from other services, and contributed to the intense competition between Charles Schwab and Merrill

Lynch. Chapter 7 presents ideas for how managers can move the traditional business to the Internet.

The third part of the book is devoted to the study of new businesses on the Internet. What strategy makes the most sense for the startup? Chapter 9 examines firms that provide complementary assets, services that help the startup (or traditional firm) enter into electronic commerce.

Adopting a new business model requires the organization to change, the topic of part IV. Chapter 10 discusses several models of the change process, and suggests a synthesized approach to change stimulated by both management and the capabilities of the technology. Chapter 11 presents alternative organization structures for the new business models discussed in the book.

Part V consists of one chapter, which discusses the opportunities and threats posed by the Internet and electronic commerce. The book concludes with a summary of the examples used throughout to analyze competitive strategy.

My hope is that the model and analysis will help managers formulate strategy in the New Economy. You can use the model to analyze your own strategy or the strategies of other companies. The model can assist you in devising a strategy; you have to identify critical resources and decide how to augment them so they become a system of resources for competitive advantage.

Electronic commerce and the Internet provide new opportunities for firms and managers willing to take advantage of them. The challenge for managers is great; they must choose a business model for the twenty-frist century, develop a competitive strategy, design an appropriate organization, and execute their strategy. The Dynamic Resource-Based Model of Strategy and the examples presented in this book are designed to provide guidance as you attempt to obtain and sustain a competitive advantage through electronic commerce and the Internet.

I wish to acknowledge the following sources for some of the material in the book: The VeriFone discussion in chapter 3 is from Garud and Lucas 1999 (1999). Parts of the discussion of airline CRS come from Duliba, Kauffman, and Lucas (2001). The experiment described in chapter 6 is from the paper by Bakos, Lucas, Oh, Simon Viswanathan, and Weber (2000). I am grateful to McGraw-Hill for permission to present some of the description of the Internet in chapter 6 from my text *Information Technology for Managers*, 2000, and to Jossey-Bass for permission to include material on Calyx and Carolla and the T-form organization in chapter 11 from my book *The T-Form Organization: Using Technology to Design Organizations for the 21st Century*, 1996. Cisco Systems granted permission to use excerpts from "The Global Networked Business: A Model for Success" from its Web site in chapter 5.

Finally, I would like to thank my new colleagues at the Robert H. Smith School of Business for their warm welcome to the University of Maryland, and my wife, Ellen, for her continued support and encouragement in writing.

Annapolis
Fall 2001

I
Strategy and New Business Models

The CEO of Megapack, a large manufacturer of packing materials, entered the conference room to attend a presentation by a consulting team from the Summit Consulting Group. The CEO had hired Summit as he became increasingly concerned about Megapak's continuing loss of market share. The strong economy masked the problem as sales and profits expanded, but he knew that Megapack had lost at least 5 percent market share in each of the last two years, and was worried that the decline would be even greater this year.

Sharon Ravenel, the lead consultant for Summit, began the presentation. "We have conducted an intensive study of the packing materials industry and interviewed a wide spectrum of people at Megapack, including the fifteen most senior executives," she said. "The results of our study suggest that Megapack has some significant challenges ahead."

The CEO interrupted, "Sharon, don't sugarcoat this—how bad are things?"

Sharon replied, "Let me put up my first slide." She pressed a couple of keys on her notebook computer, and a projector flashed her slide on a screen. "Let me talk you through the points:

1. Your largest competitor is taking orders on its Web site. This month it is opening a auction site to sell surplus goods, and it is working to develop custom Web pages for its major customers, highlighting the products they order most frequently. Custom Web sites also help it keep track of special discounts for a customer. Since they started the Web site, their sales are up 20 percent, and we estimate their market share is up three points."

The CEO stated, "They've spent a lot of money to get there I bet."

Sharon responded, "Actually, they outsourced most of the development to an Internet Service Provider who runs their site; we estimate their investment to date at around five million dollars, and that will buy them about twenty custom Web sites as well as the auction."

"Let me go on to the second point, if I may. In addition to your number one competitor, all of the top five companies in the industry except Megapack are doing something related to electronic commerce. But even more than that, we located one small firm in Omaha that has three employees. They have a plan to sell industrial packaging materials at 10 percent below going prices and still generate a large profit."

The CEO fumed, "That's impossible; margins just aren't that high in our business."

The consultant continued, "They have a new business model: they plan to sell only via the Internet, to set up custom Web pages for each customer, and to outsource all production and shipping to other companies. They have ten million dollars in start-up capital and figure they won't need any more than that. The low cost structure of their business model means they can undercut everyone else in the industry on price and still make money."

"I don't believe it," exclaimed the CEO.

Sharon added, "The really discouraging news is that in all of our discussions with you and the staff at Megapack, we have yet to find anyone able to articulate a new business model or a strategy for the Internet and electronic commerce. That is our most important point this morning. . . ."

This scenario is hypothetical, but could it describe your business? The revolution in information technology that has taken place in the last half of the twentieth century, especially the rise of the Internet, has stimulated a host of new business models and strategies. The purpose of this first section is to present a resource-based model of strategy; we will use the model to analyze a number of companies' strategies throughout the book. The model is offered as a guideline for you in formulating strategies to deal with the Internet and electronic commerce.

This book is primarily about strategy, but simply having a strategy is not enough for success. (Figure I.1 describes how a firm develops and executes a strategy). The firm first needs to develop a business model, the subject of chapter 2. The business model provides the input necessary to formulate strategy. It describes the nature of the business, markets, key

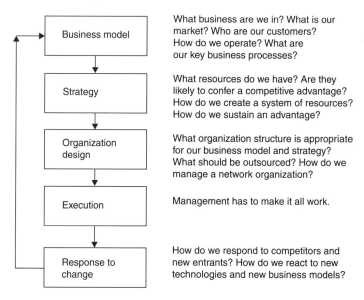

Figure I.1
Strategy Formation and Execution

constituents, customers, and business processes. Senior management uses the business model as a basis for generating corporate strategy, and this strategy is the primary focus of the book.

A firm has to do more than create a business model and strategy; it has to be successful at executing them. Successful execution requires management skills and an organization structure that facilitates the model and strategy. The subject of managerial skills is beyond the scope of this book; however, chapter 3 describes some of the characteristics of firms that have an effective Internet strategy, and chapter 11 presents in depth forms of organization that facilitate new business models. Strategies are rarely static in today's Internet economy, the organization must also respond to rapid changes in its environment; actions by competitors, the arrival of new entrants, and innovations in technology force management to revise business models and strategies.

Different chapters address the components of figure I.1, with our primary emphasis on strategy, business models, organization structures and change. Our objective is to help the reader understand and develop successful strategies for electronic commerce and the Internet.

1
Strategies Old and New

At the dawn of the Internet Age, and the United States was in the middle of a long economic expansion, business was good, the typical CEO was very contented. If anyone had suggested that his industry might be threatened, the officer would rightly have questioned the person's imagination, if not his sanity. In today's Internet Economy, threats like those listed below are very real, and senior managers are scrambling to figure out new business models and strategies.

Your Industry	The Threat
Stock brokerage	Someone figures out how to let the trading public and institutions bypass brokers and interact directly with the stock markets. (Merrill Lynch versus E*Trade)
Book retailing	A competitor is able to do a brisk volume selling books electronically without any stores. (Barnes & Noble versus Amazon)
Auto manufacturing	A competitor figures out how to build a custom automobile in five days. (Toyota versus General Motors)
Grocery retailing	An innovator offers a shopping service that allows customers to get groceries without ever leaving home. (Safeway versus Webvan)
Book publishing	A technological shift eliminates the need for paper copies of publications, and makes it possible for authors to publish without the services of a traditional publisher. (*Wall Street Journal* versus *Wall Street Journal Interactive Edition*, printed books versus e-books)

PC vendors	A competitor invents a supply chain that allows it to receive payment from customers before assembling the computer and which results in almost zero inventory. (IBM versus Dell)
Manufacturing	Another company in your industry figures out how to take most of its orders without human intervention and route them automatically to companies that manufacture its products. (Lucent versus Cisco)
Music industry	A new technology is developed that potentially eliminates the need for a record label and record stores. (CDs versus MP3)

If any of these innovations were to affect your company, it would face a strategic crisis, requiring you to formulate a new strategy to respond to the threat. The future success and even the viability of your business hang in the balance. *In the last five years, firms in all of the industries described above have faced such a strategic crisis. Only some of them have found a new strategy to compete.*

The Internet, the World Wide Web, electronic commerce, free markets, the stock market, venture capitalists, and the tremendous creativity of individuals in the United States and around the world have created these threats along with many new opportunities. The purpose of this book is to present a model of corporate strategy that describes how the firm can take advantage of new technologies, responding both to the threats and opportunities they provide. The model in this chapter is equally applicable to the Internet start-up and the traditional firm trying to cope with challenges new technology brings to its business. *Firms that fail to understand how models of strategy apply to a new economy dominated by the Internet are unlikely to survive in the twenty-first century.*

What Is Electronic Business?

It is difficult today to avoid being bombarded by stories about electronic commerce; popular business periodicals as well as the *New York Times* have special sections on e-commerce. A casual glance at the headlines would lead one to believe that e-commerce entails simply selling products and services over the Internet. However, there is much more to e-commerce than a Web site and the ability to enter orders for goods or services online.

There are two broad categories of electronic commerce—business to consumer (B2C) and business to business (B2B). The first excitement about e-commerce came from B2C; everyone can relate to buying consumer products like books and CDs over the Internet. What does this business model offer? It provides tremendous convenience for the customer who can shop from home; it is especially well-suited to commodity products like books and CDs where there is no need to examine the product, and the offerings from each vendor are identical. A motivated consumer can base a purchase on price and service. B2C electronic commerce should reduce consumer search costs and reduce the amount of friction in the marketplace. However, by the fourth quarter of 2000. The Census Bureau estimated that E-commerce was only 1% of total retail sales.

The largest potential for electronic commerce is B2B, companies buying goods from their suppliers. These purchases dwarf consumer sales. For example, a consortium of automobile manufacturers has established a Web site, Covisint, for purchasing a substantial portion of their supplies. General Motors and Ford buy about eighty billion dollars and seventy billion dollars of parts a year, respectively. One optimistic auto executive thinks Covisint could have a sales volume of five hundred billion dollars a year within three years. If the firms complete only 25 percent of their purchases on this hub, the numbers are still huge. Now think of many other industries developing similar purchasing hubs or participating in them as suppliers, and the potential for B2B commerce should be clear.

Taking an order on the Internet may let a company say that it is in e-commerce, but true electronic business is more than setting up a Web site and letting a customer order products or services via the Internet. The real advantage of e-business comes from becoming a fully electronic firm, integrating the Internet through all aspects of the firm's value chain. For a manufacturing company, being an e-business means that customers query a Web site for product availability and delivery schedules; behind the Web site supply chain, management software consults online inventory files and a production planning system to return a promised shipping date to the customer. If the product is to be manufactured rather than shipped from inventory, the customer can use the Web site to inquire about progress.

The firm uses the Internet to market its products. For example, it might offer product catalogs on the Internet, and programs that help engineers determine how best to use its products. The firm might run auctions on the Internet to dispose of obsolete or discontinued products. The manufacturing company uses the Internet to facilitate communication among its plants, and to interact with its suppliers. This electronic business uses the technology to process payments and receipts. The firm takes advantages of the option offered by technology to develop a flat organization structure, thereby increasing the span of control and delegating more responsibility to employees.

There are relatively few organizations that have achieved this vision for electronic business, but it is the direction in which leading firms are moving. An electronic business is highly efficient and flexible; it is able to respond quickly to customers and to changes in market conditions. All segments of the economy are becoming more competitive, making quickness of response an important part of a firm's strategy.

Hypercompetition

Electronic commerce and the Internet economy have stimulated much greater competition in the economy than there was in the past. In such a hypercompetitive economy, one finds the rapid creation of new, firm-specific resources. Not only do companies generate resources and assets quickly, they find that these investments depreciate rapidly. Investments in technology offer a good example of this fact. It is estimated that a personal computer depreciates at the rate of 10 percent a month.

In spite of rapid obsolescence and depreciation, one still finds firms that are rich in resources; some of these firms have large cash flows while others have the benefit of abundant venture capital and very high stock prices. With these financial resources, it is easy for firms to innovate and develop new strategic assets. New start-ups and dot.com companies expect to function in a hypercompetitive economy; some traditional firms have been caught unawares by electronic commerce and the Internet. A complex and frequently changing environment, the rapid creation of firm specific resources and rapid obsolesence are characteristics of hyper-competition.

Hypercompetition puts pressure on management in developing strategy and in the execution of the firm's business model. Time is of the essence in a hypercompetitive environment; you must respond quickly to competitors. It is unlikely that a firm in which managers make leisurely decisions will be competitive in this setting.

The manager is interested in strategies that allow the firm to sustain a competitive advantage. In a slower-paced economy, one might consider a strategy to be a success only if it conferred a competitive advantage that lasted several years. In a hypercompetitive economy a successful strategy is one that allows you sustain a competitive advantage for a year or longer.

A Dynamic Model of Competitive Advantage

Figure 1.1 presents a dynamic resource-based model of competitive advantage for firms operating in the hypercompetitive environment of the Internet and electronic commerce. In this section, I provide an overview of the model, and in the next section, review past work on strategy that has influenced its development before going into the details of the model.

The starting point for developing strategy in figure 1.1 is to identify the resources that may give a firm a competitive advantage. In order to confer such an advantage, a resource has to be *rare, valuable, inimitable, and nonsubstitutable*. If something is rare, it means that there are few other resources like it, so it is difficult for a competitor to acquire that resource. In a later chapter, I discuss airline computerized reservations systems (CRS). These very complex computer and communications systems are rare; only a small number of fully featured systems exist. A competitive resource has to be valuable as well as rare; a resource is valuable to the extent that it provides value to its owner. The CRS is extremely valuable for a number of reasons, one of which is the large, positive revenue stream it generates. A valuable resource, then, is one that enables a firm to implement strategies that increase its efficiency or effectiveness.

A strategic resource also has to be inimitable; otherwise, a competitor can create a copy or near copy of it. In theory, one could develop a new computerized reservations system. However, to reach the level of the top

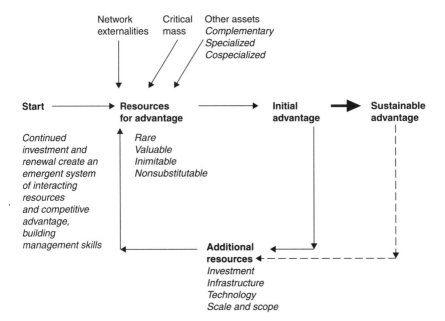

Figure 1.1
A Dynamic Resource-based Model of Competitive Advantage for the Hyper-competitive Internet Economy

three or four systems, given their links to travel agencies, would be prohibitive in time and cost. There are imitations, but the imitations are not serious threats to industry leaders. In a similar vein, a strategic resource is nonsubstitutable; that is, a competitor cannot easily find a similar resource to use in its place.

According to the model, once the firm has created or developed a resource, or bundle of resources, it can use it to obtain an initial advantage in the marketplace. In a highly competitive economy and in a period of rapid technological innovation, it is possible that some of these strategic resources will lose one of the characteristics that makes them strategic. For example, a technological breakthrough might make it possible for an innovator to create a substitute where one was not possible before.

A large brokerage firm like Merrill Lynch has hundreds of offices and about seventeen thousand financial consultants (retail stock brokers). Its formidable presence has been a strategic resource for the company for years, giving it huge coverage in the marketplace. The Internet, however, has made it possible for an online broker to reach everyone connected to the Net (well over 150 million people worldwide), with very few brokers. Size—Merrill's strategic resource—could become a liability.

The model in figure 1.1 contains a feedback loop in recognition of the fact that *in today's world, it is increasingly difficult to sustain an initial advantage.* It is likely that firms like Merrill Lynch will have to add new resources to their existing resources in order to build *and sustain* a resource-based advantage.

Value Chains and Competitive Forces

The Internet has been around since 1969 when it was a Defense Department network known as the ARPANET. University faculty and industrial researchers were the primary users of the Net then; they exchanged files and electronic-mail messages. The sponsorship of the Net moved to the National Science Foundation (NSF) and it became the Internet. In 1995, NSF phased out of financing the Net to concentrate its efforts on "second generation" networking. At this point, it became possible to use the Internet for profit-making activities, which had been prohibited when NSF was its main sponsor. The rest is history.

How does the Internet impact theories of corporate strategy? The dominant force in corporate strategy in the 1980s was Michael Porter at Harvard. While it is not correct to say that Porter's models predate the Internet, they do predate the ability to use it for profit. It would be unfair to criticize his strategy models because he developed them at a time when no one foresaw the impact of the technology. In fact, these models still have widespread applicability. Some of my students have prepared very insightful analyses of the threats to traditional businesses from the Internet using the value chain and five forces model developed by Porter nearly twenty years ago.

The Value Chain
Porter (1985) introduced the term *value chain* into the vocabulary of managers. See figure 1.2. At each stage in the chain, the firm adds value

to its products and/or services. The value chain divides activities into two types—primary and support. Primary activities are associated with the mission of the firm; they are the processes that create products and services. Inbound logistics refers to obtaining materials required for successful operations. Operations involves manufacturing, or creating a service, and outbound logistics deliver the product or service to customers. Marketing and sales are included as primary activities because they are central to customer demand. Service is responsible for after-sales support of a product.

Support activities are represented by the firm's infrastructure. Human resource management is concerned with recruiting, training, and advancing the careers of people who work for the firm. Technology development is a function that includes both information technology and research and development. Technology also applies to the support of the value chain through all of its steps. Finally, procurement deals with obtaining the raw materials needed to produce a product or service.

Today, a firm might look at the distinction between primary and support activities a little differently. For example, supply chain management is concerned with procurement, inbound logistics, operations and out-

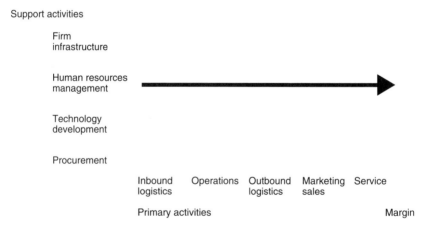

How have the Net and e-commerce affected the value chain?

Figure 1.2
The Value Chain

bound logistics. Technology applies to all of the activities described in figure 1.2, and the firm's infrastructure is increasingly characterized by its technology architecture.

What is the contribution of the value chain? It offers one way of analyzing the impact of the Internet and electronic commerce on a traditional firm and of thinking about ways to build new business models. For years, the book retailer had a procurement department that evaluated and ordered books from publishers to be shipped to the retailer's warehouses. The inbound logistics operation at the warehouse involved receiving books and then placing them in the proper location for retrieval. When a store ordered or reordered a book, the warehouse removed the appropriate number of copies from the shelf and combined all requests from the store into a single shipment. Marketing and sales used various advertising media to encourage customers to visit a store and buy books.

When Amazon.com came up with a new model, it changed the value chain in several important ways. At first, it subcontracted most inbound logistics and operations, retaining only the order processing, billing, and customer service functions. By 1999, Amazon began building its own warehouses in order to have more control over logistics. The major change to the value chain, however, was the fact that Amazon.com has no physical stores as part of its operations.

This simple change in the value chain has exerted a profound impact on the organization and its cost structure. The firm infrastructure at Amazon is considerably smaller than that of a traditional retailer, as is the effort devoted to managing it. Compared to the value chain at Borders, there is far less real estate, no investment to build or remodel stores, and no store sales personnel. Human resources has fewer people to hire and train than a bricks-and-mortar bookseller, and technology development focuses on the Web site for taking orders and not on sales systems for retail stores.

Comparing value chains can highlight the differences among business models, especially models that are built around the Internet and Web. Examples in the rest of the book will show the dramatic effect that these technological innovations have had on a variety of firms' value chains.

The Five Forces Model

Porter's second contribution is the five forces model of competition. (See figure 1.3.) This model depicts the forces that shape a firm's competition. The forces are competitive rivalry, the threat of new entrants, the bargaining power of suppliers, the bargaining power of buyers, and the threat of substitutes.

When competition is intense, management will spend more time on strategy and on monitoring competitors. Intense competition is usually good for consumers as they gain the advantage of new products and services and declining prices.

An existing firm is always concerned about new entrants who might take some of the market. The threat of new entrants sometimes keeps prices down as an industry with abnormal returns will attract other firms. What conditions attract a new entrant? If there are a number of competitors already in the market so that no one firm is dominant, entry will be easier and thus more attractive. A single firm cannot cut prices to drive out the new entrant. If it takes relatively little investment to start a business, then entry will be encouraged. If the technology required is well-known or can be easily obtained, entry will also be encouraged. It is relatively easy to start a garage, for instance, because the equipment

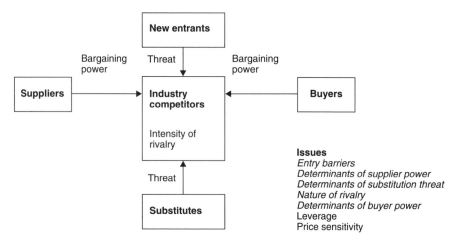

Figure 1.3
Porter's Five Forces Model

needed to repair a car is readily available; in contrast, it is very difficult to start a pharmaceuticals company due to the fact that many drugs are protected by patents; thus, a new firm may spend years in R&D before it has a product to sell.

The Internet has done much to encourage entry. If one looks at the factors that promote new entrants, the Internet has helped many new companies get started. The technology of the Internet is described in widely published standards. Vendors make inexpensive equipment that conforms to these standards, so that assembling the technology for a Web site is inexpensive and mostly available off the shelf. There are software packages for setting up a store on the Web, and a number of outsourcers who will set up and manage a firm's Web site. One needs very little in the way of a physical presence to start a business on the Internet. This technology raises the threat of new entrants for a variety of firms.

How does the bargaining power of customers affect competition? There are situations where a customer can force a company into action that it might prefer not to take. General Motors spends more than eighty billion dollars a year on its purchases. A small company must follow GM's requirements to do business with the firm; it is the automaker who sets the terms. GM has used this power to force its suppliers to adopt Electronic Data Interchange (EDI), and is now encouraging them to move EDI functions to the Internet. A small company is at the mercy of a giant like GM; in this case, the buyer has almost total power over the supplier, especially if the supplier needs its sales to GM in order to survive.

There are times when suppliers also have an advantage over their customers, though this happens less often. It is most acute when there are few or no substitutes for what the supplier has to offer. Until AMD developed competitive chips, the PC industry depended almost entirely on Intel to provide hardware, and on Microsoft for software. Both Intel and Microsoft have tremendous bargaining power as suppliers (and probably as customers as well).

The threat of substitutes is always very real. As palladium prices have increased, one electronics components manufacturer has invested millions of dollars in new equipment to substitute a less noble metal for component leads. Automobile manufacturers are substituting plastics and aluminum for steel. The recreational boat industry converted almost entirely from wood to fiberglass, and is currently in transition to composite fibers for some parts of the vessel.

How have the Internet and electronic commerce affected the five forces in the model? The first impact, as described above, is to lower entry barriers. The Internet makes it easy to start a new firm with minimal investment. The investment community was obsessed with Internet start-ups in the late 1990s; thus, capital was not a problem for the first movers on the Internet. The Net and electronic commerce are creating a huge number of substitutes for traditional businesses. One can trade stock without a broker, publish a book without a publisher, and record and distribute music without a record label; there appears to be no end in sight to Internet substitutes for existing business models.

How does the Internet affect the relationship between buyers and suppliers? Later in the book, we will discuss new kinds of business on the Web. Several of these involve brokerage and auction services. These new types of markets change the way in which buyers and suppliers interact and, thus, represent a new balance of power. It is safe to say that technological innovation like the Internet and electronic commerce affect all of the forces in the Porter model.

Core Competence

Another important view of strategy stresses the "core competencies" of the organization (Prahalad and Hamel 1990, 79). This theory states that management's task is to create an organization "capable of infusing products with irresistible functionality, or better yet, create products customers need but have not yet even imagined."

Management must combine corporate-wide technologies and production skills into competencies for competition. Core competencies are the organization's knowledge of how to integrate multiple technologies and coordinate diverse production capabilities. There are three tests to identify a core competence:

1. It should provide access to a wide variety of different markets.

2. It should make a significant contribution to the end product, especially the benefits that the customer perceives.

3. It should be difficult to imitate.

Prahalad and Hamel argue that the best a company can hope for is to be a world leader in five or six competencies. Core competence can take years to build, and companies that have failed to invest in them are not likely to enter an emerging market.

The authors feel that management should develop a corporate strategy for organizing and deploying core competencies. They envision a strategic architecture that identifies which core competencies to build and their required technologies. One option is to outsource all of the activities that are not core (Quinn and Hilmer 1994). Under this approach, management concentrates on just the firm's core competencies and leaves all other activities to others. Cisco is an excellent example of a firm that has followed this business model.

Managers have appealed to core competence in downsizing and shedding business units. It is not clear if these managers understand that competencies are intangible and are based on learning, knowledge, and management skills. You may have a lot of core competencies in one business area yet not be the number one in the market, possibly because the firm has underinvested in the business.

The resource-based model considers a core competence as a resource; later, as we will see in many of the examples in the book, management skills at a business process or technology are a key resource for competitive advantage. It is interesting to note that Internet start-ups and dot.coms are developing competencies much more quickly than Prahalad and Hamel envision. For example, Cisco converted to a major Enterprise Resource Planning software system in less than a year, and then moved aggressively to a business model based on the Web.

Resource-Based Views of Strategy

The model in figure 1.1 is drawn from a resource-based view of competitive advantage, an approach to strategy that has been discussed for a number of years. Two of the most articulate presentations of this view may be found in papers by Barney (1991) and Peteraf (1993). The theory defines firm resources as "all assets, capabilities, organizational processes, firm attributes, information, knowledge, etc. controlled by a firm." Some authors in the field divide resources into three categories—physical, human, and capital. It should be noted that this view of competitive advantage, as seen in figure 1.1, is based on combinations of resources, rather than a single resource that creates an advantage.

A firm has a competitive advantage when it creates a successful strategy that cannot be duplicated by a current or potential competitor. The advantage is sustained if competitors are unable to duplicate the benefits of the strategy, so it is important that resources be immobile. Often, a firm creates a bundle of resources by following a unique path, a path that the firm itself might not even understand. Thus, the strategy can be considered *path dependent*. If the firm with the strategic advantage cannot identify the path it has followed, than its competitor is likely to have trouble imitating its strategy.

Combine path dependence with the concept of causal ambiguity, and it can be very difficult to imitate strategy. *Causal ambiguity* refers to the difficulty of determining cause-and-effect relationships. If a particular product or service is a success, can the firm identify all of the factors responsible? If a firm is profitable overall, can it determine the reasons for its success? Oftentimes, the answer to these questions is "no" or "maybe." If the firm with a successful strategy does not understand the path it has followed and the cause of its success, competitors are unlikely to be successful with the same strategy.

An important consideration is that a competitive advantage from resources does not necessarily last forever. The theory states only that a resource-based advantage will not be competed away through the duplication of resources by other firms. There may still be "revolutions" in an industry so that resources that once sustained an advantage for a firm are no longer valuable. ". . . What were resources in a previous industry setting may be weaknesses, or simply irrelevant in a new industry setting" (Barney 1991, 103). How valuable are hundreds of branch brokerage offices today compared to pre-Internet days?

Authors call structural revolutions in an industry "Schumpeterian shocks," after the noted Harvard economist. The Internet and Web seem to qualify as Schumpeterian shocks to business and the economy. Resources that once gave a firm an advantage may no longer do so; in fact, some of those resources may now be liabilities!

The ability of a firm to gain a first-mover advantage by implementing a strategy before its competitors depends on its ability to control resources that are not controlled by other firms. In the Internet world, obtaining such control is very difficult. No one has control over understanding the technology, access to the network, or a business model, though some entrepreneurs have tried to patent aspects of e-commerce. Resource theorists discuss resource "mobility," which can be thought of as the ease with which one can obtain a resource. If resources are highly mobile, they are easily acquired and a firm cannot obtain a strategic advantage from them. Most of the resources associated with information technology, the Internet, and the Web are highly mobile.

There is one characteristic of technology that may help protect resources that are based on IT—complexity. If a resource is sufficiently complex, it can confer a competitive advantage because others cannot easily duplicate it. The first movers in e-commerce had to develop complex systems to provide storefronts for ordering and to connect the Web with mainframe, legacy transactions processing systems. However, in the IT industry, vendors frequently develop software products to automate development and to hide complexity. Today, one can find many ways to build a storefront, for example, by using software from Broadvision or Open Market, or outsourcing development and operations to US Web or US Internetworking. Resource complexity in information technology may provide a short-term resource-based advantage, but it is unlikely to do so in the long run.

In summary, Barney (1991) contends that firm resource heterogeneity (difference) and resource immobility combine to make resources rare, valuable, inimitable, and nonsubstitutable. He also suggests that one cannot expect to purchase or acquire strategic resources on the open market; they must come from within the firm. In the context of the Internet and electronic commerce, then, how does the firm obtain and sustain a resource-based advantage?

The Dynamic Model

Figure 1.1 is a resource-based view of competitive advantage in the Internet economy. This model is dynamic and contains a feedback loop to illustrate the fact that strategy and resources are not static. The firm must constantly develop and enhance resources that have the potential to provide a sustainable advantage (Teece, Pisano, and Shuen 1997). Particularly under today's conditions of hypercompetition and the speed with which events happen in the Internet economy, the firm must build and reconfigure resources to compete.

There are several aspects to this model that need further explanation in light of the discussion above on more general theories of resource-based advantage. In particular, ideas of network externalities, critical mass, and assets to enhance resources require an explanation. In addition, it is important to understand the idea of lock-in and switching costs, and to think of resources as a system in which new assets and resources emerge from the interaction among a firm's stock of resources.

Externalities and Critical Mass

Economists have developed a rich literature on *network externalities;* they explain the diffusion of many different kinds of products and services. Figure 1.4 depicts the idea behind network externalities; that is, as the number of users of a product grows, the product's value to an individual increases.

If you are the only person in the world with a personal computer and e-mail program, the value of e-mail to you is pretty low—in fact, nearly zero. As a few friends buy computers and e-mail programs, and you start to exchange messages, the value of your investment in a PC and e-mail program increases, even though you have done nothing yourself to cause this increase. As thousands and then millions of people become users of e-mail, its value for you accelerates almost exponentially until it levels

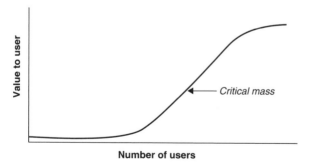

Figure 1.4
Network Externalities and Critical Mass

out at the point when everyone you want to communicate with has e-mail capabilities.

Network externalities are very important for a number of electronic-commerce initiatives. An electronic hub that matches buyers and sellers of equipment becomes more valuable to each buyer as more sellers participate. The site is more valuable to sellers if there are more buyers, so both groups gain as the site grows.

Figure 1.4 also shows an estimate of a point called "the critical mass" of an initiative. This term is borrowed from nuclear physics; when there is a critical mass of fissionable material, a chain reaction begins releasing nuclear energy. In the diffusion of an innovation, a critical mass is reached when the product or service becomes so attractive that large numbers of users acquire it. Critical mass is very important because a nuclear reaction sustains itself after reaching it. For technological innovations, a critical mass means that an accelerating number of users participate with little promotion by those offering the service. Because the incremental or marginal costs of serving another customer is very low on the Internet, achieving a critical mass is very important to Web sites. Their business increases dramatically, but their costs do not rise in proportion.

Other Assets

There are many different ways to look at the Internet and the Web, one of which is based on theories of innovation. Adding aspects of this theory to the model of figure 1.1 provides a richer understanding of strategic advantage in an Internet economy. The economist David Teece (1987) has suggested that for an innovation to succeed, it needs additional assets, including those that are complementary, specialized, or cospecialized.

A complementary asset is different from the innovation, and helps the innovation to succeed. Teece likes to use the example of the name *IBM* as a complementary asset to the PC when it was introduced in 1981. Because IBM, at the time the leading computer vendor and a vendor known for large computers, was selling a small computer for the desktop, many customers reasoned, it must be all right to buy one. In today's world, a complementary asset might consist of a special relationship with a firm that provides services. Calyx and Corolla, a nationwide floral distributor, for instance, worked for many months to reach an agreement with Federal Express to deliver flowers overnight. After the agreement, FedEx became a complementary asset for Calyx and Corolla.

A specialized asset is one that the innovation must have in order to succeed. Alternatively, the specialized asset may depend on the innovation. A specialized asset for an e-commerce vendor is an Internet Service Provider (ISP). ISPs in the form of mass-market communications services existed before there was commerce on the Net; for example, AOL, Compuserve, Prodigy, and others existed before the Net could be used for profit-making activities. Merchants on the Internet depend on their e-customers having access to the Web, and, thus, portals and ISPs become specialized assets for them.

Cospecialized assets exhibit mutual dependence with an innovation. An operating system for a computer like Windows 2000 and a browser like Internet Explorer depend on each other. Most users of a PC want to access the Web, and need a browser for that purpose. The browser has to run on a computer and interact with an operating system, so it, in turn, depends on Windows 2000.

A firm may be able to use its resources to create a highly specific or specialized asset that confers a competitive advantage. Several major airlines added resources to their computerized reservations systems, expanding them to become "travel supermarkets." These specialized assets would be very costly and time-consuming to recreate, even if an imitator was able to deal with their complexity.

Lock-in and Switching Costs

Economists have described a traditional approach to maintaining a competitive advantage—lock-in and high switching costs. If a firm offers a product or service that "locks in" customers, it may be able to sustain an advantage. By becoming a standard in the industry, Microsoft has locked in a huge number of customers for its operating systems. In addition, it has created Microsoft Office applications, which are highly integrated and work seamlessly with its operating systems. This kind of lock-in has created very high switching costs. One pays a price for not using Office; all office documents received must be converted to your own software—a task that is easy in theory but not always in practice. One strategy, then, for maintaining a competitive advantage is to use resources in such a way that you create lock-in and high switching costs for customers.

Additional Resources

Competitive advantage happens in two stages; the firm first obtains an initial advantage, and then tries to sustain that advantage. Teece (1987) describes this effort as an attempt to appropriate the value from an innovation for yourself, and speaks in terms of "regimes of appropriability." An innovation with high appropriability is one in which the innovator is likely to retain the benefits. With low appropriability, someone else has a good chance of taking your benefits. If you have an advantage based on rare, valuable, inimitable, and nonsubstitutable resources, then you should have a high regime of appropriability. One way to sustain an advantage is to protect assets (resources) so that their benefits cannot be appropriated by others.

How does one protect innovations? Traditionally, companies have employed patents and trade secrets to protect their innovations. Path dependence and causal ambiguity, discussed earlier in the chapter, offer weaker protection against those who seek the benefits of your labors. Do any of these strategies work in the Internet world? Unfortunately, it is very difficult to obtain a patent or to protect a business model. Everything is highly visible on the Internet, and it is relatively easy to copy an innovation without infringing on a patent.

A good example of trying to protect an innovation comes from Priceline.com, a "demand aggregator." It allows you to indicate how much you wish to spend on an item such as an airline ticket, and provides that demand to airlines who decide if they are willing to sell a seat at your bid price. Until recently, the company was very successful, and was selling fifty thousand airline tickets a week. Priceline has received a patent on its model for bidding, and has sued Microsoft to force it to stop offering a similar service.

Amazon.com is one of the largest merchants on the Net. On its site, the company offers something called "one-click checkout." If you have previously supplied information like shipping and billing addresses, credit card number, and so on, you can click on one button to check out. Amazon has a patent on the concept, and has sued its major rival, Barnes & Noble, to prevent it from using one-click checkout. While Amazon's attempt to protect an innovation is interesting, it is hard to see that one-click checkout is going to dramatically affect each firm's competitive position.

So for most firms, the question remains, how do you sustain an initial advantage? The model in figure 1.1 suggests that to appropriate the benefits of your innovation, your business model, it is necessary to continually add resources so that you protect and enhance existing resources that are rare, valuable, inimitable, and nonsubstitutable. By continually building on resources that first provide an advantage, it is possible to sustain that advantage. The book will discuss several examples of firms that have created and sustained such an advantage in later chapters.

A System of Resources
What the firm creates with this strategy is a system of resources[1] that interact with each other; a few resources emerge from that system to sustain an advantage. The interaction of resources creates new assets and resources that enhance one's competitive position. Later, we will look at the case of the Port of Singapore Authority (PSA). The port developed resources that interacted with those provided by the Singapore government to create a highly specialized resource in the form of an automated customer-oriented transshipment port. The PSA also exhibits one of the most valuable resources that can emerge from a system of resources—management skills. Port personnel have become skilled at developing Operations and Information Technology and operating a port—something difficult for others to imitate.

The model suggests that you can obtain and sustain a competitive advantage even in the hypercompetitive world of the Internet and electronic commerce. However, to do so requires continued investment and the addition of new resources. As shown in figure 1.1, you have to invest in technology and infrastructure, and you may have to expand the scale and scope of your operations.

Knowledge and Skills

As the organization builds its system of resources and creates assets for competitive advantage, managers gain knowledge and new skills. Consider a company like E*Trade. The firm's staff learned how to build a Web site for high-volume securities trading. This technology includes more than the customer's view of the site. E*Trade has to route trades to markets for execution, provide clearance and settlement, and handle customer records. The E*Trade staff has developed knowledge about electronic trading and skills to implement a trading system. Management knowledge and skills emerge as an important resource in their own right as they are difficult for a competitor to acquire.

There is growing recognition of the importance of knowledge and skills in obtaining and sustaining a competitive advantage (Conner and Prahalad 1996). To some extent, this view is an extension of the idea of core competence, which was introduced as "collective learning" about how to integrate multiple technological and production capabilities. In a significant number of the companies described in the rest of the book, the knowledge and skill that emerges from building resources for advantage will turn out to be key resources themselves.

Review of the Model

This chapter has introduced a dynamic resource-based model of competitive advantage in the Internet economy. In figure 1.1, the firm begins by creating resources that are rare, valuable, inimitable, and nonsubstitutable. Network externalities may contribute to creating resources with these characteristics, especially after a product or service has achieved critical mass in the marketplace. The innovative firm may also find that complementary, specialized, or cospecialized assets are required to be successful. Path dependence and causal ambiguity can help to confuse competitors, though innovations that make use of the Internet are hard to hide and to protect.

The objective of the firm is to create an initial advantage, sustain that advantage, and appropriate the benefits from its innovative activities. The model is dynamic because of its feedback loop: It is unlikely that gaining an initial advantage in the Internet economy will lead to a sustained advantage. Instead, the firm has to add additional resources to create, a system of interacting resources. From this system and its interactions emerge enough resources that are rare, valuable, inimitable, and nonsubstitutable to sustain an advantage. This cycle continues in a never-ending loop if the firm is successful.

Can this dynamic model apply to the two types of firms discussed earlier—the innovator starting a new business and the traditional firm trying to respond to the threats and opportunities of the Internet and electronic commerce? Subsequent chapters contain examples of firms that have been successful in this hypercompetitive economy. The model of figure 1.1 is used to analyze each example to show how a number of organizations have appropriated the benefits of their Internet innovations for themselves. When considered in light of the experiences of the firms in the examples, the model suggests a way for you to formulate and analyze competitive strategy in the Internet economy.

The Role of Business Models and Organization Structure

Before developing a strategy, management must devise a business model that includes the Internet and electronic commerce. Developing a new business model requires managers with vision and the ability to think creatively. Chapter 2 explores new, Internet-enabled business models; these new models also appear for the companies discussed throughout the book. The next step is to develop a strategy, hopefully with the help of the model in figure 1.1. You also need to develop an appropriate organization structure to facilitate your business model and to realize the firm's strategy. I discuss the characteristics of firms with dynamic, technology-enabled strategies in chapter 3, and organization structures facilitated by technology in chapter 11.

The final steps are to create an appropriate organization structure, and execute your business model and strategy, all the while responding to changes in the economy, environment, and technology, and, of course, to the actions of your competitors. Executing the business model is a complex challenge; it requires highly capable managers who demonstrate leadership and motivate employees. A model can provide ideas and recommendations, but success depends on skilled managers as well as business models, strategy, and the right organization structure.

Note

1. The author is indebted to Professor Ron Weber of the University of Queensland, Australia, for his insights about systems of resources and the new resources that emerge from them.

2
New Business Models

A business model is a description of how an organization functions, a general template that describes its major activities. It identifies the firm's customers and the products and services it offers them. In what markets does the firm compete? A model also provides information about how the firm is organized and how it generates revenues and profits. What are its key business processes? Business models combine with strategy to guide major decisions at a firm. The model describes products and services, customers markets, and business processes, while strategy is concerned with how to achieve the objectives of the business model.

Your business model might be to create a Web site for people to use for buying and selling houses, and your goal is to exceed the business of a competitive site operated by traditional realtors. Your strategy describes how you will execute your business model to achieve the goal of a larger market share than the traditional realtors' site. Following the advice in chapter 1, you would develop a strategy by looking at existing resources and determining what added resources would help you compete. You would then follow the dynamics of the model in figure 1.1.

The dominant business model before the Internet was a manufacturing or services company that sold its products to customers. The company had a physical location, its own employees, and used information technology in a variety of ways to make internal operations more efficient. A few leading companies had figured out how to obtain an advantage from IT, and actually used technology to generate revenue. Organizations that were most effective in using technology created networks to link themselves with their customers and suppliers, making it easier to do business with them.

The Internet and the World Wide Web have stimulated a torrent of creativity; the technology has enabled a number of new business models. Some firms have changed their existing model to adapt to this new technology. Other organizations seem to be confused by these changes and unable to cope with them. Entrepreneurs on the Internet have also created entirely new models that could not exist without this technology. The purpose of this chapter is to explore these business models. Choosing a business model is key for a new firm, and changing one's business model is an important aspect of strategy for the traditional firm that is threatened by a competitor on the Net.

The Internet

The Internet provides a worldwide communications infrastructure that brings together individuals and firms. The user of the Internet runs a browser program on a personal computer known as a *client*. The Internet provides standards for companies and individuals who want to provide information or content on the Net. Such a content provider places information or services on a computer known as a *server* that is connected to the Internet.

With a minimal communications capability, individuals and firms all over the world can access the Net with browsers, and provide content by setting up a server. For the first time, standards and the Internet make it possible for everyone in the range of a telephone to connect to the same computer network. It is very easy to become a user of the Net. There are many Internet Service Providers, and new PCs come with a browser already loaded and ready to run. It can be a little bit more complicated to set up a server and offer content or a service on the Internet. However, there are a number of companies that consult on setting up a server, or that set up and operate a server for you.

Figure 2.1 is a simplified map of the Internet and some of the many organizations associated with it. The Internet is the basic infrastructure of hardware and software that spans the globe. The World Wide Web is another set of software standards for presenting information. The standards let developers create Web sites so that anyone with a Web browser that follows those standards can access information on the site.

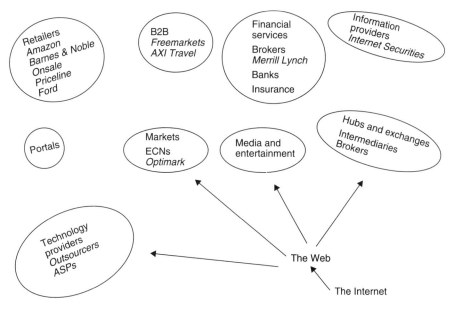

Figure 2.1
Web Map

Portals are locations that someone browsing the Web is likely to go to as a starting point for a session or to answer a question. A popular portal like Yahoo has millions of visitors, and is able to attract companies to advertise on its site. As a result, there is tremendous competition among portals for customers, with America Online being one of the most aggressive competitors. Portals compete by providing services to attract users; the major portals also provide shopping opportunities, which are both a service and a revenue producer for the portal. Other services include stock quotations, maps and directions, search engines, and similar features to encourage you to frequent the portal. Business commentators expect that only a handful of portals will survive these "portal wars."

Figure 2.1 also shows different companies and the kinds of business they do on the Internet. We have discussed B2C and B2B activities. B2C generated the first excitement about the commercial use of the Internet. Amazon.com is responsible for much of the "buzz" about selling on the Internet. This firm was very successful in attracting publicity long before it opened for business. In a consumer-oriented society, what could be more exciting than the possibility of comparison shopping and ordering from a computer in one's home or office?

The business-to-consumer companies include many name brands as conventional merchants adopt the Internet as another sales channel. Firms like L.L. Bean and Lands' End have made many products available for sale on their Web sites. Barnes & Noble has responded with bn.com to compete with Amazon.com, though it took a long time for the response.

Financial services providers are also in the B2C business. The Internet and electronic commerce impact brokerage firms, banks, and insurance companies. Retail customers (individuals rather than institutions) have flocked to the Internet to save commissions on stock trades. It is estimated that 40–50 percent of all retail stock trades will soon occur on the Internet. There are also a number of services on the Internet that collect premium and policy information and publish it on the Web for those planning to purchase insurance. Banks are interested in processing transactions over the Internet as a way to provide better service and reduce processing costs. One of the latest financial services is provided by an "aggregator" who accesses all of your various financial accounts on different Web sites, and produces a single financial statement showing all assets and liabilities.

The Internet presents a challenge to those who make and sell one of the most important and expensive retail products—the automobile. Buying services like Auto-by-Tel and Carsdirect.com work through dealers to bring the consumer a low price, or at least competing bids. The automakers would like to take advantage of electronic commerce, but in most states they cannot "own" dealers or deliver cars unless it is through an independent dealer. Ford and GM are working on plans to allow the customer to specify and order a vehicle on the Internet through dealers. One problem is that dealers offer different prices and do not have to follow the manufacturer's suggested price.

B2B, as mentioned in chapter 1, is likely to dwarf business-to-consumer purchases. With companies like the automakers buying tens of billions of dollars' worth of parts and supplies each year, shifting a small percentage to the Internet would make B2B far exceed B2C commerce. Internet purchasing allows companies to reduce the cycle time for their entire supply chain, so electronic commerce offers more than just a purchasing cost savings. A company like Cisco is built around the B2B capabilities of the Internet, both for accepting customer orders and for passing these orders to its contract manufacturers who actually build its products.

Information providers sell information to customers, or they provide it freely and obtain revenue from referrals and advertising. Information is a great Internet product because the marginal cost of producing a copy is nearly zero. Thus, once the vendor has created the basic information and infrastructure for providing it, additional sales cost nearly nothing and revenues flow directly to the bottom line.

Hubs are exchanges. For example, the site Detroit automakers have established to conduct bids and purchase supplies is a hub. Vertical hubs involve firms from the same industry or the same commodity. Covisint is a hub for the auto industry, while Avendra is a hub for hotel supplies. There can be a vertical hub for a product such as steel. Horizontal markets apply to a single firm offering its services to multiple customers— for example, a financial services company. Exchanges can be public or private depending on whether one has to be a member of a group or whether anyone can use the hub. The hub e2open.com is available to anyone in the electronics industry. An exchange that has many buyers and sellers and that is both vertical and horizontal becomes an electronic market.

There are also new markets that have been established on or with help from the Internet, for example, markets for securities trading. These Electronic Communications Networks or ECNs have created significant challenges for the traditional stock exchanges and government regulators. Electronic brokers often execute trades through this "third market," claiming that it offers greater efficiency than the established exchanges. Some financial experts feel that these exchanges will have to consolidate given that there is not enough business to sustain all of them. Electronic markets illustrate both network externalities and critical mass; there must be an adequate supply of buyers and sellers to create liquidity in the marketplace.

The Internet has generated a new industry of companies who provide technology and services. Outsourcers are companies that develop a strong core competence in some service and provide that service to others. CSC

Corporation (Computer Sciences) and EDS (Electronic Data Systems) are two outsourcers for technology services. Solectron and Celestica are contract electronic manufacturers; these firms will build electronic products like computers, routers, and cellular phones for a "manufacturer." Applications Services Providers (ASPs) run applications on their computer systems so that their customers do not have to install and operate the software internally. ASPs do a lot of business hosting Web sites for their customers. US internetworking (USi) and Digix are applications services providers.

The Internet is also an entertainment medium. AOL and other portals provide a number of entertainment services including games and chat rooms. Supposedly, the most profitable Web business are those that feature adult entertainment, although there is little written about these services. The merger of AOL and Time-Warner combines Internet and entertainment firms into a single entity that now has tremendous content and an Internet capability for delivery.

As discussed in the preface, historians will classify the last half of the Twentieth Century as the "Technology Revolution," and will compare it to the Industrial Revolution in terms of its impact on the world. There are three components of technology responsible for this revolution; then have combined, creating in the process something greater than the sum of its parts. These components are computers, databases, and telecommunications.

Computers provide vast processing power to perform computations and manipulate information. Databases are huge repositories of information and data that computers access and manipulate. Telecommunications ties everything together. You can have a client PC in New York extract information from a content server in France, and the server in France find its data on a database server in Tokyo.

Through the Internet, people have global access to over a billion pages of information. They also are all connected to each other; individuals and firms are linked via the Net. This technology provides the capability to build previously inconceivable business models, unprecedented connectivity, the ability to transform business operations and structure, and the ability to enter into electronic commerce.

Electronic Commerce

There is some controversy about the definition of electronic commerce. Most articles assume that commerce is electronic only if it involves the Internet. For years, there have been millions of electronic purchases among companies using Electronic Data Interchange. Until the Internet became available for profit-making uses, all of this traffic occurred on private networks; the companies involved created the networks themselves or they used the services of VANs (value added network providers). Much of EDI is sent in batches. For example, a computer at Ford determines which subassemblies the company needs from suppliers to build its cars the following week. The computer generates a batch of electronic orders and sends them to suppliers. The suppliers utilize their own computer programs to accept and process the batch of orders. This process may continue through the payments cycle as well. This kind of transaction today would be called business-to-business commerce.

Interest in electronic commerce on the Net first arose with retail sales when companies like Amazon.com and CDNow presented new ways to shop. Most experts expect the new forms of B2B commerce and the transition of EDI to the Internet to dwarf retail sales on the Net. The Internet offers new models for both retail and business-to-business purchasing.

The Retail Sales Model
Figure 2.2 compares the traditional model of retail sales with a new business model found on the Net. The conventional model is pretty familiar; a manufacturer sells goods to a wholesaler who, in turn, distributes the merchandise to a retail store. Customers visit the store to make a purchase, paying with cash, check, or credit card.

The Internet-based model for retailing makes some very significant changes in the traditional retailing business model. The pure model eliminates the retail store, and the distributor becomes a fulfillment partner. Instead of receiving merchandise, generally in bulk, for distribution to a small number of stores, the fulfillment partner must ship orders to the final customer. The customer does not visit the store, but instead orders over the Internet from the electronic merchant's Web site. The Web site

Manufacturer   Wholesaler's   Retail store
                      warehouse

Traditional commerce

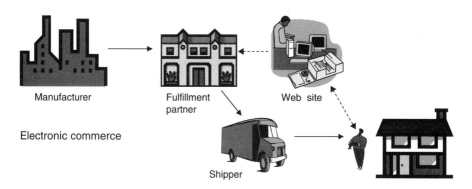

Manufacturer   Fulfillment   Web site
                      partner

Electronic commerce

Shipper

Figure 2.2
Retail Business Models

processes the order and payment via a credit card, and sends the order to the fulfillment partner.

Of course, there are variations on the new Internet business model for retailing. Amazon.com has found it necessary to build a series of warehouses around the country as it has expanded its business and product lines. Conventional retailers are adding electronic ordering capabilities, so they are faced with maintaining both retail stores and a Web ordering business.

What are the differences between the two models? The differences are more profound than appear in figure 2.2. The electronic commerce model features:

• No physical store
• No real estate purchase or lease
• No retail store employees

- No retail salaries or benefits
- No transportation between distributor and retail store
- The addition of a Web site
- The substitution of credit cards for cash and checks
- The substitution of a fulfillment partner for the distributor
- The addition of a shipping firm to deliver merchandise

The end result is that the electronic retailer faces a considerably lower cost structure than does the bricks-and-mortar retailer. The lack of a physical store and employees, and the elimination of shipments to stores all contribute to lower overhead. If the Web site actually places orders with the supplier/manufacturer, then it becomes a "virtual store" with no more overhead than its Web site. The company needs some technical support, customer service, accounting, advertising, and procurement personnel. Many of its business processes, then, are contracted out to others, thereby minimizing overhead.

The lower cost structure is the reason that traditional retailers are threatened by electronic commerce. If their strategy is to keep retail stores, most feel they must also allow online ordering. (Most of the large department stores and category firms like Toys "R" Us have Web sites for ordering.) However, they end up with a formidable challenge: they must master a new business model and pay the overhead of the traditional retailer. We explore possible strategies for these firms in a later chapter.

Business-to-Business Electronic Commerce
Because many companies and industries make heavy use of EDI, the change to B2B electronic commerce on the Internet may seem at first to be less dramatic than the changes associated with retail e-commerce. However, most experts predict that the value and volume of B2B e-commerce will vastly exceed retail electronic commerce. If you think about the number of components that an automobile manufacturer must order to build a car, compared to the one order that the end customer places for the car, the reason for this forecast is more evident. There is a tremendous volume of business-to-business transactions, and often each transaction requires more messages than the final retail sale. It is not

unusual for a B2B purchase to have an acknowledgement, a change order, an acknowledgement of the change, a shipping notice, notice of receipt, payment due, payment sent, and other miscellaneous messages associated with it. It is easy to see that B2B commerce will result in more traffic and more dollar volume on the Net than retail sales.

Figure 2.3 compares the two B2B business models—the traditional and electronic. The traditional purchasing process involves a procurement staff that negotiates with suppliers. A firm may provide an order for a specified period of time; for example, in the electronics industry, manufacturers often negotiate a price with suppliers for a commitment to buy a certain number of components a year. Then, during the year, the manufacturer provides forecasts and firm orders for the week, which the supplier ships under the blanket contract signed for the year. Other purchasing situations may require negotiation for each transaction.

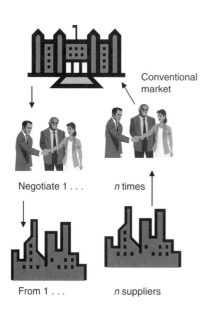

Traditional B2B commerce

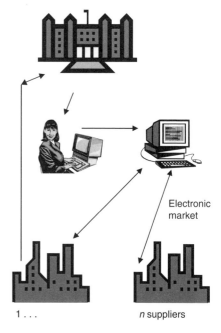

Electronic B2B commerce

Figure 2.3
B2B Models

In electronic B2B commerce, a smaller purchasing staff visits a market on the Web to procure the items it wishes to buy. One major advantage is that the buyer is able to comparison shop among a number of suppliers quickly using the Web, or through an auction offered by a company like Freemarkets.com. The Internet should facilitate finding the lowest prices available for the buyer. After locating the supplier, the purchasing process continues much as described above. The end result should be a smaller, more effective purchasing group and better prices for supplies.

Lean and Agile Manufacturing, Mass Customization

The mass manufacturing model, sometimes called "Fordist," comes from the original assembly line set up by Henry Ford. Ford produced thousands of cars with no or limited options in any color as long as it was black. This model of manufacturing has changed throughout the years, with a number of new variations. The most dramatic changes have occurred because of information technology; today one can order products with many different options.

Figure 2.4 presents the Dell Model of manufacturing, a model so popular that Michael Dell has been consulting for the Detroit automakers. Dell receives orders via phone and the Internet; currently, fifty million dollars of orders come via the Net per day, which is about half of the company's orders. As shown in the figure, Dell does not produce a computer until it has a firm order; the company orders from suppliers as it needs parts. The components that Dell does not build into the machine (an external Zip drive, for example) ship from their manufacturer directly to the customer; Dell never handles these parts. As a result, the company operates with little or no process inventory and no finished goods inventory. There are no distributors with Dell products on the shelves, and no obsolete models to sell at close-out prices. Dell also is paid for noncorporate accounts as soon as it books the order via the customer's credit card.

Even with this lean production model, Dell is able to offer a number of different computer models with different features. Given today's technology, the company appears to be about as lean as possible in terms of overhead and the manufacturing process. To encourage corporate sales, Dell sets up purchasing agreements with companies, universities, and

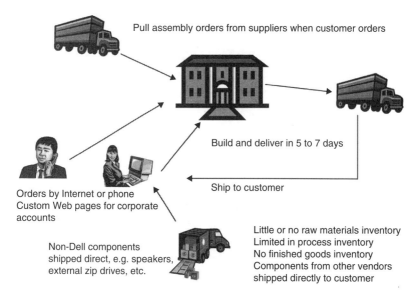

Pull assembly orders from suppliers when customer orders

Build and deliver in 5 to 7 days

Ship to customer

Orders by Internet or phone
Custom Web pages for corporate accounts

Non-Dell components shipped direct, e.g. speakers, external zip drives, etc.

Little or no raw materials inventory
Limited in process inventory
No finished goods inventory
Components from other vendors shipped directly to customer

Figure 2.4
The Dell Business Model

government agencies. It will develop custom Web pages to facilitate ordering by employees of these organizations.

Figure 2.5 presents another lean manufacturing model, this one from Cisco, an extremely successful manufacturer of communications equipment for networks. To a large extent, Cisco is a virtual manufacturer; it receives most orders on the Web and notifies contract manufactures to produce the order. The company's strength is in design and marketing. Because its customers tend to work with technology, they are quite comfortable ordering products over the Web and some 90 percent of Cisco's orders come via the Internet. An incredible 70–80 percent of customer service requests are handled by Cisco's extensive technical help information on the Web.

New Businesses on the Web

The Portal   The Internet has created a whole new series of businesses that did not exist before its creation. One example is the portal, the place

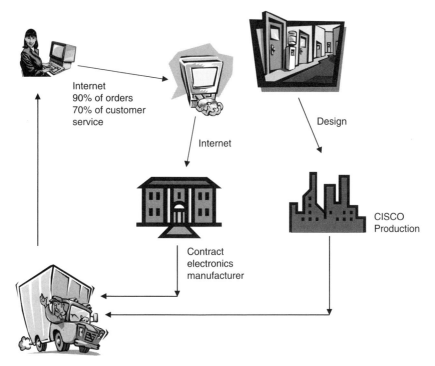

Figure 2.5
The Cisco Business Model

a person starts when connecting to the Web. Yahoo is a successful example of a portal, as it started as a search engine to locate content on the Web. However, as mentioned earlier in this chapter, the way a portal supports itself is through advertising and referrals to other sites. The more people that access the portal, the more attractive it is to advertisers and the more it can charge for ads. As the portals expanded from search engines to offer other services, they found new ways to generate revenue. If you click on "shopping" at Yahoo, follow a Yahoo link to a store, and purchase something, Yahoo gets a commission.

America Online is both an Internet Service Provider (ISP) and a portal. AOL is successful because twenty-five million people visit its portal when they log on to the Web. Portals exhibit both network externalities and critical mass. One of America Online's most popular features is its chat facility, which allows users to converse online. The more people who use AOL, the more valuable this service is.

The Hub   Figure 2.6 presents a model of an electronic hub. The hub is a kind of electronic broker or intermediary and the word *hub* is also sometimes used to describe exchanges that are vertical or horizontal marketplaces, as mentioned earlier in the chapter. While the Web threatens many intermediaries like stock brokers and real estate agents, it provides opportunities for intermediaries of a different kind. A hub connects two groups that wish to interact. The hub benefits from network externalities and critical mass. For example, a person might create a hub that matches shipping companies with excess capacity in containers with shippers who

1 . . .   Provider of service, product, information . . .   *n* providers

Web-based hub connecting
providers and customers

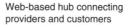

1 . . .   Customer of service, product, information . . .   *n* Consumers

Figure 2.6
Creating New Businesses: The Hub

have less than container-sized loads. A shipper would list its containers, their capacity, and destination at the hub Web site. A customer would access the hub's Web pages to locate a suitable container going to a desired location and make arrangements to rent space in it.

The hub or exchange creates a network of firms. A group of hotel chains including Marriott and Hyatt have formed a vertical exchange called Avendra. This exchange sees itself as a contracting agent, negotiating prices with suppliers and making their products available for hotels via the Internet. Avendra and all of its suppliers and hotel customers are a constantly changing network of organizations. Each supplier is a member of other networks, and the hotels are all members of a network of similarly branded hotels.

The Service Provider   America Online is a portal, but it is also an Internet Service Provider. The Internet has created a new industry dedicated to serving companies and individuals, making it easier for them to use and build applications on the Web. AOL has a private network that customers around the world can access. This private network connects to AOL's computer center in Vienna, Virginia. Vienna, in turn, is connected to the Internet so that AOL's customers can access the Web. AT&T Worldnet, @home (for cable modem users), and many other firms provide Internet access.

This class of company also includes firms like US Internetworking (USi) and US Web, which offer a wide variety of services. For example, USi develops and hosts applications for customers. Suppose that a firm wants to have a home page with the ability for customers to order products from it. An ISP will design the home page, implement electronic-commerce software, and host the entire operation on its servers. USi maintains a mirrored site in California to back up its Annapolis, Maryland site and has data centers in Europe and Japan. Intel and IBM provide services through huge "server farms," professionally managed locations that offer Web hosting.

The Applications Service Provider is similar to an ISP, but in addition offers the use of a particular application to a customer. If a firm is too small to implement a complete enterprise resource planning (ERP) system, it can access the parts it needs through an ASP for a monthly charge. This service also appeals to a company that has limited in-house expertise in implementing IT applications. Because these applications are all based on the Internet, the communications infrastructure is in place. An ASP can easily provide a sales force automation package that a sales representative with Internet access can use any place in the world.

New Markets

The Internet makes it possible to offer new kinds of markets because it provides a world-wide communications infrastructure. As an example, Avendra negotiates purchase contracts for hotel supplies and provides an Internet market for hotels and suppliers. Hotel members of Avendra like Marriott and Hyatt encourage these properties to use the exchange's market.

All one needs for a market is a central meeting place, and the Internet provides the mechanism for such a meeting; a market creator needs only a Web site. Many times, a buyer and seller do not need to interact directly or at the same time. Because the Internet is available around the clock, this technology removes time and location requirements that affect many physical markets.

Another kind of market is the auction, for example, the sealed bid auction is very common in construction. An organization wishing to undertake a construction project sends the plans for that project to prospective construction firms and requests that a sealed or secret bid be submitted by a certain date. Usually, the lowest bidder gets the job. Many government contracts, both local and federal, use the sealed bid auction in an effort to obtain a facility at the lowest possible price.

Other kinds of auctions—including most car, livestock, art, and estate auctions—employ open outcry in which an auctioneer works with an audience of potential bidders. The auctioneer opens bidding at the owner's reserve price, the minimum that the owner is willing to accept for the item for sale. The auctioneer encourages bidders to raise their bids until finally there is only the highest bidder remaining.

The Dutch auction is slightly different from the open outcry auction. In Dutch auctions, which developed in the Dutch flower markets, the auctioneer begins at a high price and decreases the price rapidly until a bidder stops the process and buys at that moment's price. Dutch flower growers believe that this kind of auction favors the seller rather than the buyer.

Except for the sealed bid auction, all of the auctions above require a bidder or representative to be physically present or connected by telephone. The Internet removes this time and place requirement. Instead, a seller posts the items to be auctioned on a Web site, and potential bidders visit the site at their leisure to review the item and decide whether or not to bid on it. One of the most popular sites for retail auctions is eBay, which has had phenomenal success. For B2B purchases, Freemarkets offers an auction service that it claims reduces purchasing costs for companies using its site and services.

Priceline.com has been successful with its "reverse auction," which its founder, Jay Walker, calls "demand aggregation." A buyer indicates on Priceline.com's Web site that she is willing to pay x dollars for an airline ticket on a certain date for a flight between two cities. Priceline has agreements with a large number of airlines who provide seats at clearance prices. Priceline determines if there is such a seat available. The buyer has to be willing to be flexible in terms of time of day and connecting cities. In addition to airline tickets, the site has a number of other products on which one can enter a bid.

The Internet has extended the auction to a large number of people and companies who could not have participated before. Network externalities and critical mass apply here as they do to other Net businesses. Because anyone on the Internet can access eBay, a potential seller has millions of potential bidders. The more sellers and bidders, the more valuable the site becomes to both groups.

Electronic Business: Pervasive Technology

The business models described in this chapter are templates that focus on the visible part of the firm; they suggest broad categories of e-commerce like B2B or B2C. In reality, the model for many organizations is more complicated. For the completely electronic business, all aspects of its strategy and operations involve information technology. A good example of the pervasiveness of technology beyond e-commerce is the auto industry.

For many years, the "Big Three" automakers have used technology heavily in their manufacturing operations. In fact, it was an industry group of auto manufacturers that encouraged early efforts at electronic data interchange. Detroit has insisted for a number of years that its suppliers accept orders electronically, though EDI takes place using batch transmission over private networks rather than the Internet. Some of the manufacturers allow suppliers to access their production planning systems to anticipate when to deliver products to factories. Chrysler has been a pioneer with this kind of just-in-time production, and electronic data interchange is a necessary technology for Just-in-Time (JIT) to work in U.S. auto plants.

GM, Ford, Daimler-Chrysler, Nissan, and Renault are cooperating to set up a Web site for purchasing supplies. They hope to save up to 10 percent of the cost of a car by purchasing through the Internet. In addition, these companies expect to gain revenue as they encourage their suppliers to use the site for their own purchases. The exact nature of electronic interaction with suppliers is not entirely clear yet. For example, will suppliers use the Web site for competitive bidding, and the conventional EDI system for releases against annual purchase contracts? Will all EDI shift to the Internet?

Because the automobile business is large and complex, the Internet and electronic commerce are having an impact in areas other than purchasing and manufacturing. Automakers do not really know the details of consumer demand; they build cars on speculation and send them to dealers. The car sits on the dealer's lot until a customer buys it; Detroit does not know which accessories the customer might ideally have wanted because many buyers are not willing to enter a custom order and wait for delivery—a time lag that automakers would like to reduce. Although shortening this time seems possible, reducing it to a few days is highly unlikely. There are over 10,000 parts in the typical car, and the source of many of these parts is subcontractors. To shorten delivery times, Detroit will have to coordinate production among a number of suppliers and find a way to reduce the time it takes to physically deliver a car from the plant to a dealer or customer.

One way to shorten cycle times is to have the customer specify and order a car over the Internet. About 55 percent of new car buyers today do some research on the Internet before visiting a dealer. Sites like Edmunds.com refer you to Auto-by-Tel to get a quote from a participating dealer, Carsdirect.com will deliver a new vehicle to your door. All of these alternatives provide a challenge for Detroit and its traditional dealership structure. It is clear that e-commerce is changing the way in which people buy cars, and that the role of dealership is evolving. It is difficult to forecast the final outcome, but the end result should benefit the consumer.

While the impact of the Internet on purchasing creates some problems as well as challenges for Detroit, automakers are excited about incorporating the Internet in cars. All of the manufacturers envision people having Internet access while driving with the ability to get and send e-mail (using voice recognition technology); inquire about traffic, obtain routing, recommendations on hotels and restaurants, and a host of other services. The auto companies have the vision of millions of customers using their cars as an Internet Service Provider and paying the companies fees of ten dollars to twenty dollars a month for the service. This kind of service would result in the automakers earning substantial amounts as ISPs.

Detroit provides a scenario for an electronic business, though it is not quite there yet. The potential exists for customers to specify and purchase their product using electronic commerce on the Internet. The companies will use B2B commerce sites to purchase and acquire their raw materials. The Internet allows them to coordinate production with suppliers, and offers an attractive service to bundle with their final product. It is also a way to stay in contact with customers throughout the life of the car. This example illustrates how the real benefits from the Internet come not just from electronic commerce, but from integrating technology throughout the firm's entire value chain.

New Business Models and Strategy

Offering opportunities that did not exist before the Web and the Internet, new business models have had a dramatic impact on strategy. The Dell model, for instance, has been so successful that it has forced IBM, the company that invented the PC, from the retail sales business for personal computers. IBM now sells its desktop PCs only via its Web site; it no longer sells through dealers and stores.

The strategist has a whole new set of models to consider. Do these models enable the firm to gain a sustainable competitive advantage? In what ways do the new models threaten existing firms and their approach to business? According to the strategy model in the last chapter, the firm needs resources that are rare, valuable, inimitable, and nonsubstitutable to obtain a competitive advantage and to appropriate the benefits of its innovations on the Internet. The problem is that none of these business models is inimitable! It is very hard to create a secret business model or to protect your model with a patent or copyright, or as a trade secret. CDNow did a great business on the Internet, but it did not take long for competitors to arrive on the scene. Soon Amazon.com branched out from books to CDs, threatening CDNow. On September 1, 2000, Bertelsmann AG, a large German publisher, acquired CDNow, providing it with the resources needed to stay in business.

3

Firm Characteristics

There are certain firm characteristics that facilitate innovation and the execution of the dynamic strategy discussed in chapter 1 and figure 1.1. The firm has to choose an organization design that meets the management challenges of the hypercompetitive Internet economy. It must decide what its core competencies should be, and whether it wishes to outsource areas that are noncore. Managers have to decide how they will provide leadership and what kind of culture they want the organization to have. We begin this chapter by looking at a technological infrastructure that facilitates electronic commerce, and then move on to discuss approaches to management within the firm that encourage innovation. Finally, we recommend a corporate culture that is well-suited to the Internet economy.

Infrastructure

Infrastructure allows an organization to operate; it consists of the underlying systems that process transactions, support decisions, and provide connectivity. Infrastructure enables and facilitates the operations of nations and of commerce. A flourishing economy depends on infrastructure like a banking system, communications networks, roads, air, rail, and often water transportation. Without such infrastructure, an economy has great difficulty functioning. In eastern Europe, in the days of central planning, infrastructure was often ignored. As a result, some people went hungry while others had to contend with food rotting in the fields. The infrastructure to transport food to the market was lacking; both the supply of trucks and the network of roads needed improvement. The modern firm needs a technology infrastructure to take advantage of the Internet and to engage in electronic commerce.

The Infrastructure of the Internet

The Internet is an excellent example of an infrastructure that facilitates new forms of commerce. It provides worldwide interconnection for anyone with access to the Net. A small firm in Nebraska can set up a Web site that is accessed by potential customers all over the world. Before the Internet, the small firm had to make a significant investment to become part of a private network, and even then it was still not accessible to vast numbers of people. Only large companies could afford extensive private networks to reach their customers. The Internet has leveled the playing field to a great extent; firm size and resources are no longer all-determining.

As mentioned in the last chapter, the U.S. government provided the initial stimulus and financing for the Net. Although the current Net is self-financing, the National Science Foundation is funding an "Internet II" initiative to plan the next generation of the Net. With the current system, the user connects to the Internet through an Internet Service Provider. The ISP provides a private network of leased lines to different points of presence. The networks of many ISPs are large enough to allow most of their customers to dial a local telephone number to reach an access point, thus saving toll telephone charges. The ISP's private network connects to its own computer center. A customer accesses an ISP server and is routed over another, high-speed leased line to an interconnection point to other networks. Here, traffic moves onto the backbone network, which offers the fastest lines of all. Internet traffic travels over the backbone and then to other more local lines until it reaches another server to complete the user's transaction. Figure 3.1 shows the global backbone network of UUNet—one of many backbone network providers—at the time of this writing, and figure 3.2 shows the North American backbone. A different line thickness indicates different capacity or bandwidth. The larger the bandwidth, the more traffic a line is able to carry.

The picture that emerges of the Internet is that of a huge network offered by different service providers using a variety of local leased lines

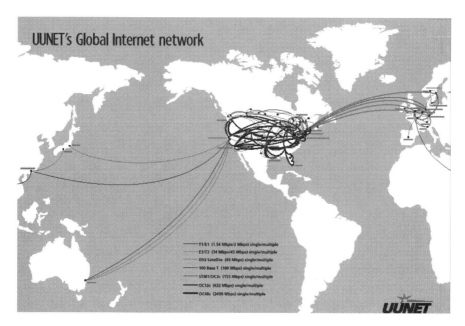

Figure 3.1
UUNET's Global Internet Network

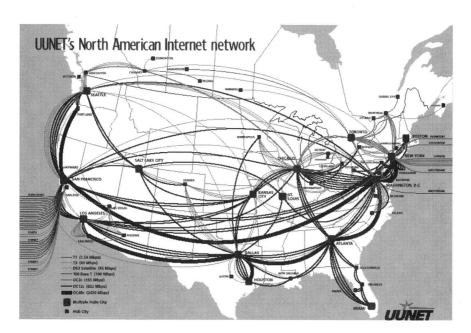

Figure 3.2
UUNET's North American Internet Network

and backbone lines from a set of common carriers. The Net is dependent on the infrastructure created by ISPs and the common carriers that provide local connectivity and leased lines to the ISPs, and on the backbone providers that speed packets across the country and around the world.

Infrastructure within the Firm

Electronic commerce depends on the Internet, and also on the information technology capabilities of firms that want to engage in e-commerce. What kind of IT does a firm need to succeed in the Internet economy? IT architecture is dependent on the firm and the nature of its business. We will examine two interesting cases—the Internet start-up and the established firm.

The Start-up   The Internet start-up begins with no technology infrastructure. It will first need to establish a domain name on the Internet and develop a Web site. This company will use one of several products that are available for designing sites. Depending on the nature of its business, it may need to purchase or design storefront software. For example, if selling to retail customers, most sites use the concept of a shopping basket. As a customer clicks on "buy," his products accumulate in a virtual shopping basket. When he has finished shopping, he moves to checkout.

Beyond the storefront, a start-up may need to develop software for logistics. If the new firm plans to operate its own warehouses, it will need programs to maintain inventory, communicate whether items are in stock or not to customers on the Web site, and handle reordering for the warehouse. While some of these programs are available for purchase, the start-up may have to write other programs that are unique to its operations. Where possible, the firm will purchase software and services in order to begin business sooner.

The Existing Firm   The major advantage of the start-up firm, paradoxically, is its lack of existing systems! It does not have to interface a Web storefront to ten or twenty year old "legacy" mainframe applications. The start-up can design a system that fits today's business model and use the latest technology to support its model. The challenges for an existing firm that wishes to embrace the Internet are different, and, in some respects, more daunting. The existing firm has an infrastructure that has been in place for years; it may or may not be up to the task of taking on electronic commerce.

A firm needs a technology base that includes:

• Transactions processing systems, possibly enterprise resource planning applications
• Decision support systems
• Desktop computing and an Intranet
• Internet connectivity

Transactions processing systems handle the basic business of the firm; they accept orders, ship products, maintain inventory, handle payments and receipts, prepare accounting and financial reports, and so on. Historically, firms have written these applications one-by-one, and they tend to lack integration. Enterprise Resource Package vendors offer solutions to these older, "stovepipe" systems. These vendors, including SAP, Baan, Peoplesoft, and Oracle, sell integrated packages.

An integrated package, for example, checks credit status on order entry; as soon as a person in the credit department updates status, it is reflected in the data seen by the person entering orders. ERP packages are expensive and difficult to implement; the customer must literally specify thousands of parameters that adapt the package for the firm's environment. It is easy to spend five million to fifty million dollars or more to implement all modules of an ERP.

Given this cost and the implementation challenge, why are these packages attractive? Many firms bought these packages in the 1990s to avoid having to change twenty-year-old programs to fix Y2K problems. Another possible reason for the appeal of such packages is that multiple locations can use the same software and, thus, coordinate activities and share data. Think of a manufacturing company with plants in the United States, South America, Europe, and Asia. It is not unusual to find such a firm with different computers and systems in each location, making it very difficult to share data. Of course, one can always transmit data, but the systems on the receiving end may not be able to integrate it. Real-time information may also be lacking.

The firm would like to have common ordering and global inventory visibility. If a customer in Asia orders a part that is out of stock locally, the system should be able to search for the part in another part of the world and easily arrange for it to be shipped. With a variety of legacy systems that use different databases, order entry systems, and inventory systems, the scenario above can be difficult or impossible to create. ERP software running on compatible computers around the world has the potential to solve these problems.

Why is this kind of transactions processing important? How does the company that lacks a common ordering system and knowledge of its global inventory offer ordering on the Web? How does it get into electronic commerce? Electronic commerce is more than ordering on the Internet; to be successful, the firm has to be able to manage everything from logistics, from locating a product to shipping it in a timely manner, to reordering so that customers receive products in time for their needs.

In addition to handling transactions, firms can gain great value from decision support (DSS) and executive information systems. A DSS is often based on transactions data; the user of the DSS manipulates the data to provide insights for decision making. A good example of a powerful DSS is revenue yield management, the systems that allow airlines, hotels, and similar businesses to maximize their revenue yield by constantly adjusting the price of available capacity, whether airline seats or hotel rooms. An executive information system provides data that is of great interest to management, for example, on-demand reports on sales and revenues.

Almost every firm today finds itself overflowing with desktop computers. The chairman of NationsBank, before it merged with Bank of America, reported that he had seventy thousand employees and eighty thousand computers. One would assume that the extra ten thousand computers are servers in a network, because a stand-alone PC is not of great value today. Desktop computing needs to be supported by a network and by an Intranet. An Intranet uses Internet protocols and software to provide the same kind of services for sharing information that one finds on the Internet. However, the Intranet is restricted to use within the firm. To complete this picture, the desktop computers should also have a connection to the Internet so that employees can exchange e-mail worldwide and access various Web sites around the world.

The challenge for the existing firm that wants to engage in electronic commerce is to find solutions when its infrastructure does not seem suited for the Internet. Many firms have connected their Web sites to old, mainframe legacy transactions-processing applications and databases. When you track a package on Federal Express or make a reservation on Travelocity, the Web pages that you complete interact with old, mainframe applications.

Why not replace these old applications? There are two reasons. One is cost, and the other is performance. Mainframe systems have always excelled at high-volume, transactions-processing applications. The Sabre system that runs Travelocity has processed over seven thousand transactions in one second. There are millions of lines of program code in these systems. The cost to redevelop them would, therefore, be staggering; the time required would delay a Web presence for years. Accordingly, the best alternative is to hide these systems through an attractive Web interface.

The firm that has invested regularly in technology and has not let its infrastructure become obsolete has the advantage. One firm that has been successful in integrating its activities with the Web is Cisco, which decided to replace all of its systems with an ERP package just before the Internet became available for profit-making activities. As a result, it was well positioned to move to the Web with a modern, integrated set of transactions-processing applications in place.

Innovation

The Internet has spawned thousands of new companies and changed the way many of us live. Many innovators have begun their own firms, both because of the freedom that provides and because of the extremely lucrative stock options that used to accompany jobs at Internet start-ups. It can be a challenge to execute the plans needed to make the innovation succeed; there are a number of start-ups in electronic commerce that have experienced difficulties in servicing their customers. Online stockbrokers have experienced downtime when customers could not trade—a potentially very costly problem if the market moves against the investor.

The traditional firm has more difficulty in encouraging innovation and changing direction. Merrill Lynch's transition to the Internet for instance, was slowed when powerful forces in the company opposed the move since it threatened the existing business model. Large, often bureaucratic, firms like Merrill Lynch often face competition from highly flexible start-ups that do not require approvals from endless committees to take action or invest funds.

When IBM started its PC division in 1981, it located the group in Florida, away from corporate headquarters in Westchester County, New York. Senior management at the time felt that the unit should be independent of existing interests in the firm, the dominant mainframe group. However, it turned out that the mainframe group had veto power over pricing decisions for personal computers! The mainframers did not want small computers to have too much advantage over mainframes in terms of price-performance ratio. As a result, IBM personal computers carried a price premium, and the company lost market share to Dell, Compaq, and others. By 1999, when IBM began to sell desktop PCs exclusively from its Web site, the division had reportedly lost one billion dollars in one year. (One advantage of the traditional firm is its ability to absorb these kinds of losses.)

One frequently used tactic to stimulate innovation is for the traditional firm to require innovators to work in a different physical location, just as IBM did with the PC. These "skunk works" have developed many new products without being burdened with the procedures of the rest of the company. Many organizations responding to the Internet have set up separate units. The former chairman of BankOne followed this strategy in setting up a completely electronic bank called Wingspan; the bank is free to compete with BankOne and is separate from it.

This approach probably makes sense for most traditional firms. However, if it becomes necessary to integrate the innovation back into the firm, problems can arise. R. R. Donnelley's first foray into digital printing failed; it began as a separate division, and existing divisions were very resistant to the kind of changes suggested. As long as Wingspan does not have to depend on BankOne, its management need not worry about integration. What about more closely coupled electronic commerce initiatives? Could Toys "R" Us build a wall between its electronic commerce activities and its physical stores? Did it make sense to have different ware-houses for each business? Do you want customers to be able to return electronically ordered merchandise to the physical store?

All of these issues confront the traditional firm as it tries to encourage innovation and move to electronic commerce. The best reason for freeing innovators from the normal constraints of the organization is "Internet time." The speed at which the Net has been adopted has exceeded all other examples of the diffusion of technology, including telephones, radio, and television. The Net and the new business it has stimulated move at a blistering pace. Traditional organizations are used to a more leisurely environment; to compete in the Internet economy, they must move faster than their procedures allow. The objective is to free innovators to inno-vate, provide them with resources, and then worry about integrating the results with the rest of the organization, if necessary.

Organizational Culture

All organizations have a culture. Some are very formal and rule-oriented; others are flexible and informal. What kind of culture facilitates the ex-ecution of strategies for the Internet and electronic commerce? Culture includes a variety of firm characteristics. I once worked at a very loosely organized consulting firm, where individual members of the firm were project leaders on one client engagement, and worked for other members of the firm on different projects. A consultant "working for you" on one project could be your supervisor on a different client engagement. Simi-lar to this consulting firm, descriptions of Internet start-up companies convey a picture of flexibility, lack of procedures, and minimum hierarchy.

One of the reasons for suggesting that the traditional firm might want to put its e-commerce group in a separate organization would be to create a flexible environment for its staff. The hierarchical firm is not well set up for team projects, and teams do much of the work in IT. The traditional manager is not comfortable in this environment with multiple teams, and overlapping memberships. The reporting relationships and layers of man-agement associated with a hierarchy are not the best structure for teamwork.

The purpose of the following section is to present an example of an organization with a culture conducive to implementing Internet-based strategies. A virtual organization offers many of the advantages that one finds with the highly flexible start-up firm.

The Virtual Organization
Our example of a virtual organization is VeriFone. Although now a subsidiary of Hewlett Packard (Garud and Lucas 1999), most of our story applies to the time when it was an independent company, that is, before HP acquired it.)

First, a definition:

A virtual organization is a type of network organization, distributed in time and space, which delegates decision rights to managers in different locations. The virtual firm uses information technology to facilitate relations with network partners and to coordinate temporary work groups.

History and Characteristics   William Melton founded VeriFone in 1981 to provide a simple check-verification system; the company's products soon expanded to include credit card verification. In 1986, Hatim Tyabji joined VeriFone from Sperry to take command of a poorly performing company. Tyabji believed in a flexible organization structure and in the importance of being close to customers to provide a fast response to their needs (Galal et al. 1995). The early history of VeriFone is described as consisting of "[f]ive people in four locations with almost no capital who grew a four hundred million dollar business world-wide." VeriFone faced strong competitors in its first days in the form of AT&T, GTE, Northern Telecom, and Mitsubishi, to name a few.

VeriFone's mission is "to create and lead the transaction automation industry worldwide." In 1996, the company's products processed an estimated 65–70 percent of credit card transactions in the world. Much of the business is in custom software that runs in the verification "boxes" and on other parts of the transactions network. VeriFone offers over one thousand six hundred programs that run on its verification devices. The firm has also formed alliances to verify and process payments on the

Internet, including agreements with Netscape, Discover, and several banks.

From Organization to Organizing   VeriFone has an ongoing structure similar to most organizations. What makes VeriFone unique, however, is the constant organizing that occurs within this structure and is accomplished through cross-functional teams. An employee participant of one of these teams stated: "If you feel passionate about something that needs to be changed at VeriFone, you can give reasons why it's not working or you can form a team and produce results" (Galal et al. 1995).

Any employee at VeriFone can form a task force to address a problem. The team makes a presentation to senior management. Blue collar workers have presented solutions to the CEO.

There are three types of teams at VeriFone:

• Ad hoc teams form frequently by themselves; often these teams employ teleconferencing systems and members never see each other.

• Formal teams employ leaders who have been through training (at VeriFone University online, or at a learning center.) The team may work short-or long-term, but it knows the assignment and its duration.

• Subunit or functional teams, such as a group of engineers trying to solve a particular problem, can be local or global.

The Asia-Pacific regional technical director described project teams that organize and disband on a routine basis. These teams tend to form into a matrix structure with one development manager responsible for up to ten products.

The picture is of teams that come into and go out of existence regularly. They are virtual in the sense that they span different organizations and members may be in different locations. The constant formation, activity, and deactivation of teams is the mechanism through which VeriFone organizes itself. The formal organization structure is static while virtual teams create a dynamic, constantly changing organization.

In addition to teams within the firm, VeriFone forms alliances with other organizations. A virtual team might span organizational boundaries. In its early days, VeriFone tried to handle only core activities and outsourced all others. Today, the company has a number of alliances.

Although organizing is a key activity at VeriFone, there is a conventional organization chart that shows reporting relationships and titles. The organization, before its acquisition by HP, was relatively flat; eight managers reported directly to the chairman while six reported to; the executive vice-president. Tyabji's corporate model is a decentralized network of locations; he refers to this structure as the "blueberry pancake": "All berries are the same size; all locations are created equal" (Galal et al. 1995). His least favorite location is corporate headquarters, and, regardless of formal structure, an employee can access any other employee directly through e-mail.

The focus at Verifone is clearly not on hierarchy and status. Rather, VeriFone defines the right organization structure as one that locates employees near customers so that they continually put the customer first. The idea is that a customer residing in a country using VeriFone products can meet with a design engineer located in the that country, and that the design engineer can make changes in the product without approval from any place else. Employees who understand local culture and customer needs are able to provide better service.

VeriFone establishes locations to take advantage of local expertise. It has a smart card R&D effort in France, which is the center of smart card activities, and a programming operation in Bangalore, where there is a large number of skilled and educated programmers. One has to constantly consider what responsibilities should be vested in local units and what decisions should be centralized. There is a "dynamic tension" between maintaining control of the company, and avoiding having headquarters dictate to local managers.

VeriFone's dynamic, organizing structure did not arise from an organization chart. What allows it to function successfully with this nontraditional approach? The answer to this question lies in the unique management culture and norms that encourage organizing activities outside the company's formal structure.

Management Culture and Norms   Two of the key characteristics of VeriFone that emerged from discussions with its employees are "fast response" and "a culture of urgency." Compared to his past jobs, the regional technical director for the Asia-Pacific region called VeriFone ". . . one hell of a place," with a "dynamic and urgent culture." It is a "face-paced life," which stresses rapid response to customers. As one employee described it, there is "never time to rejoice" after finishing a project because there is always something else to do. Lack of an organizational hierarchy makes it easier to respond quickly.

A manager who joined VeriFone from AT&T saw a new marketing program for smaller retailers develop over the VeriFone network in less than a week. By the end of the quarter, the plan had resulted in $2.7 million in new sales. The executive commented that it would have taken at least three months to come up with a similar program at any of the previous, traditionally organized companies where he had worked.

VeriFone believes that one of its main strengths is a determined focus on the customer. Managers feel that leadership comes from setting an example rather than by telling employees what to do. VeriFone's mission statement is published in the language of every country in which its employees work. The company also prepares a series of "Excellence in Action" and "Excellence in Thought" notes to communicate its philosophy to the workforce. To Tyabji, the philosophy and notes form the basic blueprint for a successful company.

Because of geographic decentralization and the existence of many virtual teams, an employee is often on his or her own; it is not unusual to be located in Atlanta and to report to a supervisor in Paris. VeriFone counts on individual initiative to achieve its goals. An Internet engineer may come up with an idea unrelated to his current assignment. He should suggest this idea to others, and he may or may not be charged with following up on his initiative. VeriFone, according to its stated corporate philosophy, believes that those who perform a job know best how it should be done. It strives to involve employees in the management of their own areas of work. There is a three-year rolling strategic plan while a calendar year plan drives work assignments.

It is clear that this culture involves mutual trust. Employees trust the company to support their actions and to encourage experimentation. VeriFone trusts its employees to take initiative and act in the best interest of the company. VeriFone tries to maintain this culture with a minimum of rules.

Geographic decentralization, decentralized decision making, virtual teams, fast response, and trust place a tremendous demand on the organization to process information and make it widely available. How does VeriFone use technology to facilitate information processing?

Information and Knowledge Sharing   Communications is a key activity at VeriFone. A corporate philosophy of distributing power to the lowest level of the organization possible reduces the amount of communications required to operate. At the same time, the global nature of VeriFone's operations creates significant demands for communications, especially for virtual project teams. Managers communicate through e-mail; there are no secretaries to print messages or enter responses. Executives in different countries might work together on the same spreadsheet in preparing a proposal. These executives can access information on bookings, shippings, and revenues from an online database with worldwide availability.

The company employs over thirty different tools for communications. Travel, face-to-face meetings, and task forces are all communications mechanisms. Frequently task forces work "around the world" with conference calls scheduled so that members take turn at getting up at 2:00 A.M. to participate. The Asia-Pacific regional technical director said that you get used to getting telephone calls in the middle of the night. To avoid overload, an effort is made to keep messages short and not bombard recipients with e-mail.

Although a virtual firm, VeriFone stresses the need for employees to interact physically on a regular basis. Large rooms in local offices facilitate group gatherings, and the firm has annual meetings of different employees who work in similar functions. Every six to eight weeks, the senior management team gets together for a meeting in a different part of the world. The manager of Support, who works out of Bangalore, visits San Francisco five to six times a year to meet with his staff there and understand their problems better. Once a year, all professional services heads meet for a week to discuss the service function. Senior managers feel it is important for employees to know each other so they can use information technology like e-mail to communicate effectively.

The cost of face-to-face communications is constant travel; Tyabji reported traveling over four hundred thousand miles in a year when he was chairman. About one-third of the company's employees are on the road at any one time, leading to an annual expenditure of over five million dollars on hotels and airfare (Galal et al. 1995).—a fact which suggests that the virtual organization does not necessarily want to substitute electronic for physical interaction completely; but rather that electronic and face-to-face (FTF) communications complement each other. At VeriFone, occasional face-to-face communications enables more regular and routine electronic communications with the advantage of reducing the constraints of time and place on interaction.

In addition to communications mechanisms, VeriFone believes in sharing information. The CIO prepares a daily "flash" report that goes to three hundred VeriFone employees daily. The report is a method for evaluating progress. Recipients can easily access the data behind the interpretation so they are not dependent on one person's view of performance. The role of the CIO is to provide information and interpretation, not just data. He is the "navigator" who keeps senior management informed on a daily basis about whether the firm is on course or not.

Plans are posted throughout the company (including restroom stalls) and employees are encouraged to add comments to them. Each quarter the company sends a video of amateur footage from various offices and countries to employees' homes. The firm provides so much information that it once registered more than 10 percent of its employees as "insiders" with the Federal Trade Commission. Employees' children are encouraged to communicate with their counterparts in other countries via e-mail.

VeriFone also shares information and knowledge with its customers and alliance partners. Before e-mail became easily available through service providers, VeriFone had suppliers and alliance partners on its own e-mail system. Today, VeriFone provides videoconferencing equipment for these firms. Before going public, when it had to be concerned about releasing information, VeriFone shared its daily flash report with some partners.

VeriFone uses "appropriate technology," not the newest equipment. It spends about 60 percent as much as comparable electronics firms on information technology. It does not try to be a leader with new technology, utilizing installed equipment until the end of its life cycle. Current technology efforts include the development of an Intranet to facilitate information sharing. The responsibility for providing content on the Internet is distributed; for example, a new product group creates and maintains pages for its product.

Self-Governance   For a VeriFone employee, the company's organizing character, management culture and norms, and information sharing result in self-governance. The employee may not have extensive physical contact with a supervisor. She is encouraged to take the initiative in coming up with new ideas for improving VeriFone, its products and service. She will communicate using a variety of media with customers, alliance partners, and other VeriFone employees. She may start a virtual, cross-functional team and be a member of several others. Her major focus will be on responsiveness and fast response to conditions in her local environment. A development group in Bangalore conceived of a new product called Omnihost and created it. This software routes payments between banks and vendors. The idea came from within the development group, not as a request from sales or marketing.

Information technology means that an employee is not constrained to local solutions; VeriFone is able to marshal its global resources to solve local problems. An example helps to illustrate this ability. Based on a VeriFone competitor's statements, a customer told a sales representative in Greece that VeriFone lacked a certain product. The sales rep sent a single e-mail to "ISales," which reached all sales reps worldwide, asking whether VeriFone had a product for this customer. A sales manager in San Francisco took on the task of heading this virtual task force. He collated one hundred-replies and constructed a Powerpoint presentation for the sales rep in Greece (while the rep slept). The sales manager had the presentation translated to Greek, and the sales rep took it to his client the next day. VeriFone won the account.

A combination of management structure, culture, and technology provide the opportunity for a virtual organization like VeriFone to manage through self-governance. At the same time, the technology makes it possible to bring the global resources of the firm to bear on local (or global) problems wherever they arise.

Summary   VeriFone's original operations provide many interesting insights on the design of virtual organizations. Information technologies serve as the backbone of such an organization form. Just as automation changed the bases of industrial production, information technologies are once again changing the nature of economic activities. In such an environment, temporally and spatially decoupled economic and social agents can connect and disconnect in fluid ways.

The term *virtual* has many other meanings, including transience, fluidity, immediacy, and extensibility. At VeriFone, one idealized mode of operation in a virtual organization is to form temporary teams incorporating various social and economic agents. These agents need not be within the administrative boundaries of a single firm, nor do they need to be in geographic proximity. Moreover, connected by information technologies, distributed economic and social agents can work in parallel.

VeriFone demonstrates characteristics that may be applicable to others. A virtual firm is constantly organizing itself through teams and alliances. Management trusts employees and encourages them to take initiative. There is a pervasive culture of urgency and fast response combined with a focus on responding to local conditions. Information technology enables the employees to communicate and react quickly. Face-to-face communications occurs "off-line," through meetings and visits; it does not become a barrier to a rapid response. Employees exercise significant self-governance, but have the ability to tap into the resources of a global firm.

The idea of local responsiveness and presence combined with the ability to use information technology to perform global searches to solve problems provides the virtual organization with a significant advantage. The example of the Greek sales rep who had a local problem but could benefit from a global solution illustrates this capability. More than technology is required to hold such a system together. As in the case of VeriFone, it requires a culture where trust among the various constituent elements is the norm rather than the exception. In the mass production world of traditional organizations, trust implies compliance at best—compliance to a set of instructions that has been generated by a manager. However, in a virtual setting, where the boundaries and nature of work are continually changing, trust as compliance is largely ineffective. Instead, the social dimensions of trust require initiative and responsiveness.

It remains to be seen if the advantages of the virtual organization are compelling enough to motivate managers to make the changes necessary in norms, culture, information technology, and organization structure to convert traditional organizations to this new form. As a postscript, Tyabji retired from VeriFone in 1999 after serving as chairman during its first years as an HP subsidiary. The latest comments from VeriFone suggest that the company is being more fully integrated into the HP structure, and that some of its "virtualness" will not survive the integration. In the fourth quarter of 2000, HP announced that VeriFone had a forty-eight million dollars loss, and there was speculation that the subsidiary was for sale. It is interesting to contrast this performance with VeriFone's results as an independent, fully virtual company.

Decision Making at High Velocity

One of the characteristics of the Internet economy that confronts both the start-up and the traditional firm is the pace of decision making. Earlier, this chapter stressed the advantages of having a modern technological infrastructure in place, given that there is not enough time to rebuild the infrastructure if that is what is required for the firm to gain a foothold in electronic commerce.

In addition to an IT infrastructure, the firm must be able to execute decisions quickly and effectively. In this respect, I favor the virtual firm over the hierarchical organization. The virtual firm allows a local decision maker to commit the organization; she does not have to wait for approval from managers in the hierarchy above. Trust is a significant part of such an organization, and, thus, senior management is able to delegate decisions to the level at which they can best be made. Generally, this level is decentralized, and a local manager makes the decision.

A study of decision making in the microcomputer industry by Eisenhardt (1989) provides insights on such "high-velocity" decisions. This study found that, contrary to popular belief, fast decision makers use more rather than less information than do slow decision makers. Somehow, those making rapid decisions had the ability to absorb and process more information than their slower counterparts. The fast decision makers tended to use real-time information on the competitive environment and operations rather than forecasts of future events. Fast strategic decision makers looked at quantitative indicators like daily and weekly tracking of bookings, cash flow, engineering milestones, and competitors' moves. They preferred these operating statistics to accounting data like profits.

Eisenhardt believes that using real-time data speeds the identification of issues, making it easier to spot problems and opportunities. These data may help executives sharpen their intuition and develop insights into how their company functions. Chapter 1 introduced the notion of causal ambiguity, the difficulty of understanding cause-and-effect relationships in business. Real-time data helps managers develop hypotheses about causal relationships, and sets the stage for strategic decision making. Forecasts and planning information, in contrast, do not seem to provide an intimate knowledge of the business.

Fast decision makers are able to consider multiple alternatives at the same time. These managers want the opportunity to consider multiple choices; they do not spend time debating a single alternative, only to reject it and then move on to another choice. With multiple alternatives, people tend not to become committed too early to a single choice; decision makers also have alternatives to fall back on when they reject one or two choices.

An experienced counselor often plays an important role for the fast decision makers; he provides advice that helps the decision makers understand their choices. The counselor is a sounding board for ideas, and tends to be a respected, long-term employee of the firm. The decision makers could be very open with these individuals, and the counselors, in turn, felt safe offering advice and opinions.

Overall, the results of the study failed to support the idea that centralized power is associated with fast decision making. Centralization leads to procrastination and delay, and often to an information-restrictive, highly political culture. Fast teams also were able to deal with conflict within the team; conflict did not prove disruptive.

Although the study involved multiple cases making generalization difficult, the results support the observation that faster decision making is associated with better performance in high velocity environments. The argument for a virtual organization and project teams is based upon a belief that the flexibility they provide contributes to performance when speed is important. The flexibility of Internet start-ups provides some evidence to support this view. The challenge for the traditional company is to develop a culture and decision-making routines so that it can compete in the high velocity environment of Internet time.

The Role of the Leader

The role of the leader or senior manager is hotly debated in the management literature. In the case of VeriFone, one observer suggested that the organization was a mirror of Tyabji; his strong views were reflected throughout the firm. Whether employees felt this was true is unclear. Our research left no doubts that he was a forceful leader, and it may well be that organizations do better with strong leadership.

Being a strong leader is not synonymous with being a dictator or being mean-spirited. A strong leader provides guidance and leadership; he or she is skilled at monitoring progress and executing strategy. The effective leader may have good ideas, but she also recognizes good ideas from others and provides the support needed to take advantage of them. It is not so much that the senior manager has to come up with a strategy, but rather, as Henry Mintzberg has suggested, she must recognize strategies and opportunities as they arise and take advantage of them.

The story is told that Thomas Watson became convinced that the computer had a future in business early after the first computers appeared in research laboratories. Managers at IBM, a well-performing office products and typewriter company, were not so sure. Watson campaigned to get IBM into the computer business, a leadership move that changed the fortunes of the company and kept it competitive. As enthusiasm for mainframe computers declined, Louis Gerstner, a nontechnical manager, became convinced that electronic commerce was the wave of the future. He has successfully turned IBM into an e-commerce company.

The dramatic changes in direction and fortune of IBM are due to the leadership of two different chairmen at two very different points in history. Leaders can make a difference, and both the start-up and the traditional firm need to consider leadership carefully as a part of their strategies.

Summary

To be successful, the organization has to choose an appropriate strategy for e-commerce and the Internet, and then execute it. The nature of the organization has a significant influence on the ability of the firm to execute such a strategy. The firm needs an appropriate technological infrastructure. It also needs an organizational culture that encourages innovation and risk-taking. One kind of organization that provides this kind of culture is the virtual organization, which encourages individual initiative through decentralized decision making and employee teams and is constantly organizing so that it can adapt to the hypercompetitive Internet economy.

II

Internet Strategies for Mostly Traditional Firms

Most managers work for traditional firms, not dot.com companies or start-ups. Traditional firms face a tremendous challenge in adapting their business models and strategies to the Internet and electronic commerce. Not only do managers have to come up with new models, they must generate enthusiasm for changing the traditional model that has served the firm well for years.

Part II of the book features four chapters devoted to examples and includes an analysis of the strategies of traditional companies. The analysis uses the dynamic, resource-based strategy model from chapter 1 to compare and contrast firms. Some of these organizations appear to have made a successful transition to becoming "Net companies" while others have yet to figure out a successful business model or strategy for the Internet.

Chapter 4 presents examples of companies that have added resources to their original set of strategic resources, as suggested by the model in figure 1.1. All these firms' resources combined to form a system, and from this system emerged new assets and resources that helped the firms sustain a competitive advantage. For two of the key examples, airline computerized-reservations systems and the Port of Singapore, the Internet was not a major factor. However, the experiences of these organizations with information technology provide evidence to support the strategy model in chapter 1 and show the impact of adding resources to those that provide an initial competitive advantage.

In chapter 5, we look at manufacturing firms that have been successful at integrating the Web and the Internet into their operations. Both Dell and Cisco have invented very successful business models. A resource-based review of their strategies helps us understand how these new manufacturing models work.

New business models in the services industry are the subject of chapter 6. Here, the dynamic strategy model is used to highlight a struggle between two firms and their business models. Schwab is a brokerage firm that developed an early understanding of the Internet and its potential. Merrill Lynch, the largest U.S. brokerage firm, on the other hand, stayed with its traditional business model until, 1999, when it was forced by the success of electronic trading to undertake a searching reexamination of its approach to business. Right now, the company is a study of the transition to a new business model, a model that impacts its entire philosophy as a brokerage firm.

In chapter 7, we look at strategies for moving a traditional firm to a business model that embraces the Internet. The chapter covers some of the arguments offered for why the Internet and electronic commerce do not apply to a particular business, and offers ways to counter these arguments. We also look at two examples of firms that have radically restructured themselves to do business solely on the Internet.

4

Adding Resources to Sustain an Advantage

According to the dynamic resource-based model of competitive advantage, a firm needs resources that are rare, valuable, inimitable, and nonsubstitutable in order to obtain a competitive advantage. It turns out to be very difficult to find resources that fit all of these criteria. If an organization does have a basis for an advantage from its unique resources, the advantage may depend on network externalities and the development of critical mass. An advantage could require or be enhanced by the presence of other assets that are complementary, specialized, or cospecialized. The original resource-based view suggests that the firm will be able to sustain its advantage because competitors cannot create the same unique bundle of resources.

However, the characteristics of a firm's resources can change over time; that is, a resource that was valuable can lose some of its value. The resources that traditional steel mills have in blast furnaces and production facilities have, for example, become less valuable with the advent of the minimill, which makes steel at a much lower cost, using a completely different production process. The model in figure 1.1 is dynamic because it recognizes that the characteristics of resources change over time, and that a resource bundle that once provided a competitive advantage may not always do so.

How, then, does the firm sustain a resource-based advantage? The model suggests that the organization, once it has obtained an initial advantage, must continue to invest in building additional resources that keep its bundle of resources rare, valuable, inimitable, and nonsubstitutable in the face of competition. In particular, the firm would like to reach a position in which the various resources in a bundle interact and reinforce the characteristics that provided an advantage in the first place.

Microsoft has a tremendous resource in its operating systems that are used on IBM compatible computers. That resource provides a constant stream of income that the company can use to build on its original operating system resource. Microsoft Office is a product that integrates with Windows 98, NT, and 2000; Office and the operating systems are co-specialized assets. Each brings in significant revenue that is used to enhance the product, creating an even more formidable bundle of resources for sustaining an advantage.

We should distinguish between physical and knowledge-based resources. Most people are familiar with physical resources—things like capital, a state-of-the-art manufacturing facility, and other resources that can be touched. Knowledge and skills are another type of resource. Superior knowledge may confer a competitive advantage, given that it can be rare, valuable, inimitable, and nonsubstitutable. Intel, for example, considers the knowledge of how to build and operate a large chip fabrication plant a competitive advantage. In many of the examples in this and succeeding chapters, we will see different types of knowledge that serve as resources for the organizations that possess them. We will also see how a firm may be able to keep hard-won knowledge proprietary despite the mobility of its employees.

We will examine three organizations in some depth, each of which has first used resources to gain an initial advantage and then used additional resources to enhance and strengthen the bundle of resources that provided an advantage in the first place. The three organizations are American Airlines, the Port of Singapore Authority, and Amazon.com. (Although Amazon is obviously not a traditional firm, it is included in this section because it has continually added resources to its business.)

American Airlines

The airline industry provides a unique opportunity to examine a resource-based competitive advantage attained by appropriating a variety of benefits from a technological innovation. The bulk of these innovations occurred before the Internet, but the examples illustrate the model in figure 1.1 well. The Internet also presents computerized reservations system (CRS) vendors with new challenges and opportunities.

The Early Days of Airline CRSs

American Airlines developed the first airline computerized reservations system in order to prevent an uncontrolled escalation in costs that would have resulted if forced to use a manual reservations system when jet travel began (Copeland and McKenney 1988). The company chose to solve its reservations problems by applying financial, human, and knowledge resources to develop a new technology; it began to move along a path that provided major benefits at each step.

After the initial investment, the Sabre system became a technological resource for American that was valuable and rare (Barney 1991). Unfortunately, however, it was imitable and eventually substitutable. American's CRS had extremely *weak value appropriability* and a group of other airlines, including United, quickly imitated it. Later, IBM offered any airline a packaged system called "PARS", which was based on its joint work with American in developing the SABRE system. The challenge was clear: How could American and other CRS developers both create and sustain an advantage from their reservations systems and appropriate high levels of business value in the process? The reservations systems were a resource, but they were imitable and substitutable at this point in time.

Acquiring a Cospecialized Asset

One way for the CRS developer to protect its innovation, to make it more difficult for competitors to imitate or substitute for its CRS resource, was to offer the system to a select group of travel agents and lock-in this distribution channel. Through this strategy, the CRS vendor "acquired" a cospecialized asset, which it denied to competing CRS vendors, thus making its reservation system less imitable and less substitutable.

The airlines also created very high switching costs so that, once acquired, the travel agent could not easily move to another vendor. Five-year service contracts that were extended for another five years each time new equipment was installed were not unusual, and liquidated damages clauses in the CRS contracts made it very expensive for a travel agency to switch CRS vendors. The CRS vendors also came to recognize the channel power they could affect by developing markets that were biased in their favor, for example, by listing their flights first on the reservations screens (Copeland and McKenney 1988).

Thus, as an airline CRS vendor acquired more and more travel agencies, the travel agencies helped to make its reservations system more valuable and less imitable and substitutable. The agencies that signed up with American were no longer available for a competing carrier because at the time the airlines did not allow more than one CRS per agency. The general counsel of Eastern Airlines complained to me in a phone conversation that the other CRS vendors had "signed up all the good agencies," leaving Eastern with small, low-volume agents. What kind of agent would interest an airline the most? American and United sought large agents with a high volume of tickets. They were happy to leave the small tourist-oriented agency for their competitors.

Expanding the system to travel agents also created economies of scope through the inclusion of more capabilities in the system; the capabilities came to include those that are common in most industry global distribution systems today. These capabilities include the ability to reserve rental cars and hotel rooms. As airlines with CRSs invested more resources in the technology, the CRS system itself became a highly specialized asset that an airline needed as a platform to offer further innovative travel services. This continued path of development and enhancements helped the CRS resource become more rare, valuable, and difficult to imitate or substitute for, and these characteristics turned the reservations system into a resource for competitive advantage. Reflecting the value in the marketplace that was being contested, the competition among CRS vendors and nonvendor airlines has been intense and at times even bitter; there have been many lawsuits and appeals for regulation during the history of these systems.

In 1976, United and American Airlines began installing terminals, which were connected to the airlines' CRSs, in travel agents' offices (Copeland and McKenney 1988). Several other airlines quickly imitated this tactic. Some observers argue that CRS vendor airlines installed terminals at travel agencies to protect their innovations and to keep competitors from imitating them. The CRS vendors received immediate benefits from booking fees and charges to travel agents. And, if the various lawsuits and legislative directives of the early 1980s are any indication, the vendors also obtained other unpredicted but highly valuable benefits through the biased markets made possible with their CRSs. As a result, the airlines strengthened their *appropriability regime* (i.e., their ability to appropriate the benefits of technological innovation) through their influence on travel agencies (the cospecialized assets, in this instance), while turning their reservations systems into highly specialized resources for further travel-related innovation. These CRS vendor airlines followed a unique path in applying their resources; once the majority of travel agents had chosen a CRS vendor, another airline would have great difficulty following the same path to obtain or equalize the competitive advantage of the first-movers (Barney 1991, Mata, Fuerst, and Barney 1995).

Many of the benefits described above are enjoyed by all airlines whose flights are listed in a CRS. What are the benefits to the *owner* of a system? The economics literature on externalities suggests that the value of a network increases as the number of its locations increases. How might benefits accrue to a CRS vendor as its number of agency locations reaches a critical mass? One example is extra bookings due to screen bias for the vendor with a large installed base of terminals. Until it was eliminated by government regulation in 1984, CRS vendors routinely listed their own flights first on the reservations display. Copeland and McKenney (1988) report that by 1983 over 70 percent of flights were booked from the first screen and more recent estimates put this number at 90 percent to 95 percent. Screen bias favored the CRS host airline that displayed its flights first. Even though rules by the Civil Aeronautics Board (CAB) and later by the Department of Transportation (DOT) attempted to eliminate screen bias, non-CRS vendors have continued to assert that subtle biases in systems favor CRS vendors.

Analysis

Table 4.1 presents an analysis of the airline CRS industry using the dynamic resource-based model of figure 1.1. The table shows that American obtained its initial advantage with the Sabre CRS and the technical and managerial skills it developed building the system. However, while these

Table 4.1
CRS Resource Analysis

Resource	Rare	Valuable	Inimitable	Nonsubstitutable	Other Model Components
Initial Advantage					
Sabre system	Yes	Yes	No	No	
IT skills	Yes	Yes	No	No (use consultants)	
IT management	Yes	Yes	No	No	
Knowledge of CRS	Yes	Yes	Gradual	Gradual	
Additional Resources					
Agencies automated	No	Yes	Partially	Partially	Agencies a cospecialized asset; critical mass, network externalities, lock-in
Continued investment	Yes	Yes	No	No	Built CRS into more valuable asset—harder to duplicate
Extended features to create a travel supermarket	Yes	Yes	Partially	Yes, harder to find substitute	Features made CRS harder to duplicate
Interactions					
CRS ↔ agencies	No	Yes	Gradual	Gradual	Cospecialized assets grew in value
CRS ↔ revenue, investment	Yes	Yes	Gradual	Gradual	
Decision support → revenue	Yes	Yes	Possibly	Possibly	
CRS ↔ Internet	Yes	Yes	No	No	New technology challenges existing resource base

skills were rare and valuable, they were largely imitable and substitutable. The CRS served an important role as an operating system for American, but other airlines had similar systems and Sabre did not offer a competitive advantage over airlines that had access to a CRS.

Sabre added to these initial resources to gain a sustainable advantage through agency automation. American as a CRS vendor obtained significant revenues in the form of booking fees. A study we conducted also suggests that the CRS helped increase American's market share (Duliba, Kauffman, and Lucas; forthcoming 2001). These revenues helped American invest more in building up its CRS. The enhanced CRS became a more valuable resource, and one more difficult to imitate or substitute for. *Resources may be built over time; they do not always start out conferring a competitive advantage.* In the case of American (and, to some extent, United), continued investment in and enhancements to a CRS created a system that was rare, valuable, inimitable, and nonsubstitutable. Why the latter two characteristics? As Sabre became more complex, the knowledge and investment needed to replicate it became a significant barrier to entry. Some statistics indicate the capabilities of the Sabre resource:

• Sabre books over seventy billion dollars in travel annually.

• It makes four hundred million reservations annually, 40 percent of the world's total.

• The average reservation takes less than three seconds to make.

• The system is connected to 210,000 terminals worldwide and to 42,000 travel agents.

• It processes 270 million messages a day with a peak of 7500 per second.

• The system can make reservations with 440 airlines, 45,000 hotels and 50 rental car agencies.

As Sabre has grown, it has collected a rich set of data for further analysis. American used Sabre's database to create sophisticated yield management systems. These systems provide decision support to a group of yield management analysts who decide how many seats to make available in what fare classes on each flight. The objective is to maximize the revenue or "yield" on each flight. If there are a large number of empty coach seats compared to historical data for a flight, yield management software increases the number of discount fares in order to fill the plane.

In addition to yield management, American uses Sabre's data to try to optimize its flight network, a complex problem involving a number of aircraft fleets and routes. To evaluate yield management and network scheduling for senior management, Sabre Decision Technologies wrote several simulation programs. The results indicate that, instead of being profitable in the ten-year period up until 1999, American would have had losses in every year but 1998 had it not been for these two systems. In other words, the revenue created through yield management and network scheduling is responsible for American's profits for nine years out of ten!

There are a number of interactions among American's system of resources. The CRS made it possible to obtain benefits from agency automation, and the revenue from agencies helped to provide investment funds for American to spend on Sabre. Agency automation also required the airline to expand the features of the system, making it attractive to more agencies and generating more revenue from them. The rich database in Sabre facilitated the creation of yield management and network scheduling programs, contributing further revenue for investment. This is one example of interactions of a system of resources.

Summary

To obtain benefits from Sabre required strong management leadership. Even though American Airlines was healthy, its decision to undertake the Sabre system was difficult and risky, as Max Hopper, then senior vice-president of American Airlines, pointed out:[1]

The initial investment in development costs was $40 million. . . . the figure was equivalent to the cost of four Boeing 707s, which was the largest plane flying in those days . . . If we had bought aircraft instead, it would have been a 20 percent increase in the existing jet fleet. So, diverting our capital from jets to exotic technology . . . was a very major commitment and a significant financial risk for us as a company.

This comment is consistent with the view of Mata, Fuerst, and Barney (1995) that only IT management skills meet the requirements for obtaining a resource-based advantage. However, other paths to a resource-based advantage exist, for example, appropriating cospecialized assets and leveraging network externalities and critical mass in the marketplace so that competitors are at a disadvantage.

American obtained direct benefits in the form of travel agent charges and booking fees, and other market share benefits. The airlines also turned their CRSs into highly successful specialized assets by investing more resources in them. CRS platforms became travel "supermarkets" that were valuable, rare, imperfectly imitable, and, to a great extent, nonsubstitutable resources. It would indeed be difficult for an imitator today to create the specialized asset of a Sabre reservations system on which to offer more travel-related services. The path that the first-movers in CRS agency automation followed in applying resources to technology is no longer available to others. The value of the CRS specialized asset became clear in August 1996 when American turned Sabre into a subsidiary and sold part of it to the public. The overall market value of American Airlines at that time was $6.2 billion and the initial public offering of SABRE valued the subsidiary at about $3 billion, nearly half of the airline's market value. In late 1999, American announced plans to spin off its remaining stock in Sabre Decision Technologies to its shareholders; at that time, Sabre was valued at over $6 billion. In 2001, Sabre Decision Technologies signed an outsourcing agreement with EDS to take over the operation of much of its technology and systems.

The Internet: A New Business Model?

Sabre Decision Technologies faces a major challenge with the rise of Internet travel agents. It is estimated that U.S. airline customers booked seven billion dollars of travel on the Internet in 1999, or about 3 percent of all travel purchased, up from $2.6 in 1998 (*Wall Street Journal*, January 19, 2000). One estimate is that this total will reach $20 billion or 8 percent of total travel in 2001. Travelocity is one of the most successful of the Internet travel sites; it is "powered by Sabre." One of the reasons that American wanted to spin off Sabre is the competition that exists between Travelocity and American's own travel site where only American flights are listed. The Internet presents a new channel for making travel reservations. Sabre saw this challenge and invested in technology to become one of the early Internet travel sites. Sabre added major resources to its existing system to build the Travelocity site and to become a service provider for a number of airline travel sites.

A Sabre is free of its association with American should be able to gain business from other airlines that might be reluctant to deal with a competitor. With no reporting relationship to American, Sabre will respond more quickly to the marketplace, especially the changing channels for distribution stimulated by the Internet. Airlines that are not CRS vendors (which includes American now) have invested one hundred million dollars to create a shared Internet site because customers resist going to sites that only provide reservations for one airline. The twenty-three carriers that are joining forces hope to avoid paying fees to CRS vendors like Sabre or Web sites like Travelocity and Expedia (*Wall Street Journal*, April 11, 2000).

The fact remains that American has now spun off one of its most valuable systems of resources—its prized reservation system—a move motivated in part by changing technology. American's stockholders gain as they now will own a significant part of the Sabre system, and Sabre will have no restrictions on its ability to compete in the marketplace. However, will American be as well-off? Sabre, after all, has been a mainstay of its operations since 1962—almost forty years. When American's former combative chairman, Robert Crandall, testified in Congress about the role of reservations systems, he commented that if the government forced him to sell something, he might just keep the reservations system and sell the airline!

The development of strategic resources that provide a competitive advantage is dependent on a path that cannot be easily duplicated; an advantage does not last forever, however, and characteristics of resources change over time.

The Port of Singapore Authority

Singapore's most important natural resources include its large, protected harbor, its location on major trade routes, and the skills of its well-educated workforce. The location advantage is clear in figure 4.1, which

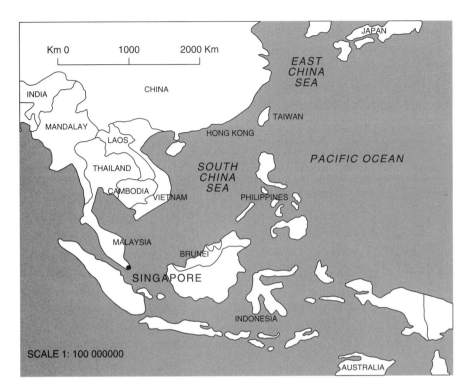

Figure 4.1
Singapore's Locational Advantage

has been taken from the Singapore Web site. Note that Singapore is located where ship traffic between Europe and Southeast Asia and the U.S. West Coast and Southeast Asia must pass; it is a natural entry for products shipped to and from neighboring countries.

A port, requires massive infrastructure development including berths, cranes, trucks, storage and warehousing, anchorages, tugboats, and pilot launches, particularly after shipping becomes containerized. Early in its history, Singapore opened its economy to foreign investment. As its economy grew, it allocated significant amounts of capital to developing its port:

On 1 April 1964, the Port of Singapore Authority (PSA) was formed to take over the functions, assets and liabilities of the Singapore Harbour Board. At that time, its facilities were confined to some five kilometres of wharves and 160,000 square metres of transit sheds and warehouses at Telok Ayer and Keppel Harbour. The main type of cargo then handled was break-bulk general cargo, with small volumes of bulk vegetable oil and latex.

The most significant port development took place on 23 June 1972, when a container berth was opened at Tanjong Pagar (at the East Lagoon). With that, Singapore became the first port in Southeast Asia to accommodate a third generation container vessel, making it an important link in the new chain of global container ports.

The 1997 Annual Report reviews the development of the modern port; the portion since developing container facilities is the most significant:

The Beginning of Containerisation:
PSA boldly proceeded to design and construct a container terminal in the late 1960s. The first 300-metre berth was completed in 1972, and the first container vessel, "m.v. Nihon," arrived in June that year. Productivity took a quantum leap. With goods packed in metal containers and handled by quay cranes, 53 tonnes of cargo per man hour were handled, representing a 136-fold increase in productivity when compared to the days before 1972.

Tanjong Pagar Terminal (TPT) ended the landmark year of 1972 by handling 24,515 TEUs,[2] using two quay cranes. For the next ten years, an average of 100,000 TEUs were added to PSA's container volume every year. The additional volume had to be accommodated by building new capacity—berths were progressively added to TPT. By 1981, another milestone was reached, with TPT celebrating the record of its first million TEUs within a year.

Container Transhipment Hub Port
As significant as PSA's achievements in the 1970s were, they were surpassed by the meteoric growth which characterised the 1980s—the result of the pioneering of the hub-and-spoke container shipping concept in the region. By investing in massive berth facilities and sophisticated equipment and computer systems, PSA began to attract large container ships on global trade routes. From the mega-carriers, large numbers of containers were discharged on each call at PSA, for distribution to the region, while large numbers of containers, which had arrived from regional countries for consolidation at PSA, were also loaded on the same call. PSA had become the container transhipment hub port of the region. Such a wide network of connections has enhanced PSA's value as a hub port for container transhipment, and has been made possible because of the support of the global ocean carriers and the common-user feeder operators serving the region. The network of feeder services ensures cost-effective, reliable and frequent services for mainline operators, ultimately benefiting the entire logistics chain in the region.

As the 1980s progressed, container volume poured in. From one million TEUs in 1981, our volume grew quickly to 4.36 million TEUs by 1989. By then, our value-added per employee had increased 13 percent per annum from $39,056 in 1980 to $116,613. PSA once again determined to innovate and improve in order to stay at the forefront of the industry, in the face of greater demands on its container-handling capacity. The conventional wharves at Keppel Terminal were converted into container berths on a large scale. The unprecedented volume also increased the scale and complexity of operations so tremendously that manual terminal operations were no longer possible. PSA adapted to the changing situation by taking another major step: introducing computer systems linking both terminal and marine operations, based on real-time information, to direct every job by every worker and every piece of equipment. By 1995, PSA achieved more than 10 times the container throughput of 1982.

Path Followed

Figure 4.2 shows Singapore's path in creating its system of resources. Singapore recognized that its location was a natural resource that could give it a competitive advantage in economic development. The country has little agriculture, and in the 1960s, the industrial base was relatively small. Singapore has to be sure that its port remains viable to safeguard its manufacturing base and export-oriented policy. There are other locations astride or near the major Europe-Asia trade routes, and other harbors could be developed.

Singapore has developed a system of resources for competitive advantage. The country opened its economy to foreign investment, resulting in economic growth and the ability to allocate significant amounts of capital to developing its port. Foreign investment also created demand for a transportation infrastructure, including ocean shipping. Singapore's location and the harbor itself made a compelling case for applying capital to the port. TradeNet and other IT initiatives, described later, became high priority applications to make it easier to route cargo through Singapore. We can see that investment and technology interact with location and harbor in this system of resources.

The advantages of Singapore's port are matched by several disadvantages, the most significant being the small size of the island. Space is at a premium, which creates operational problems for loading and unloading containers. Singapore applied Operations and Information Technology to minimize this physical disadvantage. For example, the PSA uses technology to track, assign and locate containers in the yard. It uses planning heuristics to stack and retrieve containers higher than other ports, while minimizing handling. The PSA also exhibits significant IT and operations

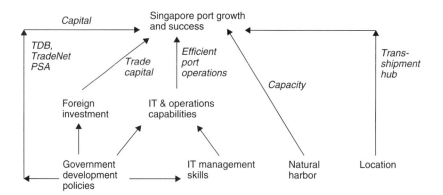

Figure 4.2
Singapore's Interacting Resources

management skills, which Mata et al., contend provide a resource-based advantage.

The PSA also has other strategies that contribute to its competitive advantage. The first is a constant focus on customer service; the objective is to minimize ship turnaround times and to produce high-quality handling (minimum container shipping errors). Second is the development of other ports and hubs to feed traffic to Singapore along with the creation of value-added services to maintain shipper loyalty, for example, systems to manage empty containers and to provide warehousing services.

Critical Success Factors
The following are the critical success factors for Singapore's port:

• Recognition of the potential for a resource-based strategic advantage

• The presence of few competing areas for investment

• A highly focused government industrial policy

• The availability of capital and openness to foreign investment

• Education of port personnel (government focus on education)

• IT risk taking, for example, deploying expert systems

• Use of IT/operations technology to make up for resource-based disadvantages, notably lack of space

- PSA's focus on customer service
- The creation of a system of interacting resources

Operations at the Port

A brief discussion of port Operations and Information Technology demonstrates how the PSA developed resources to supplement the port's attributes and location. Port operations have always been a key success factor for the PSA. Being situated in a strategic geographic location has its advantage but it is not the determining factor for the PSA to become the number one transshipment port in the world. The East-West sea lanes have many strategically located ports, such as Hong Kong, Port Klang (Malaysia), Colombo (Sri Lankan) and Kaohsiung (Taiwan). However, more than one hundred container shipping lines choose to call at the PSA. On an average day, there are three sailings to the United States, four to Japan, five to Europe and twenty-two to South Asia and South-East Asia. The PSA is connected to 740 ports in 130 countries. This kind of high-volume traffic requires efficient port operations.

Key customer requirements in port operations include freight rates, frequency of services, shipping options, turnaround time, port charges (about 20 percent of freight charges), support services (ship maintenance, ship supplies), and feeder operations. The port customers are essentially the shipping lines; however, it must be noted that shipping lines often take their cue from manufacturers, exporters, and the large buyers of goods and raw materials.

As Singapore is a transshipment hub for shippers, port operations are very demanding. Arriving containers destined for other port destinations have to be transferred to other ships or stacked for later shipment, while containers destined for Singapore are placed on trailers for local delivery. These operations have to be well coordinated to maximize port resources and minimize ship turnaround times.

Before ships arrive in Singapore, the shipping companies send a message to the PSA through the PortNet system. The company indicates when the ship will be arriving and applies for berthing spaces. Information sent to PortNet includes the number of containers on board, their arrangement, destination, and promised arrival date. Application for port call can be made between one month and twenty-four hours before the ship arrives.

Once PSA receives the application, operations planning begins. Port personnel use the Computer Integrated Terminal Operations System (CITOS) to create plans for ship berthing and for unloading containers. Unloading plans have to specify whether the container will be picked up from the terminal, transferred to another ship immediately, or stacked for later shipment. The system also has to handle imports and exports for the domestic market.

When the ship arrives, it docks at a specified time at its assigned berth. A specific number of quay cranes are assigned to service the ship based on the number of containers to be unloaded and loaded. Prime movers (special trucks that carry two containers) in the port move the containers from the ship to the stacking yard.

At the stacking yard, cranes stack and unstack the containers. Containers in the yard are placed in an initial holding area. Internal yard operations restack the containers in appropriate places and sequence to await eventual loading onto another ship or for pickup for domestic delivery by freight forwarders. Containers originating from Singapore exporters are handled by gate operations and routed to the stacking yard first, before eventual loading onto ships. CITOS determines the stack locations.

The PSA anticipated global containerization in the late 1960s and built the first container port in the region. It also made early preparations to harness IT on a major scale and used it strategically in its port operations in the 1980s. The PSA is expanding its terminal facilities to meet the challenges of globalization, and concomitant anticipated cross-border trade growth. To attain the objective of becoming a major transshipment hub requires more than fast turnaround of containers.

Although loading and unloading containers is the key operation in shaping the success of the PSA, there are a number of support features or *enablers* that make the port operations highly effective and help sustain its competitive edge.

First, Singapore has the eighth largest merchant fleet in the world, 3,380 ships with 20.77 million gross tons (*The Business Times*, August 21,

1998). Singapore had total external trade amounting to S$382 billion in 1997 (approximately U.S. $224 billion, based on 1997 exchange rates), and the country is a major oil refinery center. Second, the PSA is the largest owner of warehouse space in Singapore, managing over 500,000 square meters of space. With its warehouse business, the PSA attempts to provide value added services to its traditional port operations, including the storage of goods and empty containers, labeling, repackaging, tagging, sampling and testing, quality control, and billing. The aim is to establish an integrated global logistics network that connects Singapore to major regions such as Asia, Western Europe, China, India, and the U.S.

Third, the PSA's workforce is trained to focus on customers. A quality culture is prevalent in the organization. The port has programs such as "Key Customer Managers" and "Chat Time." The Key Customer Managers program provides regular dialogue sessions with customers, helping PSA staff to better understand and attend to customer's operational and contractual needs. To promote a quality culture in the workforce, the PSA has widespread quality circles (QC) and encourages staff suggestions. Staff suggestions and QC projects have saved PSA about ten million Singapore dollars over the last five years. In 1999, the PSA won the Singapore Quality Award (SQA), which is given annually to an organization that has shown consistent business excellence in achieving world-class quality standards in its operations.

The PSA has been able to harness these enablers and integrate them into its overall information and operations technology strategy to transform itself into a major regional transshipment hub for container shipping. The PSA has invested heavily in information and operations technology, both to solve immediate operating problems and to remove constraints on the growth of traffic.

TradeNet   One of the first trade-related technological innovations in Singapore was TradeNet. The Trade Development Board (TDB) sponsored the design of this EDI system to facilitate the processing of trade documents. Prior to the development of the system, a large number of clerks processed batches of forms to clear shipments in and out of Singapore. The EDI system links the TDB, customs, shipping agents, ports, freight forwarders, traders and others. After the system was installed, the turnaround time for documents that formerly had taken two days to process dropped to fifteen minutes, while documents that used to require four days could normally be handled in four hours (Teo, Tan, and Wei 1997).

TradeNet has greatly facilitated document processing, and it has removed time considerations for most of the parties who use it. Port operations, on the other hand, impose severe, real-time requirements on information processing. Effective customer service, which is measured by minimum ship turnaround time and error-free container handling, imposes significant constraints on information processing and port operations.

The PSA, in combination with various partners, developed an integrated set of traditional and expert systems to provide customer service to shipping lines. There are two major systems and many subsystems that allow the port to provide superb service despite the shortage of land area for storing and moving containers.

CITOS   The Computer Integrated Terminal Operations System, or CITOS, supports the planning and management of all port operations. The subsystems in CITOS process information for allocating berths to ships, planning the stowage of containers, allocating resources in general, reading container numbers, and operating trucking gates.

Prior to the arrival of a ship, shippers notify the port authority of the containers that will be loaded using PortNet, an online system with about fifteen hundred subscribers. The PSA replies with a window of time for the shipper's trucks to appear at an entry gate to the port. Its objective is to have trucks go to the right stack of containers and to have a yard crane available to offload the container on the truck. Such scheduling minimizes the need to handle containers.

The Container Number Recognition System uses a video camera for each letter and number of the eleven-character container ID. A neural net recognizes each character, and the system checks it against its record of the container that was expected. The gate automation subsystem also records the weight and directs the driver to the container's location within forty-five seconds. This system has reduced the number of individuals manually checking IDs from sixteen, one per lane, to three.

The Ship Planning Subsystem deals with the loading and unloading of containers, positioning the containers inside a vessel, the allocation of quay cranes alongside the vessel, and the sequence in which the cranes will operate. This problem is complex because ships typically carry cargo for several destinations; it is important to minimize handling by loading containers in the right sequence. As an example, one of the new large container ships, the 6,600 TEU *Sally Maersk*, recently made her maiden voyage to Singapore. The PSA achieved a rate of 203 container moves per hour for this vessel, exceeding its 1997 average of 88 moves per hour (the fastest in the world). The Port handled 1,700 boxes and turned the ship around in less than 8.5 hours. The ship loaded containers from 44 other vessels and discharged containers to another 38 during her visit.

The Yard Planning Expert Subsystem sorts containers to support fast turnaround. One of its objectives is to use space efficiently and keep yard activities orderly. It must be sure that containers are accessible to avoid unnecessary handling and movements.

The Resource Allocation Subsystem assigns all operations staff and container handling equipment with the exception of the quay cranes.

CIMOS   The Computer-Integrated Marine Operations System helps to manage shipping traffic and the activities of the port. It includes a Vessel Traffic Information Subsystem that watches the Singapore Straits and approaches to the port using five remote radars. Another set of four radars monitors port waters; this subsystem sends information to expert systems that plan the deployment of tugboats, pilots, and launches. All of this information is available in a database that shippers access via PortNet to learn the status of vessels in the port.

There are five expert systems used for planning including applications to assign ships to anchorages, schedule the movement of vessels through channels to terminals, deploy pilots to tugs and launches, route launches, and deploy tugboats.

Note that these systems are highly asset-specific; they have almost no applicability outside a port, and the size of Singapore's port makes them inappropriate for many smaller port locations. As an example, the PSA will sell the CITOS system, but few ports are complex enough to use it.

The systems also interact to strengthen port resources. TradeNet reduces the cycle time for processing trade documents, which encourages shippers to use the port. CITOS reduces the cycle time for loading and unloading ships, a further benefit to customers. Readily available capital to invest in the port made the most extensive use of technology possible and provided physical equipment (docks, quay cranes, prime movers, etc.) to handle cargo. *It is not only the resources, but it is their interaction that has helped the PSA create a sustained competitive advantage over other ports.*

Key Performance Data
Singapore is the busiest port in the world in terms of shipping tonnage, and compares quite favorably on metrics of port operations. At any one time, there are more than 800 ships in port. In 1997, Singapore received 130,333 vessels with a shipping tonnage of 808.3 million gross tons. Singapore is Asia's main transhipment hub and is one of the world's largest container terminal operators, handling a throughput of 14.12 million TEUs in its container terminals in 1997.

PSA facilities can provide on average 88 container moves per hour; it holds the world record for 229 containers moves per hour in 1995 with the ship *Mette Maersk*. The PSA Marine, a wholly-owned subsidiary, performed 108,048 pilotage jobs and 94,904 tug jobs in 1997. The company provides high standards of service as 99 percent of pilotage jobs were serviced within thirty minutes and 96 percent of tug jobs were serviced within fifteen minutes.

Figures 4.3 and 4.4 present some annual operating statistics for the PSA. Note that measures of volume have been steadily increasing, while the workforce has peaked and is decreasing. The data show that Operations and Information Technology help substitute for labor. It is also clear that technology helps to compensate for the relative lack of physical space at the port. Efficient operations and support from information technology allow Singapore to increase the number of containers handled without a proportionate increase in space. Income per employee has shown steady increases, as has the number of TEU container moves per hectare of port space.

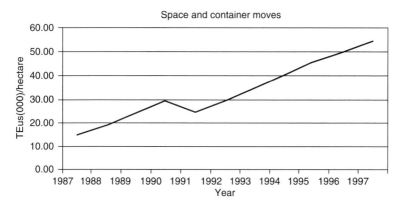

Figure 4.3
PSA Container Moves/Hectar

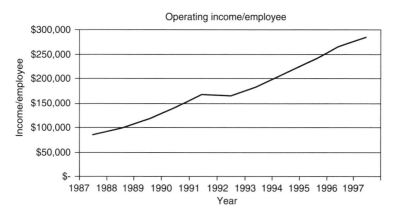

Figure 4.4
PSA Operating Income/Employee

In comparison, China's ports handled a total of 10.77 million TEUs in international container services in 1997. Hong Kong had 14.5 million TEUs in 1997 while South Korea handled about 6 million TEUs in 1996. Taiwan's main port at Kaoshiung had 7.87 million TEUs in 1996. However, these are all larger countries than Singapore, and the containers in the country are handled by more than one port operator.

Analysis

Singapore began with two natural resources—strategic location and a large, protected, deep-water port. These resources, although rare and valuable, are imitable and substitutable. By creating a system of resources, adding man-made resources to natural ones, Singapore was able to create one of the world's leading ports that, as a whole, is rare, valuable, inimitable, and nonsubstitutable. The PSA follows a strategy of focused customer service, continued planning, and the expansion of capacity to keep up with demand. It is unlikely, in a highly competitive world economy, that an organization can sustain a resource-based competitive advantage without such continuous improvement.

The Resources

Table 4.2 presents a system of two natural and three man-made resources that have contributed to the success of the port and the Port of Singapore Authority. The interaction of natural resources and man-made resources has contributed to Singapore's ability to sustain a resource-based competitive advantage (Gordon, Lee, and Lucas 1999).

The Singapore example illustrates well the emergent system of interacting resources described in figure 1.1. This system of resources may be found in table 4.2. The first interesting interactions occur between location, harbor, capital for infrastructure, and foreign investment. Singapore built an infrastructure to attract foreign capital, and this capital, in turn, generated economic activity that paid for further infrastructure development.

A strong norm against corruption has given Singapore a reputation as one of the least corrupt places in the world to do business, making it even more attractive to companies. The government has consciously tried to raise living standards with government housing and a pension plan, which both benefits citizens and makes the country more attractive for investment. Singapore places great importance on education, and an educated workforce attracts investments.

The second important interaction includes Singapore's infrastructure, IT, operations, and specialized port equipment. Singapore's infrastructure, including the Trade Development Board, distriparks (warehouses), and highway system, make the port attractive to shippers. It is easy to tranship goods in Singapore, and there is a great deal of truck traffic moving shipments down the Malay Peninsula to Singapore's port. The efficiency of the port is enhanced by IT and Operational systems, and by the infrastructure Singapore provides in general.

The third interaction occurs between IT management skills and port operations and information technology. One example, described later, in more detail, is the PSA's successful implementation of a number of expert systems. IT professionals from Kent Ridge Digital Laboratories worked closely with PSA staff members to develop these applications, and both groups developed skills in technology and port operations. As a result, the PSA has the IT management skills to undertake a variety of development projects for a major port, and these skills have contributed a series of key systems.

As table 4.2 shows, all of the resources directly applicable to the port are rare and valuable. However, for the most part, the resources are imitable and substitutable. How, then, has Singapore created a sustained competitive advantage? The *interaction* among these resources has produced a system of resources that is valuable, rare, inimitable, and nonsubstitutable. Although another location might be attractive, nearby ports are not as conveniently located and lack the capital, infrastructure, and Operations and Information Technology to provide service to shippers. In addition, other countries may lack the IT management skills to create an equivalent facility to Singapore.

Singapore's strategy of supplementing its location and harbor with man-made resources has overcome the limitations of its natural resources to create a port whose location, harbor, infrastructure, and operations and information technology are rare, valuable, inimitable, and nonsubstitutable. This system displays emergent properties that enhance the competitiveness of the port. The interaction among system components has

Table 4.2
PSA Resource Analysis

Resource	Rare	Valuable	Inimitable	Nonsubstitutable	Other Model Components
Initial Resources					
Singapore's location	Yes, few other sites as convenient for transhipping	Yes, high volume shipping route Asia-Europe	No, other locations in SE Asia can expand their ports	No, there are nearby ports capable of development	
The natural harbor	Yes	Yes	No, possible to create at high cost	No, shippers could in principle use another port	
Additional Resources					
Capital for infrastructure—foreign investment	Yes, relatively so for Asia	Yes	No, funding might be possible from taxes, world agencies	No, capital may be available from other sources	A complementary asset, especially a road system
IT and operations capabilities for a port	Yes, due to size and scale of port operations	Yes	No, in principle, but few ports have this scale	No, if another port is to provide acceptable service	Create many specialized assets; software and equipment
IT management skills	Yes	Yes	No, in general; yes, for running a large port	Yes, outsourcers do not have experience with this scale	

Interactions

Location and harbor ↔ island infrastructure and foreign capital	Yes	Yes	Difficult	Difficult	Create more specialized assets
Infrastructure ↔ IT, operations, and port equipment	Yes	Yes	Difficult	Difficult	
IT management skills ↔ port systems	Yes	Yes	Difficult	Difficult	
IT management skills ↔ port technology and operations	Yes	Yes	No, in general; yes, for running a large port	Yes, outsourcers do not have experience with this scale	

increased the asset specificity of PSA's resources. For example, investment-generated growth requiring more quay cranes and the technology that allocates these cranes to ships is highly specific to a port the size of Singapore. Because of the increased specificity, this system of resources would be difficult or impossible for another port to duplicate; it creates a sustainable competitive advantage for Singapore. In addition, other nearby ports face a tremendous task in creating Singapore's level of infrastructure and skilled labor while building a comparable port.

Amazon.com

One of the best-known electronic commerce sites on the Web is Amazon.com. Through an advertising campaign that began well before the company took its first order, Jeff Bezos created a brand name that people associate with purchasing books on the Internet. By 1997, Amazon had sales that exceeded firms that had previously started selling books on the Web (Ghemawat and Baird 1998). Amazon is a new company, and certainly not a traditional one. However, it illustrates the strategy of continually adding new resources to old to try to create a competitive advantage.

Amazon.com developed a new business model for the Internet. Bezos studied a number of products and decided that books offered one of the best opportunities to open a store on the Net. New books are commodities; one that you purchase from Barnes & Noble is the same as one that you purchase from Borders or your local bookstore. In addition, the industry is not dominated by one firm; there appeared to be room for an Internet start-up.

Amazon.com's business model is similar to the retail electronic commerce model in chapter 2. There are no physical stores, only an ordering site. Amazon features over a million book titles and now sells a variety of other products; it has alliances with other firms and direct investments in companies like drugstore.com and gear.com. Initially, Amazon relied on book wholesalers like Ingram to fill all of its orders, so that it did not need to have more than a very small number of books on hand. In 1999, the company began a three hundred million dollars program to build large, highly automated warehouses in Nevada, Kentucky, and Kansas—

all low-cost labor states. Amazon, like a number of other Web retailers, feared losing customers due to lack of product and poor service.

The Internet allows a different kind of business model for retailing, and Amazon has taken advantage of what the Web offers. The company encourages readers to write reviews of books they have purchased and post them to the Web page about the book. A prospective buyer can read these reviews to determine whether to make a purchase. Amazon provides access to top sellers, makes personalized recommendations based on prior purchases, and lists other books that customers who have bought the book you are interested in acquiring have bought. After a customer makes a purchase, Amazon periodically sends the customer new book recommendations via e-mail based on his buying behavior. Many of these features are automated, saving tremendous amounts of labor over the traditional models of retail promotion.

As of this writing, Amazon claims seventeen million customers in 160 countries, and it operates additional sites in the United Kingdom and Germany. Jeff Bezos believes that Amazon has reached a critical mass of customers so that a large number of people will want to associate with the site (*Business Week*, February 21, 2000). It sells for a discounted, posted price, and offers auctions as well. Products on the site include free greeting cards, and millions of books, CDs, DVDs, toys, games, and electronics. Most recently, Amazon has started selling tools. Some analysts regard Amazon's customer base as one of its greatest assets; over 70 percent of sales come from repeat customers. In addition, the company's e-commerce platform makes expansion into new product offerings easy.

Analysis
Table 4.3 is an analysis of Amazon.com using the dynamic resource model from the first chapter. Amazon began with strong financial backing, and had no trouble raising money when it went public. Bezos concentrated on brand awareness before opening for business in 1997. As a result, customers associated Amazon with selling books on the Internet, and flocked to this new site despite the fact that other Web booksellers existed, and despite the fact that Amazon did not necessarily have the lowest prices. The company has a program with associates who list Amazon on

Table 4.3
Amazon.com Resource Analysis

Resource	Rare	Valuable	Inimitable	Nonsubstitutable	Other Model Components
Initial Resources					
Capital	No	Yes	No	No	
Brand	Yes (on Net)	Yes	No	No	
Alliances	No	Yes	No	No	
Virtual store, one million titles	Yes	Yes	No	No	
Additional Resources					
More capital, no requirement to make a profit	Yes	Yes	No	No	
Expand range of products	Yes	Yes	Moving toward	Moving toward	Attempt to establish critical mass; customers think of Amazon first
Build own warehouses	No	Yes	No	No	A necessary complementary asset?
The Amazon site	Yes	Yes	Possibly	Possibly	
Interactions					
Capital → virtual store and expanded range of products ↔ customer base	Yes	Yes	Moving toward / Yes	No	Virtual store with huge selection of titles, more products harder to imitate; can substitute category stores, critical mass of customers
Expanded product line → alliances	Yes	Yes	No	No	Network externalities for alliances—the more business at Amazon, the better for them

their site and refer customers to the bookseller. The associate gets from 8 percent to 15 percent of the first sale to a customer whom it has referred. Finally, the Net made it possible for Amazon to begin business with a huge number of titles and quickly become a virtual store much larger than any physical store. (A Barnes & Noble superstore might offer 60,000 to 175,000 titles as compared to over a million at Amazon.)

Table 4.3 shows that although some of Amazon's resources are rare and valuable, another competitor could imitate them or find a substitute. How, then, has the company sustained its advantage? First, it has added capital and, until recently, not worried about breaking even. It has expanded its range of products and built warehouses, a complementary asset to its site. This system of resources has resulted in a site that becomes difficult to imitate or substitute for. The site and its large customer base have become rare, valuable, and possibly inimitable and nonsubstitutable. These characteristics, however, could change quickly if another firm finds a new approach to retailing on the Web.

In order to appropriate benefit from its technology, Amazon patented its technology for "one-click checkout," and so far has successfully sued to stop Barnes & Noble from using the same technique. Amazon continues to expand the range of products its sells, and to invest in other retailers. Bezos' dream is to become the largest merchant on the Net, a goal that pits Amazon against some fairly impressive bricks-and-mortar stores like Wal-Mart.

Amazon's resources demonstrate some interaction. Capital allowed it to create the virtual store in the first place and expand the range of products. These resources, in turn, have created a large and loyal customer base, which is a resource in its own right. The lack of need to make a profit (while still keeping investors satisfied) gives the Web merchant a significant advantage over physical merchants who are expected to make a profit. By expanding its product lines, an association with Amazon becomes more valuable for an alliance partner.

Amazon has been very successful as a Web store, if one discounts the fact that it has yet to make a profit. The company is positioning itself to become *the* Web merchant for a variety of products. This approach makes the site itself a significant resource. The challenge for Amazon is to keep this resource rare, valuable, and relatively inimitable and nonsubstitutable. Brand recognition and customer satisfaction are key to keeping the site popular. Amazon seems very vulnerable to a competitor with different resources and a slightly different business model. For example, Random House offers electronic versions of one hundred classic works of literature online. One can buy from a Web site and download an electronic copy of Dickens's *David Copperfield* for $4.95. Will publishers eventually disintermediate booksellers? Amazon and other B2C e-commerce merchants must be constantly alert for new business models that impact their operations.

Conclusions

The three organizations discussed in this chapter—American, the PSA, and Amazon—illustrate the dynamic resource-based model of the first chapter. Each tried to create a resource-based advantage not by beginning with resources that are rare, valuable, inimitable, and nonsubstitutable, but rather by building resources. American, the PSA, and Amazon have more than a bundle of resources; the resources they bring to bear on the competition interact with each other. From this interaction, American built a travel supermarket and network that would be very hard to imitate, the PSA built a smoothly operating port with highly specialized equipment and systems, and Amazon built a Web site with products and services that give it an advantage.

Of the three organizations, the PSA has the clearest sustainable advantage. American's advantage has been challenged by the Internet, which has changed the model and channel for selling travel and forced American to spin off Sabre Decision Technologies and its CRS. Amazon appears the most vulnerable of the three as there is little about its site that cannot be imitated, given the right amount of investment capital and a slightly different business model to attract a critical mass of customers.

Notes

1. Videotaped comments at an NYU seminar on 3 November 1992.

2. *TEU* stands for "twenty-foot equivalent unit." Some containers are larger, so operations are measured in the number of twenty-foot equivalent units that the port handles.

5
New Manufacturing Models: A Resource for Advantage

Can a business model be a resource for competitive advantage? A lean manufacturing model like the one followed by Dell and Cisco offers these firms an advantage, but to what extent is it rare, valuable, inimitable, and nonsubstitutable? There is no doubt that the model is rare, because few firms are able to execute it as well as Dell and Cisco. It is also valuable due to the outstanding performance of both companies.

The model is certainly imitable, or is it? The Dell and Cisco models cannot be patented or protected as a trade secret. However, each company's model has proven very hard to imitate because others lack the knowledge of how to make it work, or have conflicts between the new model and their existing business model. Compaq, for instance, has tried to adopt Dell's model with limited success because while the model is obvious, how to implement it and make it successful are not; this skill is difficult to imitate and provides the basis for a competitive advantage.

Can another firm find a substitute? So far, the literature has not presented any manufacturing models that offers higher performance than lean manufacturing; it seems to be the basis for several models like agile manufacturing or mass customization. These latter models use technology to customize products to some degree even though they are manufactured using mass technology.

This chapter discusses Dell and Cisco and their manufacturing models, which were first introduced in chapter 2, in figures 2.4 and 2.5 respectively. The discussion focuses on the path that each company has followed to implement its current business model, and the role of the Internet and electronic commerce in realizing these models. These manufacturing firms offer examples of what a successful manufacturing company looks like in the first part of the twenty-first century.

Dell

Dell is currently the second largest computer systems company worldwide, and it claims to be the fastest growing. Its most recent four-quarters sales were almost $24 billion. The company has 33,2000 employees and ranks number one in the United States in PC sales.

History
In 1983, Michael Dell, then an eighteen-year-old freshman at the University of Texas at Austin, spent his spare time formatting hard disks for IBM PC upgrades. Soon, he had dropped out of college to manage his business, a venture with sales of six million dollars by 1985 (Rangan and Bell 1998). That same year, Dell's company moved from upgrading computers to assembling its own brand; by the end of the year, sales had increased to a rate of seventy million dollars a year. In 1990, sales hit five hundred million dollars, and Dell had secured a place as a major supplier to Fortune 500 companies, offering a broad product line of office and home desktop computers and laptops.

In 1992, Dell had its first loss, generated partially by its efforts to sell products through retail channels. The company also experienced quality problems with laptop computers. Dell acted quickly to exit the retail channel and to withdraw from the laptop market until it could offer a machine up to its quality standards.

Dell Direct
With its decision to abandon retail sales, Dell became a direct seller, its model being an efficient, made-to-order, high velocity, and low cost distribution system. From 1992 until it launched its Web site in 1996, customers ordered via toll free phone numbers, fax, or mail. With only one way to sell its products, Dell concentrated on a direct, lean manufacturing model.

After order-entry personnel check an order for completeness and accounting does a credit check, the order goes to manufacturing. There, the order is broken down electronically into a list of parts needed to build the computer; this process generates a specification sheet with a bar code linking the spec sheet to the original order. If a customer calls to check order status, her order number is linked to the spec number, and Dell can tell where the computer is in the manufacturing process. The spec sheet contains a bill of materials, special instructions, and the software to be loaded on the new computer, and it travels with the computer chassis during manufacture.

The spec sheet is generated from a computer file that has information about the specific components installed and the employees performing assembly at each step in building the computer (Kraemer et al. 1999). Workers use the spec sheet to assemble the computer, beginning with the motherboard containing the central processor that the customer ordered, and the amount of RAM specified. Factory workers put other assembly parts into a bin—disk drives, CD ROMS, and so on—and they forward the motherboard and parts bin to an assembly cell.

The five-person assembly cell is responsible for the final assembly of the PC. Members of the cell constitute a team; their job is to assemble a properly configured computer and test it before the machine leaves their area.

The next stop for the computer is the software loading area where the operating system, applications, and the customer's custom software are loaded onto the disk. (Corporate accounts provide proprietary software that Dell downloads to their computers.) Dell uses an Ethernet connection and fiber optics to download software in about ten minutes, a task that used to take forty-five minutes with standard cables.

After software download, the PC is transferred to an area where it is powered up and "burned-in" for four to eight hours. After passing this test, workers put the computer in a box and send it to the packaging area where components such as the keyboard, mouse, and manuals are packed.

Dell does not handle the monitor that goes with the system. Instead, the company sends an e-mail message to a shipper who pulls the appropriate monitor from supplier stocks, and schedules an arrival date that coincides with that of the PC. This process saves about thirty dollars in shipping costs and reduces the number of times someone handles the monitor; it reduces Dell's overhead as well.

Enter the Internet

Given its direct sales model, Dell viewed the Internet as a natural step. In the early 1990s, the company began experimenting with the Internet, prompted by requests from its customers to deliver online technical support and order status information. Dell established a small group to explore the use of the Net for communicating with customers. The group found that most Fortune 500 companies provided employees with Internet access while slightly fewer had Intranets that could be set up to allow external customs access as "extra-nets."

In July 1996, Dell opened up its Web site for ordering and immediately began selling one million dollars of computers a week through the Net. Customers could order and track their computers through links from dell.com to shipping partners. The site also contained service and support data, some thirty-five-thousand pages of information, which is the same information used by Dell's technical representatives.

Because initially only 20 percent of electronic orders were complete, they did not flow directly to manufacturing, but rather were directed to a member of the order processing department who reviewed them with a sales representative. The electronic order was then keyed into Dell's existing order processing system. (The most frequent missing information was the credit card number, reflecting consumer fears of sending credit data over the Internet.)

Sales on the site have grown rapidly, within six months, the rate was one million dollar a day. Three months later, sales hit two million dollars a day, and in six more months, three million dollars. By January 1999, sales at the Dell Web site were at the rate of ten million dollars a day and by December, over thirty-five million dollars a day. As of this writing, 50 percent of Dell's sales, averaging fifty million dollars a day, are through the Web; 40 percent of technical support activities take place on the Web, and 50 percent of order status inquiries are online.

The site has a number of important features (see figure 5.1). The Web pages help direct customers to their appropriate category, individual/ home users, small businesses, and large organizations. The customer chooses a computer model, and the site helps with the configuration. There is a base system with CPU and memory and recommended components. However, as shown in the figure, you can change the components and reprice the computer: the user can evaluate a variety of configurations before choosing to submit an order.

Dell has also established custom Web sites for its "premier" partnerships with over two hundred of its largest customers; these sites contain more than nineteen thousand pages. The sites reflect negotiated prices with each customer. Because Dell handles all the PC sales of some customers, it knows the configuration and location of each of these clients' computers worldwide; customers can access Dell's site to learn how much they have spent and what products are in place.

Direct Ordering, the Internet, and Manufacturing

The original direct ordering strategy and the Internet have had a major impact on Dell's business model. Because Dell made the decision in 1992 to move to direct ordering and not to sell in retail stores, it was well positioned to adopt electronic commerce and take advantage of the Internet. All orders come directly to Dell, so the Internet became another channel for the customer to use to place an order. As a result, its business model has become widely emulated.

How lean is Dell's lean production? Dell uses a "pull" system to obtain parts from its suppliers who warehouse their components within fifteen minutes of the Dell factories. Suppliers must ensure two hours of inventory in the plant at all times. In 1992, Dell reduced its number of suppliers from over two hundred to forty-seven (twenty-five suppliers account for 85 percent of parts and materials). Dell provides suppliers with real-time access to its production systems, allowing them to track demand and resupply factories faster than if they had to wait for Dell to issue an order.

Dell has also worked with its suppliers to reduce defects per hundred units to 1.53 percent. Dell believes that components fail because they are "touched" too much in production; the company has thus reduced the number of machine touches during assembly from 126 to 56 by redesigning assembly processes. Dell has outsourced its inbound logistics to one firm, and its outbound transportation operations to another.

CUSTOMIZE YOUR DESKTOP

Dimension 8100 Series

- Cutting Edge Technology
- NEW! 1.7GHz Intel® Pentium® 4 processor
- Dual-channel RDRAM memory technology

click here

Select the options below and then select Configure This System

1. Intel Pentium 4 Processor   ?Learn More

   [NEW Pentium 4 processor 1.7GHz ⬍]

2. Microsoft Productivity Software   ?Learn More

⦿ MS Office XP Professional or Small Business Edition
  Includes Microsoft Word 2002, Excel 2002, and Outlook 2002
○ Microsoft Works Suite 2001

3. Multi-Media   ?Learn More

⦿ Premium Sound (Sound card)
○ THX - Certified Solution (Click Here for Details)

4. Networking Options

⦿ Integrated 10/100 Ethernet
○ No Integrated Option

Figure 5.1
An Example from Dell's Web Site

Remember that Dell does not start ordering components and assembling a computer until it has a firm order. A company building to a forecast and selling through retail sores may have thirty to forty-five days of inventory in plant and another forty-five days in the distribution channel. Dell has an average of eleven days of inventory, including inbound supplier goods in transit, outbound customer goods in transit, and spare parts. It is estimated that PC components fall 30 percent a year in value, and that a PC sitting on a shelf loses about 10 percent of its value per month in obsolescence. Dell avoids all these costs because it owns minimal inventory, and it does not build computers on speculation.

Dell's cycle time for building a computer is impressive. In 2000, the company connected its suppliers to Dell over the Internet so that they could see the parts Dell needs. Its most efficient plants order only the supplies needed to keep production running for two hours. The company notifies suppliers electronically of what it needs for the next two hours, and they must deliver from nearby warehouses. In some cases, a plant finishes and loads a PC for shipment just fifteen hours after a customer orders; Prior to the Internet hookups with suppliers, the process took thirty hours (*Business Week*, September 18, 2000).

From the beginning of the building process to loading the product on a delivery truck takes an estimated seven hours. At the new Austin plant, workers can sometimes build a PC, load software, test the machine, and package it in five hours. As a result, Dell's inventory turns over nearly 42 times a year, compared to an average of 14.3 times in the industry as a whole. Its "days cost of goods sold in inventory" is 9 compared to an average of 25 in the industry.

Dell's cash conversion cycle is minus-five days as it frequently receives payment from a customer before it has to pay suppliers for the components of the computer! For retail transactions, Dell converts the order into cash within twenty-four hours. Compare this cash cycle to the build-to-forecast manufacturer who must buy components to build a PC, send the PC into a distribution channel for sale, and wait to receive payment.

Dell also knows its customers because all orders come from a customer, not a wholesaler or retail store. The manufacturer selling at retail has no idea who bought the machine unless the customer completes all of the information on a warranty card and returns the card to the manufacturer. Even then, Dell knows more as the warranty card does not include the actual price that the customer paid for the PC.

One of the reasons that Dell can follow its business model is because technology, both from the Internet and from its internal systems, allows it to substitute information for physical parts and buffer stocks. IT processes the order and makes it possible to track production and shipping. The technology produces a bill of materials and instructions for assembling the computer. Dell has interfaced internal systems to the Web so that customers can follow production and shipping. Overall, the statistics suggest that 40–50 percent of all Dell transactions are made via customer entry on the Web. How many employees, how much labor, is thus saved? Estimates are that Dell has a 6 percent cost advantage over manufacturers who follow the traditional build-to-forecast model.

The success of the Dell business model has made Michael Dell a popular speaker in Detroit where automobile manufacturers see a major change coming in the way their distribution channels work. Of course, a car has many more parts than a PC, but many of the principles should apply to any assembly operation.

Analysis

Dell exhibits interesting path dependencies in the development of its competitive advantage and business model. (See table 5.1.) A loss in 1992 shocked the company and forced it to reexamine the way it was doing business; that event led Dell to withdraw from the build-to-forecast business and concentrate on direct sales. It applied resources to implement lean manufacturing and direct ordering by phone and fax. Although direct sales and lean manufacturing can be imitated, and substitute resources found to implement them, other PC firms like IBM and Compaq have had trouble following this model. Dell has developed the requisite management skills to integrate direct ordering with lean manufacturing, and these skills may be its most important resource.

When Web ordering came along, Dell invested in the new technology. Although in principle the individual resources of Web site ordering and lean manufacturing are imitable and substitutable, Dell has protected its advantage through critical mass, network externalities, and lock-in. A critical mass of customers place orders on the Web site, helping to feed the lean manufacturing production system and reduce labor costs for Dell. A critical mass of premier companies work with Dell, justifying the resources that Dell devotes to them. Within the premier companies, employees experience some degree of lock-in, depending on whether the firm has an exclusive purchase agreement with Dell. Within any organization,

Table 5.1
Dell Computer Resource Analysis

Resource	Rare	Valuable	Inimitable	Nonsubstitutable	Other Model Components
Initial Resources					
Lean production 1992	Yes	Yes	No, cannot protect model	No, similar models exist	
Dell Direct	Yes	Yes	No	No	
Original skills at direct ordering and lean production	Yes	Yes	Yes	Yes	Dell became skilled in management approach: a cospecialized asset
Additional Resources					
Investment in IT	No	Yes	No	No	
Web site ordering 1996	Yes	Yes	No, originally, hard to catch up now → Yes	No, could substitute a similar resource, premier programs and customer lock in → Yes	Web ordering quickly reached critical mass, provides network externalities within premier companies
Skills at managing direct, Web ordering and lean manufacturing	Yes	Yes	Yes	Yes	Dell executes its model well; others have had trouble trying to adopt; management a co-specialized asset
Interactions					
Lean production model ↔ direct and Web ordering, a new business model	Yes	Yes	No, but few have demonstrated skills → Yes	Yes, can substitute model, but can a competitor execute it?	Interaction has created new business model that is based on technology investment, Internet infrastructure, some customer lock-in

there are network externalities due to everyone using the same brand of computer; common technology and software greatly ease support. Dell has demonstrated skills in managing its business model as it has moved to the Internet.

The major interaction in this system of resources takes place between the lean production model, direct ordering, and the Web. This interaction has created a new business model arising from an investment in IT, the Internet, direct sales, and lean production. Few other organizations have been able to imitate this model or substitute an equivalent one; the model and Dell's management skills provide a sustainable competitive advantage.

Cisco

Cisco Systems was founded in 1984 and went public in 1990. The company has been extremely successful in selling networking equipment; it has grown with the rapid expansion of corporate networks and the Internet. One of its primary products is a router, a hardware and software package that determines where traffic is to go on corporate Intranets and the Internet.

The Internet was originally designed to link together disparate networks, often built by the lowest bidder on a government contract. These networks might use different communications protocols to communicate. A protocol is a standard that describes how messages on a network should be handled. An example of a simple protocol is answering the phone with "hello." If someone deviates from this protocol, it can confuse the other party and lead to unexpected outcomes.

Internet engineers developed a protocol, TCP/IP, that could encompass existing protocols; it is a packet-switched network protocol. Communications hardware and software break each message up into a series of packets; computers and routers send these packets around the network. Internet Protocol (IP) is responsible for moving packets of data from note to node in a network; IP uses a four-byte destination number or IP address to determine where to send the packet; all computers connected to the Internet must have an IP address. Transmission Control Protocol (TCP) verifies the correct delivery of data from a client computer to and from a server, and it must check to see that data are not lost someplace on the Network. (When data are lost, TCP ensures that they are retransmitted.) TCP is concerned with error correction as well.

The Internet stimulated manufacturers to develop products for packet switching that follow the TCP/IP protocol. The browser and Web made it easy to post and retrieve information on servers, and companies developed Intranets. The Intranet uses Internet protocols, hardware and software to create a private network within a firm. A company like Ford has hundreds of applications that run internally on its Intranet, working to coordinate different groups. As an example, automakers "tear down" competing automobiles. By posting the results of a teardown on the Ford Intranet, engineers all over the world can review parts of other makers' cars. Because all the components for an Intranet follow standards, it is easy for firms to build on this infrastructure.

Combined with the explosive growth of the Internet, the corporate Intranet model creates a large demand for devices like routers that work with the TCP/IP protocol. Cisco is thus in an enviable position with its Internet-based products.

History and Strategy

An excerpt from Cisco's Web site describes the company's rapid growth:

Since shipping its first product in 1986, the company has grown into a global market leader that holds No. 1 or No. 2 market share in virtually every market segment in which it participates. Cisco Systems shipped its first product in 1986. Since then, Cisco has grown into a multinational corporation with more than 20,000 employees in more than 200 offices in 55 countries. Since becoming a public company in 1990, Cisco's annual revenues have increased from $69 million in that year to $12.2 billion in fiscal 1999. As measured by market capitalization, Cisco is among the largest in the world.

Cisco has enjoyed incredible growth; the company focuses on large corporations, small- to medium-sized business, service providers, and education. The company makes products for a variety of network applications, including hubs, switches, and a variety of routers. It also has a line of equipment for local area networks (LANS), which generally use Ethernet as their protocol.

Sections of the chairman's letter from the 1999 annual report provide insight on Cisco's strategy:

A recent study by the University of Texas found that in 1998 alone, the Internet economy in the United States generated more than $300 billion in revenue and was responsible for more than 1.2 million jobs. In just five years since the introduction of the World Wide Web, the Internet economy already rivals the size of century-old sectors such as energy, automotive, and telecommunications. Milestones that took up to 100 years to achieve in the Industrial Age are occurring at a staggering pace in this new economy.

Cisco's number one priority . . . continues to be customer focus. We are committed to helping our customers become agile by implementing Internet business models that will position them for success in today's fast-paced business environment. Our . . . customers are deploying networks for the next century that deliver data, voice, and video capabilities over a single network.

Our strategy . . . is to focus on internal product development and blend that with acquisitions and partnerships. This strategy has allowed us to add more than 65 new products, acquire 11 companies, and develop dozens of partnerships to help us pursue emerging markets and achieve market share leadership over the last year. Cisco holds the number one market share position in 16 of the 20 key markets in which we compete. We hold the number two position in the remaining four areas. Some of these new emerging market opportunities include broadband access, voice over IP, and optical internetworking.

Cisco has developed its own business model, which it calls "the Global Networked Business." Because it is in the networking business, Cisco also advises its customer and others to consider this model. Later in this chapter, we will describe the model in more detail. Before doing so, this it is important to look at the development of information technology within Cisco, the technology that paved the way for it to become a Web-oriented company.

Internal Information Technology at Cisco

In 1993, Cisco was a five hundred million dollars a year company running a Unix-based software package to support basic transactions processing like order entry, financial reporting, and manufacturing (Cotteleer, 1999). The package and systems in general were having trouble keeping up with an 80 percent annual company growth rate. In January of 1994, the legacy systems failed, shutting the company down for two days.

As a result of that experience, Cisco began a crash project to locate an ERP vendor and install a standard solution for its core processing requirements. Within two days, a team had narrowed the candidate packages to five, and a week later to two. The final choice was Oracle, due to its size and capabilities, and the quality of its manufacturing package.

Cisco viewed the Oracle implementation as a strategic project and set up an ambitious nine-month timetable for completion of the project. The total cost was estimated at fifteen million dollars, Cisco's largest capital investment to date. There was no formal justification for the project. The project ended up with one hundred people assigned to it at a time when employment at Cisco was about twenty-five hundred people.

After an intensive effort with several prototypes, Cisco cut over to the new system on schedule. Although the transfer was eventually considered a success, on-time shipping at first fell from 95 to 75 percent; it took several months to stabilize the system and begin to realize its benefits. Cisco now had a scalable IT infrastructure in place to support future growth.

"Webifying" Cisco

The ERP project provided for future growth because of its modern architecture and Oracle's commitment to browser and Internet access, and Cisco took the next step of moving its business to the Net. Cisco customers order most of their products over the Internet, saving order-processing costs for Cisco. They also use its Web site to answer some 70 percent of their questions. This use of the Internet saves a considerable amount of expense, compared to the costs of having a Cisco employee field and answer a phone inquiries from customers. The company recruits and screens job candidates over the Web; information is available for managers on staff and competitors. Cisco is planning to become the first company that can essentially close its books on any day of the quarter to study financial results. See figure 5.2.

The Net has become an integral part of Cisco's order entry and manufacturing operations. Most of Cicso's production is outsourced to companies like Flextronics, and 90 percent of its orders, worth one billion dollars a month, come in through the Net with over half being forwarded to the contract electronics manufacturers. The contractor ships to the customer, and Cisco never touches the product. Employees do not handle paper until a check arrives, and soon checks should be replaced with electronic payments.

Cisco had revenues per employee in 1999 of $650,000 compared to an average of $396,000 for the S&P 500 and $253,000 for rival Lucent

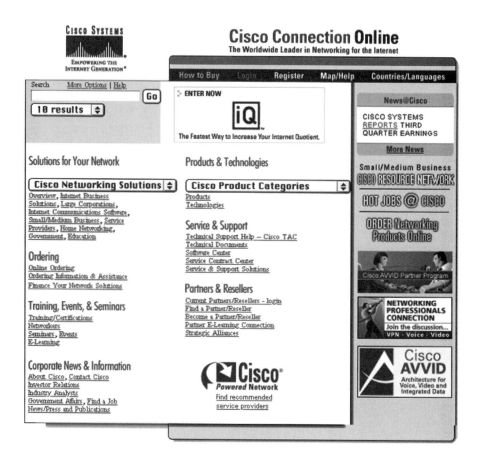

Figure 5.2
An Example of Cisco's Web Site

Technologies. Cisco figures that going on the Web has cut $1.5 billion in costs in the past three years.

The Global Business Model

Cisco has been so pleased with its move to the Web that it is promoting its model to customers. From a white paper on Cisco's Web site, the company describes its view of the model:

The pace of business worldwide is accelerating rapidly. Product cycles are shrinking. Just-in-time manufacturing abounds. Decisions are made on the fly. In this environment, access to relevant information is essential to remaining competitive and will mean the difference between survival and extinction for many companies. Yet many organizations still cling to an outdated model of information technology that builds walls around corporate information and systems, limiting access to a select few.

The level of competition has been stepped up in today's global, networked market. Businesses that fail to take advantage of what the network has to offer are missing opportunities and allowing competitors to gain important economic advantages. Companies must foster interactive relationships with their many constituencies (prospects, customers, partners, suppliers, and employees) opening up internal systems and the flow of information. Achievement of this higher level of competitiveness requires the openness and information accessibility of a new model—the Global Networked Business.

The Global Networked Business model is based on three core assumptions:

• The relationships a company maintains with its key constituencies can be as much of a competitive differentiator as its core products or services.

• The manner in which a company shares information and systems is a critical element in the strength of its relationships.

• Being "connected" is no longer adequate. Business relationships and the communications that support them must exist in a "networked" fabric. . . .

. . . A Global Networked Business is an open, collaborative environment that transcends the traditional barriers to business relationships and between geographies, allowing diverse constituents to access information, resources, and services in ways that work best for them . . .

The new Global Networked Business model seeks to maximize the value of information by sharing it, cultivating ongoing relationships between all parties. Employees have access to information and tools that allow them to do their jobs more proficiently, and prospects have ready access to information that aids in purchasing decisions. Partners have ready access to a variety of information and interactive applications that help them sell more effectively. Customers have better access to support capabilities that enable them to resolve problems in less time, and suppliers have improved access to inventory levels and manufacturing needs . . .

But simply throwing money at technology is not the answer. . . . As the investment in IT continues to grow, chief information officers come under increasing pressure from management to justify expenditures. The Global Networked Business views the network as a means of generating revenue, reducing costs, and improving customer/supplier relationships. Cisco, for example, will save $250 million a year in business expenses through its networked applications.

Networked applications in a Global Networked Business provide a wide range of benefits to the company and to its prospects, customers, partners, suppliers, and employees. As a successful Global Networked Business, Cisco can point to numerous examples of networked applications that help Cisco meet the needs of all its constituencies.

When facing a buying decision, organizations are often presented with many choices. A key competitive differentiator is the ease with which prospects can access company information to simplify and facilitate their purchasing processes. Cisco's prospects can use the Cisco Connection Online (CCO) Web site. CCO is the foundation of the Cisco Connection suite of interactive, electronic services that provide immediate, open access to Cisco's information, resources, and systems anytime, anywhere, allowing all constituents to streamline business processes and improve their productivity.

Through CCO, prospects gain immediate access to information on Cisco's products, services, and partners. Nearly a quarter-million prospects log in to CCO monthly. CCO allows prospects to register for seminars, purchase promotional merchandise and Internet software, read technical documentation, and download public software files. In 1996, for example, nearly one-fourth of all seminar registrations were completed via CCO, streamlining the registration process for users.

With expenses rising and qualified sales people in short supply in many industries, many companies are studying ways to reduce the cost of sales while maintaining closer relationships with customers. Cisco's dramatic growth caused it to evaluate alternatives to traditional sales ordering methods. One solution was to create the Networking Products MarketPlace, available through CCO, which enables users to place and manage orders for Cisco networking products and services on line. In its first six months of operation, the ordering Tool, one of the Internet Commerce Applications available through the Networking Products MarketPlace, processed more than $100 million in orders, and Cisco continues to see dramatic increases in the percentage of orders received through the application. The ordering Tool assists direct customers and partners in configuring equipment, leading to shorter delivery intervals and more accurate orders than those typically received through traditional sales methods. The end result: customers receive exactly what they need in less time . . .

Cisco also provides technical assistance to its customers worldwide through the CCO Internet Web site. Over 20,000 support cases are opened or queried each month. The online service improves the support process, speeds resolution of problems, and provides immediate global access to Cisco's support systems and engineers around the clock.

Cisco has improved access to critical information systems and tools in yet another way, allowing customers to simply download software electronically via the Internet. Through CCO, customers and partners download more than 70,000 pieces of software each month, drastically lowering distribution costs while giving users immediate global access to mission-critical information 24 hours a day, seven days a week. Users also receive interactive guidance in selecting software, simple interfaces for downloading, extensive documentation, proactive defect alerts, and access to updates and new releases . . .

The purchasing function—ordering, delivery, and billing—can be time and labor intensive as well as expensive. EDI is one networked application that can benefit both suppliers and customers. Suppliers networked to Cisco, for example, have a competitive edge over other firms, potentially leading to increased sales.

They are also able to better manage manufacturing schedules, improve cash management, and respond more quickly to Cisco's needs.

Cisco, as a customer, benefits from EDI. Cisco has leveraged its networking expertise to create EDI links to a growing number of its suppliers, resulting in more than $80 million in purchases per month processed electronically as of January 1997. As a customer, Cisco has gained real-time access to supplier information, experienced lower business costs in processing orders (an estimated $46 per order), improved the productivity of its employees involved in purchasing (78 percent increase), and seen order cycles reduced substantially. Deploying networked applications such as EDI allows suppliers and customers to truly become partners . . .

Information must be readily available to employees if companies are going to compete successfully. Intranet applications provide the backbone for immediate access to current information and services. Cisco's Intranet Web site, known as Cisco Employee Connection (CEC), addresses the unique needs of its 10,000 networked employees, providing instant global communications. Cisco's marketing department, for example, uses CEC to distribute the latest product and pricing information, saving many thousands of dollars in printing and mailing costs and decreasing time to market. CEC also streamlines business processes, reducing the time employees spend handling repetitive tasks. Employees can use CEC to enroll in internal training courses on line anytime from anywhere without ever speaking with a training department employee. Another networked application enables Cisco employees to view meetings broadcast over the network backbone. All employees, regardless of where they are located, can share the same information simultaneously through the power of networking.

Posted: Tue Jul 20 13:51:36 PDT 1999

Analysis

Cisco's path to a new business model started with a crisis; legacy systems shut down the company. The ERP implementation provided a new resource that could grow with the company; fortunately, it also prepared the internal IT infrastructure to move to the Internet. Although the Oracle software fit well with a lean production environment, there was no way for Cisco to gain a competitive advantage from it. The software and the business model are available to all, and unlike Web integration and ordering, it does not take special management skills to implement them. (See table 5.2.)

The additional resource of a major Web presence, moved Cisco to an extended business model, reducing overhead while providing better customer service. Many of Cisco's clients are individuals concerned with the design and operation of networks; it is very natural for them to interact

Table 5.2
Cisco Resource Analysis

Resource	Rare	Valuable	Inimitable	Nonsubstitutable	Other Model Components
Initial Resources					
ERP infrastructure	No	Yes	No	No	
Cisco business model: lean production and outsourcing	No	Yes	No	No	
Additional Resources					
Move company to the Web	Yes	Yes	No	Yes, hard to substitute for the Internet and Web	Quickly achieved critical mass of customers ordering online, and accessing customer service; customers' Web knowledge a complementary asset
Web IT management skills	Yes	Yes	Yes, hard to imitate currently, less so in future	Yes (difficult to find substitutes)	
Interactions					
Web ↔ business model	Yes	Yes	Yes, but not easily imitated; Cisco encourages others to adopt its model	Yes, there are no viable substitutes for the Internet	Lock-in from dominant product position?

with a supplier over the Internet. These customers and their orientation are a complementary asset for Cisco, and have helped them achieve critical mass with their Web applications in a short period of time. Cisco has also developed critical IT Web management skills that are hard to imitate or substitute for, given today's labor market and the shortage of IT personnel.

Cisco has benefited greatly from the interaction of the resources it has developed, especially the natural fit between the Web and its business model. The Web enhanced and extended a lean manufacturing model to become Cisco's Global Networked Business Model, a concept it sells to customers based on its own experience. The Web and IT management skills at Cisco are hard to imitate or substitute for. Given a critical mass of customers ordering on its site and the popularity of its products, this business model looks for now as if it provides Cisco with a sustainable advantage.

Detroit: Figuring Out the Internet

The Detroit automakers have a history of massive change, much of which has been forced on them. In the late 1960s and early 1970s they built large, gas-guzzling cars only to find their customers flocking to Japanese imports when the energy crisis hit. Consumers found the quality of these imports better than Detroit's, and continued to buy foreign cars even after the crisis was over. Detroit had to redesign most of its products, turning to front-wheel-drive cars that had better gas mileage, and above all else, it had to improve product quality. During this period, the auto industry became truly global. Daimler-Benz and Chrysler have merged; GM has supplemented its European operations by buying the Swedish automaker Saab, and Ford has purchased Jaguar and Volvo.

Detroit is fascinated by the Internet and electronic commerce, though most of its activity at this point is in the planning stages. GM believes that it can cut up to 10 percent of the cost of a car by using the Internet. It and other automakers have established a purchasing site for suppliers to bid on the billions of dollars of parts the automakers purchase each year. At least one GM official thinks the company can build cars the way Dell builds computers. The idea is to manufacture a car using modules manufactured by different subcontractors. A customer orders a car over the Internet, and GM puts it together from different modules in about a week. Toyota announced in 1999 that it had figured out how to make a custom car in five days, and Detroit does not want to be left behind.

Detroit's retail channels are an area of great concern. A variety of Net services work with dealers to help customers get the lowest price on a car. Carsdirect.com has developed a new model; a user finds all information about a vehicle on its site, including the manufacturer's suggested retail price. Other sites offer the same information, but then refer you to dealers who bid for your business. CarsDirect also lists the price it can provide for each vehicle, a price it has determined by consulting with a group of dealers that have signed on to the service. If the customer accepts the price, Carsdirect delivers the vehicle and the buyer has minimal interaction with a dealer.

Detroit is a threat to the traditional dealer distribution channel for vehicles. In some states, automakers are prohibited by law from selling cars directly to consumers in order to protect the auto dealer, who is likely to have political influence in the state legislature. Detroit could easily take Internet orders for cars, and deliver them through a few centers in each state. If the automakers could find an easy way to perform maintenance at local sites and provide test drives, possibly by subcontracting with existing repair facilities, the manufacturers could consider closing almost all dealerships. Of course, such an action would raise a storm of protest, but certainly must attract the interest of Detroit executives.

These automakers epitomize the large-scale, mass-production manufacturing company. The fact that these firms see the Internet as a way to make major changes in their business indicates the power of this technology. Detroit has the profits and the capital to embrace Internet technology; automakers can easily acquire or create the resources they need to weave the Net into all aspects of their business.

Conclusions

Both Dell and Cisco demonstrate the powerful interaction that can occur among resources in a system; each company created synergies when its basic business model interacted with the resources of the Web. The companies began by taking orders on the Internet, but soon the Web became a way of doing business. Although other companies would like to imitate Dell and Cisco's business models, they will have trouble doing so. Dell and Cisco have created a new resource—the ability to manage lean Internet-enabled business models. Until competitors find a substitute, or develop or acquire their own IT and management skills, Dell and Cisco will be able to sustain their resource-based competitive advantage.

6

New Business Models in Services: The Brokerage Industry

Projections for electronic commerce from Jupiter Communications are that 11 percent of books and 9 percent of music will be ordered over the Internet by 2002. Its estimate for the largest Internet share of commerce is software at 35 percent, a natural for ordering or downloading over the Net. Given these projections, one of the greatest successes in e-commerce must be Internet stock trading; it is estimated that nearly 20 percent of retail stock trades took place online at the end of 1998, and that online trades will grow to 49 percent by the end of 2000 (*Business Week*, November 15, 1999). As of this writing, the ten largest Net brokers have seventeen million accounts and a billion dollars in assets and make one million trades a day (*Business Week*, November 20, 2000).

The retail brokerage industry in the United States has traditionally been characterized by two types of brokers—full service brokers like Merrill Lynch and Dean Witter, and discount brokers like Fidelity or Charles Schwab. Until the mid-1990s, full service brokers typically charged commissions of $150 or higher even for small trades of one hundred shares, while the discount brokers often charged one half that amount or less.

The late 1990s saw the increasing popularity of online brokers like E*Trade, Datek, and Accutrade, which use the Internet as the primary delivery channel for their services. These online brokers have substantially changed the competitive landscape; one of their most noticeable impacts has been the availability of deeply discounted commissions, as low as seven dollars per trade, which contrasts with the one hundred dollars and higher typical commission charged by full service brokers.

How has the Internet affected the traditional brokerage model? Before the advent of the Internet, and well before the arrival of discount brokers, the full service brokerage model consisted of research, brokers, and stock commissions. A full service firm like Merrill Lynch employs a significant number of analysts who study companies and industries. The analysts write reports and make recommendations on stocks, which brokers communicate to clients. The broker presents and interprets the research, and hopefully the customer will make trades with her. In the retail market, which is the market for individuals trading stock, revenue comes from the commissions that the brokerage firm charges on the purchase or sale of stocks.

It should be noted that this model differs substantially from the approach to investing advocated by most academic finance faculty and economists. These researchers believe that the stock market follows a random walk and that an individual cannot do better, over the long term, than the market averages. This work has led to the large number of index funds that seek to follow the market, rather than outperform it.

Commissions vary greatly among brokers and might run as high as one hundred dollars for buying or selling a hundred shares of stock. Discount brokers offer fewer advisory services than full service brokers, and charge lower commissions. The Internet made it possible for new services like E*Trade, as well as for existing companies like Schwab, to offer trading online. Because the cost structure for online trading is much lower than for a bricks-and-mortar broker, online trading commissions tend to be lower than the commissions of the discounters. Which model is likely to be the most successful? Which kind of firm has a competitive advantage?

An Experiment

There are wide differences in advertised commissions, especially among electronic brokers and traditional full-service brokers. In the summer of 1999, we conducted a carefully designed experiment to better understand the impact of the Internet and electronic commerce on brokerage firm business models and strategy. We asked whether differences in commissions among brokers are offset by the quality of execution of a trade. Do brokers with higher commissions save customers money on trade execution? Are the total costs of trading, commission plus execution quality, comparable across brokers? How has the Internet and electronic commerce impacted the retail brokerage business model?

A broker obtains a price improvement when the execution price of a trade is better than the bid price for a sale or the ask price for a buy. For example, consider a stock that is quoted as $30 bid, $30¼ asked. This spread means that the specialist or market maker will buy shares of the stock for $30 and will sell them for $30.25 each. Assume two brokers have "buy" orders at the market price, and the first broker buys the stock at $30 ¼. The second broker is able to get a price of $30 ³⁄₁₆ths, and thus offers the customer a better execution. This second broker has obtained a "price improvement" of ¹⁄₁₆th or 0.0625 per share. On a one hundred share order, the improvement is $6.25. In this example, the second broker has obtained a better execution price for the customer than the first. An improvement like this occurs, for example, when a floor broker offers to sell at a better (lower) price than the specialist's ask price in order to sell stock.

Experimental Design
Comparing execution prices implies that one must execute identical trades at different brokers nearly simultaneously so that each broker faces the same market conditions and bid/ask spread executing the trade. Our strategy was to compare several types of brokers, full service brokers using human intermediaries, and two different types of online brokers. The experiment includes NYSE and NASDAQ listed stocks.

The Salomon Brothers Center at NYU agreed to provide financing and working capital, sixty thousand dollars in total, for a controlled experiment. We opened six brokerage accounts for three different kinds of brokers: (1) two "voice brokers" who take orders the traditional way with the investor calling and speaking to a human broker, (2) two "expensive" online brokers, and (3) two "inexpensive" online brokers. The voice brokers were designated A and B; the expensive online brokers, J and K; and the inexpensive online brokers, Y and Z. Commissions for trading one hundred shares were in the fifty dollars range for the voice brokers, the fifteen dollars range for the expensive electronic brokers, and under ten dollars for the inexpensive electronic brokers.

The experimental design involved sixty-four trials, each placing three simultaneous buy or sell orders for one hundred shares of the same stock, using a voice broker, a medium-priced online broker and an inexpensive online broker. In other words, each trial involved one of brokers A and B, one of brokers J and K, and one of brokers Y and Z. Out of the total sixty-four trials in the experiment, thirty-two were buy orders and thirty-two were sell orders for thirty-two different stocks. (Note that only had the ability to choose stocks for purchase; we had to sell stocks purchased in the morning that afternoon.)

We conducted the experiment over an eleven-day period during July and August 1999. The experimenters worked in a room with a telephone and two computers with high-speed connections to the Internet. In the morning between 10:00 and 10:30, we selected stocks to purchase as specified in the experimental design. The selection came from the stocks in Standard & Poor's Platinum and Fair Value Portfolios as listed in its newsletter *Investor's Monthly;* the criteria for choosing a stock involved price, volume, and spread. We chose securities priced under fifty dollars so as not to exhaust our working capital at any one broker on a given day, and we selected stocks that showed active trading volume. We chose stocks with a spread of at least ⅛th, so that there was some potential for price improvement. All transactions were for a lot of one hundred shares, a lot size that retail customers frequently trade. Each trial comparing three brokers involved a different stock to remove any variation caused by the security being purchased, and all trades were "at market." There were a total of 64 trials involving three brokers per trial for a total of 192 trades.

Each trial involved one voice broker, one expensive online broker, and one inexpensive online broker. An experimenter at each computer completed the purchase screen for an online broker, stopping just before clicking on the button to submit the trade. The experimenter talking to the voice broker signaled when the broker indicated that he had submitted the order, and the experimenters at each computer clicked to submit their trades. All three transactions were thus identical ("buy 100 shares of PRQ Corporation at the market") and were as close as humanly and electronically possible to being simultaneous.

Beginning at approximately 3:30 P.M., we simultaneously sold the stocks purchased in the morning so that we held no position longer than six hours. We recorded data identifying each broker, the bid/ask spread from the online brokers' real-time quotes and the voice broker's bid/ask spread just before the transaction. We also recorded the execution price and the commissions, which we verified when we received the printed trade confirmations.

Results

The Bloomberg system provides a trace of each transaction so it was possible to see if the trades actually executed simultaneously. An analysis of the Bloomberg data showed that 66 percent of the trades executed during the same minute and 87 percent within a two-minute period. Each trade, except two that reflected problems with the market makers, faced the same bid/ask spread.

The results indicated that there were no statistically significant differences in price improvements among the brokers. The most frequent price improvement was zero (see figure 6.1). Our conclusion was that none of the brokers had significantly better execution than others; the greatest average improvement was about $0.04 per share. Looking at just NYSE

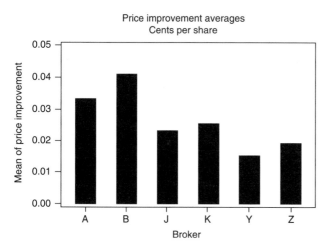

Figure 6.1
Average Price Improvements by Broker

listed securities, however, we did find that there was a pattern of more expensive, full-service brokers obtaining more price improvements. However, these improvements were not enough to offset these brokers' higher commissions.

Next, we calculated something called the "liquidity premium," which is the difference between the midprice of the bid ask spread and the execution price. For example, if the bid ask spread is 30 to 30 ¼, then the midprice is 30 ⅛th. If your broker buys a share for 30 ³⁄₁₆ths, the liquidity premium is 30 ³⁄₁₆ths–30 ⅛th or ¹⁄₁₆th per share. If the broker buys at the bid price of 30 ¼, then the liquidity premium is 30 ¼–30 ⅛th or ⅛th per share. In the first case, the broker has obtained a price improvement of ¹⁄₁₆th per share; price improvements reduce the liquidity premium. (For a sell, the logic is the same with the signs reversed.)

To compute the total cost of a trade, we used the commission cost + one hundred shares × the liquidity premium. With commissions included, there are statistically significant differences among brokers. The mean differences seen in table 6.1 result from subtracting the total cost of the broker in the column from the total cost of the broker in the row for the sixteen trials in which the pair participated together. The table shows that there are statistically significant differences between the brokers on total

Table 6.1
Comparison of Mean Total Trading Costs

	J	K	Y	Z
A	−30.69 [2.77] (−44.39)***	−42.80 [2.78] (61.66)***	−51.86 [5.80] (−35.74)***	−52.08 [4.09] (−50.88)***
B	−0.82 [12.7] (−0.26)	−13.32 [3.57] (−14.91)***	−21.20 [12.65] (−6.71)***	−24.55 [3.76] (−26.09)***
J			−20.39 [5.35] (−15.24)***	−21.00 [3.00] (−28.07)***
K			−9.84 [2.65] (−14.85)***	−10.84 [3.50] (−12.40)***

Notes: *$p \leq .10$, **$p \leq .05$, ***$p \leq .01$
Mean differences for 16 matched trades, [standard deviation], (t statistic)
Positive differences favor the broker in the row
Negative differences favor the broker in the column

trade cost. The magnitude of the differences shows that the total costs of a trade for one hundred shares with expensive online brokers is less than the total costs of voice brokers, with the exception of broker B versus broker J. Total trading costs for inexpensive online brokers are significantly less than total trading costs either for the two voice brokers or the two expensive online brokers. All differences except those between broker B and broker J are highly significant statistically. These same data are presented graphically in figure 6.2.

Funding allowed trading only in one hundred share blocks; what would be the results for larger block sizes? There are different commission structures for the brokers in our study depending on the number of shares traded. The differences in commissions raise an interesting question: What kind of price improvement would be necessary for a broker charging a higher commission to have a total trade cost less than the total cost for a broker with lower commissions? To be precise, we are interested in a differential price improvement as the lower commission broker might also provide a price improvement on an order.

Figure 6.3 shows the price improvement needed by each of the five brokers to offset their higher commissions when compared with broker Z, the lowest commission electronic broker in our sample (assuming broker Z obtains no price improvement). The highest average price improvement in our study was $0.041 per share for voice broker B. When we compare average improvements for one hundred shares, only the electronic brokers are within the range of the lowest cost electronic broker Z in figure 6.3. The figures indicate that for retail trades of one hundred to one thousand shares, it will be difficult for the more costly brokers (A and B) to offset their higher commissions through price improvements.

Implications

Although price improvements tend to reduce the differences among voice brokers and expensive and inexpensive online brokers, price improvements do not appear sufficient to change the rankings of the brokers on total cost up to a volume of 2,500 shares. The data suggest that voice brokers will be the most expensive in terms of total trading cost followed by expensive online brokers followed by inexpensive online brokers.

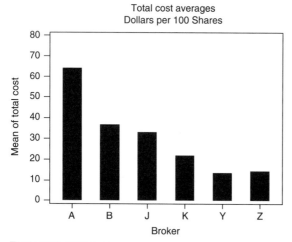

Total cost is defined as
commission + 100 X (liquidity premium per share)

Figure 6.2
Total Trading Costs by Broker

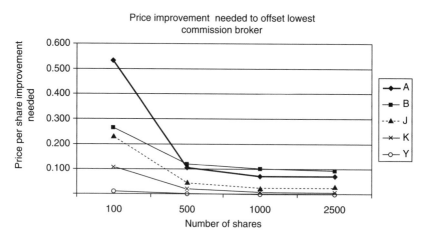

Figure 6.3
Price Improvement to Offset Commissions

The results of the study favor the online broker for retail trading. There is no way to tell if the extrapolation to twenty-five-hundred shares is valid because there may be some reason why price improvements are more frequent with larger trades. However, even with this warning, it looks as if the lowest cost trading will be found with Internet brokers.

Why, then, would a customer remain with a full-service broker? It is possible that he values the advice and research that he can obtain from such a broker. A medium-priced electronic broker like Schwab, however, makes research available on its site. He might remain with a full-service broker due to switching costs; it is not easy to move one's portfolio among brokers, and having accounts at three or four places makes it difficult to get a consolidated financial position. There may be a substantial number of customers who remain with full-service brokers because of these factors, but as more investors become aware of the price differences, they are likely to turn to lower cost brokers on the Net.

How has the surge in Internet trading affected the brokerage industry? What impact has it had on strategy? Electronic commerce in the brokerage business has made the trading component of the traditional bundle of services provided by brokers very visible. It appears that in return for lower trading costs, many retail customers are willing to forsake the other parts of the brokerage bundle of products and services, or obtain them elsewhere. The Internet has forced most full-service brokers to offer unbundled trading online.

Two brokerage firms illustrate quite different strategies for offering retail trading on the Internet. Charles Schwab embraced the Net early and moved to make it a major part of its business. Merrill Lynch resisted online trading, calling it bad for investors, until it was forced to adopt a completely new business model.

Charles Schwab

Schwab began business in 1971 in California as a retail brokerage firm providing services for the individual investor. Following the deregulation of fixed commissions in 1975, Schwab became a "discount" broker, one of a group of firms that reduced their commissions to almost half of the commissions of full-service firms. From 1980 to 1994, discounters went from 1.3 percent to 14.5 percent of industry commissions, and their share of transactions was close to twice their share of commissions (Maggion-calda 1996). The rise of discounters coincided with a move to 401k, self-managed plans and the greater availability of investment information.

Schwab invested heavily in technology from its inception in an effort to keep its costs down. With a cost-effective operation, Schwab had funds to pay for marketing campaigns and advertising. The firm's strategy was successful: From 1990 to 1995, customer assets grew from $31 billion to $182 billion. Schwab's income increased as number of its customers increased.

Schwab undertook a number of initiatives that enhanced its market share. First, the company offered back office services for fee-based advisors, independent advisors who do not make a commission from their advice to investors. An advisor might handle accounts for a large number of clients; the Schwab service allowed him to outsource this record-keeping activity. Schwab charges a fee based on transactions and asset size; in addition, the advisors become a virtual sales force for Schwab as it is easy for them to use the firm for trading. By 1995, Schwab had fifty-six-hundred advisors who contributed fifty-two billion dollars in assets and generated 13 percent of Schwab's commissions.

OneSource has become one of Schwab's most valuable assets. One-Source is a mutual fund supermarket, offering customers the ability to purchase Schwab and non-Schwab no-load mutual funds easily and without transactions fees. This service greatly simplified the process of purchasing shares in a mutual fund. Schwab charged fund providers a fee to be included in its supermarket. Schwab also controlled the customer relationship; the fund did not receive information on individual holders.

The technology required for OneSource required a major investment of more than $150 million. The company provides each fund with a computer and a direct communications line to Schwab's computers. The investment has paid off handsomely; from 1993 to 1995, OneSource assets generated almost 25 percent of the broker's money management revenues. Nearly half of the money flowing into Onesource came from the network of fifty-six-hundred fee-based advisors (Maggioncalda 1996).

Internet Trading Strategy

In 1995, electronic brokers started to attract the industry's attention. Within four months of deciding that the Internet was a high priority, Schwab had a Web site running from which its customers could enter trades. The site began charging $39 for trades of up to one thousand shares, and then reduced that price to the current $29.95 for up to one thousand shares. Schwab found that the cost of delivering brokerage services over the Web was substantially lower than building proprietary trading systems.

In January 1998, Schwab merged its separate online and offline services into a single business. Regular customers paid the same $29.95 commission as charged on the Web; whether in person, on the phone, or over the Web, a client received the same service. Responding to competition in early 2000, Schwab cut its trading fees to $14.95 for customers making thirty to sixty trades a quarter and who maintained an account balance of at least fifty thousand dollars. A page from the Schwab Web site explains the strategy:

> For 25 years, Schwab has worked hard to demystify investing and empower individual investors, providing them with the tools, access, and information they need to become better investors. With its singular focus on customer service, Schwab's mission is to provide the most useful and ethical financial services in the world. . . .
>
> Through the . . . execution of a single idea—low-cost stock transactions without sales pressure or conflict of interest—Schwab defined discount brokerage. Then, with the creation of the Mutual Fund Marketplace, Schwab created its ground breaking mutual fund supermarket, making it easy and economical to invest in mutual funds. Next, it pioneered the delivery of financial services through multiple points of access (on the Internet, in-person at more than 300 branches, or interactively by telephone day or night)—what Schwab calls "high-tech and high-touch."
>
> Today, led by its customers, Schwab is creating a new model of full-service investing in which information flows freely, investors make their own decisions with objective help and advice when they need it, and fees are fair. Full-service investing today, fueled by the incredible power and reach of the internet, and built on a foundation of people, is open, accessible and ultimately empowering.

Has this mixed strategy been successful? Earnings for the quarter ending September 30, 1999 showed 27 percent growth to $124.5 million with online trades accounting for 67 percent of all customer trades. Schwab's average online account is $90,000 whereas E*Trade's is

$17,000. Over the last three quarters, Schwab attracted $75 billion in assets, compared to $34 billion for Merrill Lynch. Gideon Sasson, the executive in charge of electronic brokerage at Schwab, describes the company's strategy as bringing people and technology together, or "clicks and mortar," or high-click and high-touch (*Internet World*, December 1, 1999). By the third quarter of 2000, Schwab had over 4 million on line investors and about 80% of its trades were via the Internet.

By late 1999, Schwab had moved into the position of leader rather than a upstart; other firms were targeting it. At the end of the third quarter, Schwab's market share of all online trades per day had fallen to 23 percent from 28 percent six months earlier. Some full service competitors were rolling out fee-based trading accounts, partially aimed at the independent financial advisors that use Schwab's services. In 1999, these advisors provided 30 percent of Schwab's assets, which are growing at 65 percent a year. A new Merrill fee-based account charges 1 percent of asset value compared to a typical 1.5 percent at Schwab. Morgan Stanley offers an account with a range of fees from 0.2 percent to 2.25 percent annually. These fee-based accounts offer unlimited trading online or through a broker at no additional charge. Schwab is given credit for forcing full service brokers to adopt this new business model (*Wall Street Journal*, December 18, 1999).

In early 2000, Schwab bought U.S. Trust, an investment bank serving wealthy individuals. Schwab has some clients with large accounts; 175,000 customers out of 6.6 million have investable assets of more than $1 million, and 25,000 have assets over $5 million. The company expects some of its customers to see their assets grow to these levels in the future. Schwab had claimed that it was losing money to trust companies. Now, it had the task of integrating U.S. Trust, with an average customer portfolio of $7 million, into the Schwab organization. The "do it yourself" customers of Schwab would be able to get help if they became nervous as portfolios grew (*Business Week*, January 31, 2000).

It is interesting to note that the purchase of U.S. Trust threatened one of Schwab's existing resources—its independent financial advisors. These individuals control about $243 billion of Schwab's $1 trillion in assets, and they feared that Schwab might use U.S. Trust to compete with them.

Schwab now had a presence at both ends of the financial market—investors with fairly small asset bases and investors with a high net worth; they lacked investors in the middle, say, those with $250,000 to $5 million. To reach this market, Schwab depends on its financial advisors (*Wall Street Journal*, September 12, 2000).

What is the next challenge from the Internet for Schwab and other brokerage firms? It is called "direct trading." The Web site accepting the order bypasses a market maker and goes directly to the ECN that offers the best price. These sites appeal to day traders who might make eight or more trades a day, where as Schwab's average client trades eight times a year. It is expected that direct access to the market will work for securities that have large trading volumes so that there is adequate liquidity without a market maker, stocks like Microsoft, Cisco, and Yahoo. Schwab purchased Cybercorp for $488 million in 2000 to provide an entry into this kind of trading, and at the same time cut its commissions for frequent traders (*Internet World*, March 15, 2000).

Analysis

Table 6.2 contains an analysis of Schwab that uses the dynamic resource-based model of competitive advantage. Schwab was very successful with its financial advisor network. The company captured a large number of advisors, preventing them from doing business with competitors. (It does not make sense for an advisor to have more than one brokerage firm process its statements and provide back office support.) The financial advisor network is similar in this respect to the airline CRS vendor that deploys a system to travel agencies. Schwab has captured a cospecialized asset.

OneSource has also been a tremendous success, making it far easier for a customer to invest in mutual funds. Schwab's site has a free application that ranks mutual funds on a number of indicators to help the investor choose a fund. A supermarket has to feature many products, and the success of OneSource is based on having a large number of funds; Schwab quickly achieved a critical mass with this product. However, the idea is certainly imitable, and competitors have established substitutes. E*Trade, for example, offers a large number of mutual funds to its customers.

Table 6.2
Schwab Resource Analysis

Resource	Rare	Valuable	Inimitable	Nonsubstitutable	Other Model Components
Initial Resources					
Financial advisor network	Yes	Yes	Yes, to the extent that Schwab has locked in the advisors	Partially, competitor can look for unaffiliated advisors	Advisors become a co-specialized asset like CRS agency; they depend on Schwab and provide it with assets and revenue
OneSource mutual fund supermarket	Yes	Yes	No, but no one else has tried	No	Has reached critical mass of funds,
Brand	No	Yes	No	No	
Additional Resources					
Internet brokerage services	No	Yes	No	No	
New business model of on-line and physical presence	No	Yes	No	No	
Buys U.S. Trust	Yes	Yes	No	No	A complementary asset for high net-worth customers; a threat to independent advisors?
Purchase of CyberCorp	No	Yes	No	No	Provides entry into direct routing of orders to ECN—a complementary asset

Interactions

Advisors ↔ OneSource	Yes	Yes	Maybe, but very difficult	Possibly substitute another product or group of advisors	May have created lock-in for advisors, but threatened by competitors with lower fees
Online trading, physical presence (new business model), brand ↔OneSource, advisor network	Yes	Yes	Possibly	Possibly	Investment in technology and infrastructure, expanded scale and scope of products all interacting as a system, coming close to creating a sustainable advantage

Finally, Schwab has invested in building its brand, which has become a resource. Through advertising and promotion, a large number of investors recognize Schwab, and it has positioned itself as a leader in the brokerage industry.

Schwab had to add resources and technology to enter the Internet brokerage business. It was not the first mover, and others have imitated and substituted for its Web site. There is no competitive advantage from entering this field; firms have to offer online access or lose customers. Schwab has also merged its offline and online operations, creating a new business model which entails treating all customers equally. This model is not unique; it appears that some full service brokerage firms are being forced to adopt it, too. Schwab has purchased U.S. Trust to expand the supply of its products and services, however U.S. Trust is not unique, and there are substitutes. It also purchased Cybercorp, continuing its strategy of adding resources to sustain an advantage, to have a presence in the direct sales arena.

Do the interactions in Schwab's system of resources provide a sustainable advantage? The financial advisor network interacts with OneSource, generating assets and revenue for Schwab. It would be difficult for a competitor to create this kind of interaction: It would need a network of advisors and a mutual funds supermarket. As long as Schwab can keep up its relationship with advisors and mutual funds, the resource created by the interaction of advisors and OneSource looks sustainable. However, Schwab must carefully manage its acquisition of U.S. Trust and its relationship with independent advisors.

Can Schwab gain an advantage from the interaction of its new business model with OneSource and the advisor network? Certainly, the combination of these resources and their interaction is rare and valuable. Will other full service brokers moving to the Internet be able to imitate it? Will they be able to create a substitute resource? Schwab's success in sustaining an advantage requires it to protect its system of resources, and to find ways to enhance their value. It might do this by developing new services for advisors, continuing to provide sales for mutual funds in OneSource, and keeping customers loyal through a business model that combines physical and online brokerage services.

Merrill Lynch Strikes Back

Background

Before the rise of online stock trading, Merrill Lynch occupied a comfortable position as the largest brokerage firm in the world. Merrill has over sixty thousand employees in forty countries, and has a relationship with more than five million households. As a full service firm, Merrill offers far more than retail brokerage services; it provides institutional trading and investment banking services, among others. The company has over $1.5 trillion of assets under management; institutional trading amounts to over $30 billion a day. The company is the world's leading underwriter of debt and securities, and is first in mergers and acquisitions. Merrill has an extremely large research group—nearly eight hundred analysts in twenty-six countries.

Merrill's business model defined the full service brokerage industry: A research department produces research products for the brokerage workforce. Brokers provide clients with research and encourage them to place trades with Merrill Lynch. The firm earns revenues from commissions, underwriting, fee-based account management, and a number of other sources. Online brokers threaten this business model.

Merrill's Initial Response

Merrill executives saw the publicity and interest in e-brokers, but they did not "get the Internet" as Schwab did. On September 23, 1998 the *Wall Street Journal* printed an article that quoted John "Launny" Steffens, a Merrill vice-chairman in charge of the firm's seventeen thousand retail stock brokers:

Steffens. . . . has waged an unusually public campaign over the last few months to dramatize what he calls the dangers of buying and selling stocks unassisted over the Internet . . . Mr. Steffens has badmouthed low-priced cyber-trading, saying it encourages people to trade too much at the expense of long-term returns . . . "The do-it-yourself model of investing, centered on Internet trading, should be regarded as a serious threat to Americans' financial lives. This approach to financial decision-making does not serve clients well and it is a business model that won't deliver lasting value."

For one hundred shares of IBM at this time, Charles Schwab would charge $29.95, and it would charge the same for one thousand shares. Merrill would have charged about $100 for one hundred shares and nearly $1000 for buying one thousand shares.

Merrill's first response to electronic trading was to offer the public free access to its stock research over the Web for a four-month trial period. Mr. Steffens announced this initiative on October 15, 1998. Merrill had provided access to research for its clients on the Internet earlier; this effort was intended to generate new leads by making research available to the public, according to the company.

Why did Merrill hesitate so long? One view is that seventeen thousand brokers have a lot of influence in the company; these individuals are used to six-, sometimes seven-, figure incomes. Trading on the Internet has the potential to drastically reduce commissions and incomes. However, the *Wall Street Journal* estimated that in 1998, only about $2 billion of Merrill's $17.5 billion in revenues came from commissions paid by individual investors.

Merrill Embraces the Internet

On June 1, 1999, Merrill announced that it would offer online trading at fees of $29.95, matching Schwab and worrying its seventeen thousand brokers. The Web service allowed individuals to set up online accounts, and trade stocks, bonds, and mutual funds, and, eventually, stock options. Customers can obtain complete reports of their holdings and transactions, pay bills, and handle other financial tasks through Merrill.

Although Merrill's assets have been increasing 15 percent annually, this amount pales in comparison to Schwab's growth rate of almost 40 percent a year. Merrill Lynch will trade for a fixed commission, but the firm wants to convert customers to a new account called "Unlimited Advantage." For a percentage of the assets in the account, starting at fifteen hundred dollars per year, Unlimited Advantage account holders can access all of Merrill's online services and will be able to make as many trades as they want, electronically or through a broker. At the time of the announcement, less than 10 percent of Merrill's retail customers had fee-based accounts (*New York Times*, October 8, 1999).

Transforming a Business Model

What motivated the change? How did Merrill decide to overcome the resistance of its brokers? A cover story in the November 15, 1999 *Business Week* offers a behind-the-scenes analysis of Merrill's conversion to an e-broker. The first indication of a problem occured in late 1998 when Schwab's market value exceeded Merrill's. By every other metric, Merrill was considerably larger than Schwab. But investors feared that it did not understand the Internet. As customers flocked to e-brokers, the firm faced an 85 percent compression in its margins, much more than retailers of toys and books. Not only did this change concern the retail brokerage division, the huge corporate division began to panic as well.

The big news is the retail site, but on the corporate side Merrill is also building an institutional portal referencing an array of Web sites for its corporate clients. The system moves Merrill's global capital markets business with seventeen thousand employees and $6.5 billion in revenues onto the Web. This move could cannibalize Merrill's existing business, or it could generate new business by being the first mover in this segment.

Several key executives and strategists at Merrill (including Mr. Steffens) became convinced that Merrill had to embrace the Internet, and change its business model accordingly. Bringing about such change is difficult in a firm that is on top of the industry and extremely successful. The change in Schwab's business model to embrace the Web was relatively small; for Merrill, the changes are gigantic. It expects to lose one billion in equity commissions, but hopes to make it up in fees and assets under management. Merrill also fears the loss of key brokers to rival firms, but this fear may be misplaced as others adopt Merrill's or E*Trade's model. In a few years, there will be no place left for the full commission broker; the stockbroker will have to adapt to low commission trades or fee-based services if he is to survive.

The next challenge for Merrill is to reduce its cost structure; electronic brokers, especially those that are totally online, face costs that are a fraction of those at Merrill. Merrill's offerings of research and services at $29.95 a trade are probably richer than those of Schwab, but it lacks a OneSource and the network of financial advisors. In addition to financial services, Merrill has signed up four hundred retailers to sell through its portal, although some experts question whether mixing all kinds of e-commerce with its site will be a success.

What has been the result of this transformation on the retail side? Merrill regained its edge over Schwab in absolute dollars; its inflow in the first quarter of 2000 topped Schwab's at $48.1 billion to $44 billion (*Wall Street Journal*, July 17, 2000). However, there are still more Merrill customers transferring to Schwab than vice versa.

Institutional customers have already been linked to Merrill electronically; at the end of 1998, 26 percent of equity trading for institutions was electronic and the number is expected to rise to 44 percent by 2000. How will the portal approach impact institutional customers, customers who tend to be professionals rather than occasional retail investors? The company hopes the portal will allow it to expand institutional business to twenty thousand middle-market corporations, well beyond its two thousand current institutional clients.

Analysis

Table 6.3 summarizes an analysis of Merrill Lynch's strategy from a resource-based view. In the beginning, Merrill's name and its successful execution of the full service brokerage model were very valuable assets. However, there were formidable substitutes and potential imitators, firms like Morgan Stanley Dean Witter come to mind. The full service brokerage model worked fine for many years, but it is an example of an asset that has turned into a liability. Retail customers, and possibly corporate customers as well, could and did substitute electronic brokers for Merrill's services.

When Merrill switched course, it embraced a new business model. Will this model be a strategic resource? Will Merrill be able to execute this new model as well as it did the old one? The most obvious change is the addition of electronic brokerage services and portals for both the retail and corporate client. Given that other companies are following this model, and it is easy to imitate or substitute for, the portals and new business model do not appear to provide a resource-based advantage for Merrill.

Table 6.3
Merrill Lynch Resource Analysis

Resource	Rare	Valuable	Inimitable	Nonsubstitutable	Other Model Components
Initial Resources					
Merrill Lynch name	Yes	Yes	No	No	A complementary asset
Full service brokerage model	No	Yes, but threatened	No	No, e-brokers substitute for retail nonadvice trades	
Additional Resources					
Internet brokerage services—retail and institutional	No	Yes	No	No	
New business model of online and physical presence	No	Yes	No, Merrill is imitating Schwab	No	
Interactions					
Internet brokerage services ↔ Merrill Lynch name	Yes	Yes	Possibly	Possibly	Merrill's leadership combined with the Internet could turn out to be sustainable; switching costs for current customers

The hope for gaining and sustaining an advantage comes from the interaction among Merrill's Internet brokerage services and the Merrill Lynch brand name. Merrill has an impressive group of clients and outstanding performance in almost all the markets in which it competes. It needs to retain their business and convince these clients to interact with it, at least partially through the Internet. If successful the move to the Net and Merrill's new business model, combined with its brand name, may provide the basis for a sustainable advantage.

Conclusions

This chapter presents a tale of two firms, one of which embraced the Internet and electronic commerce early, and one that was forced into a new business model. The brokerage market is highly competitive; stocks are commodity items, and it does not matter where one buys or sells them. Advice and research are not commodities, and customers differ in their levels of interest in these products. At first, observers suggested that the market for brokerage and financial services would become segmented between the do-it-yourself faction and those who wanted more service. Schwab's success and Merrill's move to a new business model suggest that major brokerage firms plan to compete in both markets; they will not differentiate but will let customers choose the services they want.

The online customer can choose to look at research without having to pay for it through fees or higher than average commissions. It is clear that the individual investor has gained from electronic brokerage operations; the same probably holds true for corporate customers, especially those who have been utilizing electronic connections to brokers from pre-Internet time.

The most interesting question is whether the new resources that brokers have created and enhanced, their product offerings, Web technology and brand names, and the interaction among these resources, will allow one broker to obtain a sustainable competitive advantage over the others. Time and the quality of execution of each firm's business model will answer this question.

7

Moving the Traditional Business to the Internet

This section of the book concerns the traditional firm as it faces challenges from the Internet and electronic commerce. The Internet is a technological masterpiece, but it is surrounded by exaggerated claims that have made some senior managers skeptical of its value. This chapter explores the Internet as a resource for the traditional business, attempting to present a balanced view of what is possible using this worldwide network. All of the new business models discussed to date involve the Internet in some form. What is this technological innovation and how has it changed the way in which the world does business? What are the implications for the traditional firm trying to develop a strategy for electronic commerce?

The Internet as a New Resource

The Internet is a major resource for both individuals and firms. Because it is available to anyone, it alone cannot create a sustainable advantage. Rather, it is the creative application of the Internet that may allow a firm to use it for competitive advantage. Even if one cannot sustain such an advantage, the Internet offers the traditional firm many opportunities to improve operations, provide better customer service, and reduce costs.

Key Characteristics of the Net

The appendix to this chapter provides an overview of the Internet and how it works. The Department of Defense sponsored the initial network that became the Internet; the government was interested in connecting a variety of disparate networks, each built by a different contractor using different standards. The idea was to allow networks to *interoperate*, that is, for data to be able to flow from one network to another without users having to take any particular action to translate their data to work on another network. The Defense Department wanted a robust network that would keep operating if some part of it became unavailable or was destroyed.

All communications involve protocols so that network devices are able to process data. If you think of the post office as a network, one protocol is that addresses go on the front of an envelope and another is that a stamp goes in the upper right-hand corner. The Internet developed a set of protocols called "TCP/IP" that are capable of transmitting any data that adhere to the protocol. All that a proprietary network has to do is put its data into the TCP/IP format, and the data can travel anyplace on the Internet.

The next major innovation with the Internet is packet switching. Conventional phone systems are circuit-switched. When you make a phone call, there is a dedicated path between your phone and the one you are calling. No one else can call you because your line is tied up on the first call. You can actually trace the connection from your home phone to the central office, to other central offices, and to the home of the person you are calling. This entire circuit is dedicated to your call.

Packet switching resembles a freeway; packets of data travel over a shared network to their destination. Each packet has to have an address for its destination, and each computer on the network must have a unique address to which packets are sent (known as the computer's "IP address"). Envision the Internet as a giant road system; each car has an address for its destination as it travels over the road system. Because the cars only have room for so many passengers, there may be convoys of cars all headed for the same destination (an office, an apartment building). At various intersections or nodes, there are traffic signals that look at the car's address, and direct it on a road to its destination. These signals are intelligent and know if a path is congested or blocked; they route the car the best way possible to its destination. Cars in a convoy may get separated, but all of them will eventually arrive at the same destination.

On the Internet, the cars are packets, and the traffic directors are special computers called "routers." The router looks at the packet's address and sends it on the best path to its destination. Just as on the highway, the packets share the road or communications lines in the network. A message or file may require many packets, and like the car convoy, different packets may take different routes. However, all of the packets eventually arrive at their destination. Because of packet switching, your computer can perform a number of tasks using the Internet at one time; the line is capable of sending and receiving packets that contain e-mail, data from a Web site, and so forth.

Packet switching was first implemented with what was then a radically new charging mechanism. Until its development, communications charges had always been based on time and distance. Providers of packet switching began charging for the packet transmitted, no matter where it was going on the network.

By 1995, the government was no longer providing any funding for the Internet, and it became possible to use the network for profit-making activities. The invention of the World Wide Web and then the graphical browser interface, turned the Net into a remarkable innovation for all kinds of commerce. The Web is a way of presenting information on a server, a computer that is connected to the Internet. (Your personal computer is a client that connects to the server via the Internet.) The information on a server uses a standard set of codes or links to point to other related information. The author of a document has to insert these links in her documents on the server. If you were to look at my home page on the Web, you would find links to the courses I teach; each course page has a link to the course outline, and each outline has a link to each company discussed in a teaching case.

The invention of the browser was the final feature that opened the Web up for widespread use. By publishing information in a standard format, a browser like Netscape or Internet Explorer running on your client computer can access documents on the server and present them in a rich graphics format (as compared to a typed page of text). As a user, you do not need to know about links or where documents exist on the Web. You simply use a mouse to click on the highlighted text on the screen, and the browser connects you to that information wherever it resides on the Internet.

What Does the Internet Provide?

Table 7.1 presents some of the characteristics of the Internet that are most important for firms. In pre-Internet days, a firm wanting to deploy an application that featured communications had to design its own private network, or make use of a network provider's proprietary network. American Airlines, for example, was responsible for configuring its own network for Sabre, and for connecting tens of thousands of terminals in airports and travel agencies around the world to it. This network was American's alone, and no other firm could use it for another purpose; Chase Manhattan Bank could not develop an ATM network using American's network. The Internet is a worldwide shared network that makes use of standards. Anyone who adheres to the standards can access and use the Internet.

The Sabre system network has some capability to exchange messages with other airlines. However, it would not work very well trying to handle your company's e-mail. It certainly does not connect to a banking network so that you can review your accounts after making a plane reservation! The Internet, however, provides interoperability among a variety of networks; you can access any Web site that is connected to the network. Thus, you can use Travelocity (which runs on Sabre) to make a reservation while, at the same time, you are moving funds among different accounts in your bank using the bank's Web site.

As the discussion above implies, in pre-Internet days, you had to build your own network infrastructure to deploy applications of the technology. Thousands of firms around the world developed countless private networks each time they implemented new systems with remote or interactive access. Today, the Internet makes it possible to plug into an existing network infrastructure.

The proprietary network has controlled and limited access. To add another user, a person must configure the network, possibly extending it to a new location. With the Internet, one can connect in a variety of ways through an industry of Internet Service Providers. Because browsers are available without charge, there is no need to write an interface program for the client computer. Because the client's interface software is standard and used for a variety of applications, there is much less training required when the user connects to a new application. All Web sites used by individual customers have to be simple enough not to require training, as the cost of training for each application on the Web would be prohibitive. As a result, the interface to purchasing goods at Amazon.com is simple and intuitive, as is the reservations application on Travelocity or Cheaptickets.com. The company using the Internet for an application does not have to write nearly as much custom software for the end user compared system developed using technology that predates the Internet.

What is the bottom line? With the Internet, companies can:

• Make a technology innovation available to over 150 million people by setting it up on a server connected to the Internet.

Table 7.1
Internet Characteristics

Characteristic	Pre-Internet Technology	The Internet	Implications
Standards	Proprietary to network, vendors	Open standard worldwide	Plug any device or application into the Internet anywhere
Interoperability	Limited or none	Yes	Worldwide communications and connectivity
Infrastructure	Build your own	In place worldwide	Not necessary to build network for each application
Access	Closed; limited to locations you choose to provide connection	Well over one hundred million people globally; rapidly growing	There is no need to configure a network or write programs to allow access
Interface	Custom	Browser	No need to write or distribute interface software
Software	Custom	Standards: TCP/IP, HTML, Java, XML	Less programming to develop applications; faster implementation

• Reduce development time because there is no need to configure a private communications network or elaborate interface programs.

• Connect with companies all over the world just as it can connect to individuals.

• Place applications on the Internet and limit access to them to specific individuals through log-in names and passwords (an Extranet).

• Connect a variety of applications and computers anyplace in the world; the location of hardware no longer matters.

• Develop more innovative products and services.

• Substantially reduce communications costs while expanding the reach of network applications.

• Link closely with customers and suppliers, shifting certain tasks like order tracking and production monitoring to them.

• Enjoy a level playing field; the small firm can have the same connectivity as the large firm without needing to make a huge investment in technology.

All of these features make it easy to develop new business models. They also make it possible for your competitor to develop a new model and to become the first mover before you realize what is happening.

The Net and New Business Models

Chapter 2 presented examples of new business models made possible by information technology. What is the role of the Internet in each of these models?

1. Retail electronic commerce: The Internet eliminates the need for a physical store; the e-retailer's Web site becomes a virtual store and a delivery service replaces a trip to a physical store. (This model has suffered lately as dot.com merchants have failed to attract a critical mass of customers and traditional stores have fought back.)

2. Business-to-business commerce: The Internet replaces physical and phone contacts with suppliers with an electronic market, reducing search costs and speeding procurement.

3. The Dell Model: Customers order through the Internet, and Dell uses the Net to help fill the order. Dell has no retail sales outlets or distributors; the Net replaces them all.

4. Cisco: Similar to Dell, Cisco has integrated the Internet throughout its entire business, from order entry to customer service to coordinating production with its contract manufacturers. The Internet is the instrument that coordinates the company.

5. Portals: A portal is a new business on the Internet; it is the starting point for a session on the Net, providing access to a variety of services along with search engines to help the user locate a desired site.

6. Hubs: the Internet becomes a new market, facilitating communications and buyer-supplier relationships around a special interest area.

The Internet's many facets enable these business models. It provides communications and coordination while linking over 150 million people to hundreds of thousands of Web sites. The Internet creates an electronic world for individuals and for business, a global community that communicates with ease and at relatively low cost. It expands the realm of the possible, and stimulates new ideas for business and leisure. The challenge for management is to understand the Net and figure out how to use it to build a competitive advantage.

Impediments To New Business Models

A number of traditional firms have been surprised by the success of start-up competitors taking advantage of the Internet. A few of these firms have been successful in fighting back; for example, Toys "R" Us was very competitive with eToys until eToys failed. The outcome of electronic trading in the brokerage industry, however, is still in doubt. Will Merrill Lynch succeed with electronic trading and a new revenue model? What has kept some firms from acknowledging the Internet and responding to new business models?

Current Success Does Not Predict Future Success
Companies like Merrill Lynch have been very successful historically, and it is easy to be lulled into the belief that past success will continue in the future. In today's hypercompetitive environment, such a belief is very dangerous. Not only do you have to worry about known competitors, but also about the new entrant who leverages the power of the Internet to become a major factor in your industry. E*Trade's business model did

not exist before the Internet; its growth and success caught traditional brokerage firms flat-footed. Now, with their franchise threatened, they are responding.

The Internet Does Not Apply to Our Business

The president of one company stated that because his firm sells to man-ufacturers rather than to retail customers, ordering on the Internet did not apply to his company. I responded with the example of Intel, another firm that sells to manufacturers rather than end-users, which offered ordering over the Web and soon found itself booking one billion dollars a month of business on the Internet. The company president said that Intel was a special case given that all of its customers would be very famil-iar with the Internet. A manager can deny the importance of moving to the Web and find a number of rationalizations for such a position. *The Internet, however, has implications for everyone's business, and a man-ager in the twenty-first century needs to understand how to use it effectively.*

Vested Interests in a Current Business Model and Channel Conflict

This impediment is best illustrated again with Merrill Lynch: The firm has a business model that has been in use for decades. A new model integrating the Internet threatens the firm's seventeen thousand retail bro-kers and its revenue model. Sometimes, this problem is described as "channel conflict" by marketing experts. The stockbroker is the historical channel for conducting business; the Internet is another channel that threatens the existing one. For all businesses that involve sales represen-tatives, taking orders over the Internet runs the risk of stealing business from the sales rep. A bricks-and-mortar store is threatened by an Internet business that sells the same products. A challenge for management is fig-uring out what to do with existing channels and vested interests when moving to a new business model and the Internet.

There are creative solutions to this problem. Some companies give com-missions to the sales representative of a client who places an order on the Web, even though the sales rep was not directly involved in the order. Remember that if you do not solve the channel problem, you are likely

to face a start-up on the Net that is unencumbered by the historical channel that is the source of your immediate problem. How much business do
you want to cede to this competitor?

We Don't Understand the Internet

Not all firms have the in-house talent to develop applications for the
Internet. Small firms may have very limited technology resources. Even
firms that have a lot of IT staff members may have managers who lack
an understanding of the technology. In 1999, a story circulated about the
chairman of a company who became convinced that his firm had at least
to look into the possibilities of the Internet only after he finally figured
out that the presents that he received from his children and grand-
children via UPS and Federal Express had been ordered on the Net! It is
hard to imagine a senior manager in 2000 not realizing that consumers
order a lot of goods over the Internet, but the chairman may not be
alone!

We Lack Infrastructure and Talent

Many firms have underinvested in information technology so they are not
in a position to take advantage of what the Internet offers. Electronic
commerce is more than just ordering over the Internet; the firm taking
the order must have internal systems in place that allow it to fill the order.
Customers expect to be able to track the progress of their orders over the
Internet after having placed them. One company wants to let customers
order on the Internet, but its manufacturing process is not well-controlled;
the fear is that the Web site will tell every customer that the company
cannot meet their desired delivery date. It is critical for the company to
implement supply chain management software to better utilize its capacity
before opening itself up to Web orders. Many firms do not have the systems in place for electronic commerce, and they may lack skilled technology staff members to develop them.

The good news is that an industry exists to help firms move to the
Internet and to set up and host Web sites. You can buy much of the
software needed to set up an electronic store, or you can outsource development and operations. The lack of internal infrastructure and talent

can be compensated for through outsourcing, and this is a particularly good strategy when you are behind and need to move quickly with a Net-enabled application.

Strategy and the Move to the Internet

The traditional firm has some disadvantages compared to the start-up when it considers moving to the Internet and participating in electronic commerce. The start-up's entire business plan is to take advantage of the Net and technology. The traditional firm has to consider its existing business model and organizational structure; there will be employees who are not enthusiastic about an Internet initiative. The firm also has to consider how to organize: Does it start a separate division, an entirely new subsidiary, or try to integrate Net activities into the existing structure of the organization?

Successful companies like Dell and Cisco have integrated electronic commerce and the Internet into their existing operations. By doing so, they have become "Net companies," as the Internet pervades all that they do. Other companies have adopted the subsidiary solution, both to stimulate new ideas and thinking and to provide incentives to employees working on new technology initiatives. Toys "R" Us established a separate Internet subsidiary when it decided to sell toys online in competition with eToys and others. This division was expected to go public at some time; such a move would unlock value for the parent company and provide employees of the subsidiary with the same financial opportunities that people working for a pure dot.com enjoy. (Toys "R" Us has recently formed an alliance with Amazon.com, which provides the ordering Web site and fulfillment for its online toy sales.)

Which alternative is best? If you want to see the Internet as a part of the way a company operates, it will be hard to diffuse this technology through the firm if it is being promoted by a separate division or subsidiary. If the Internet/electronic commerce initiative is not dependent on the rest of the organization, it can safely be placed in a subsidiary with a clear mission.

Toys "R" Us's e-commerce move has minimum dependencies on the rest of the business, though now it is dependent on Amazon. One could establish the electronic business with changes in the warehouse to ship directly to customers, and establish procedures in the store to accept returned merchandise ordered on the Net. However, electronic commerce does not require any changes in the core business of selecting and ordering products or the process of running physical stores.

The First Mover Strategy

There are firms that have gained a competitive advantage by being the first mover with a new idea. The number of these firms is small, and the duration of the advantage is often not long. In the 1970s, Merrill Lynch "invented" the cash management account, a brokerage account that swept cash into Merrill mutual funds at the end of each day. The account also had a number of additional features for the customer like check-writing privileges and a credit card. At the time, liquid assets mutual funds were paying very high interest rates, much higher than individual investors could obtain with CDs from a bank. The account turned out to be a big hit with investors. Although Merrill gave up the interest it earned on customers' balances, it gained a huge inflow of cash into its Mutual Funds, generating significant management fees for the firm. The cash management account also attracted a number of new customers.

Merrill tried to protect the cash management account with a patent as others rushed to develop the same kind of service. Merrill was unable to enforce the patent, and accounts that automatically sweep idle funds into higher interest paying accounts are now found at almost every financial institution. Merrill still enjoys market leadership and is believed to have the largest number of such accounts among brokerage firms. The cash management account has provided a partially sustainable advantage, but this move did not preclude competitors from imitating the idea.

Obtaining an Initial Advantage   The first challenge is to obtain an initial advantage using the firm's resources. Remember that, according to the model in figure 1.1, these resources need to be rare, valuable, inimitable, and nonsubstitutable. To try to obtain an advantage by being the first mover, you must come up with an idea and implement it quickly.

Critical Mass and the Hunt for Other Assets   The next step according to our strategy model is to achieve critical mass, especially if network externalities are likely. For Covisint, the automakers' joint purchasing site, to be successful, a critical mass of suppliers must participate. To encourage suppliers, the "big three" Detroit car companies along with Nissan and Renault cooperate, thus creating a critical mass of buyers. An auction site like this has network externalities; the more companies offering goods at auction and the more customers, the more attractive the site is to everyone.

Adding Resources to Sustain an Advantage   According to the model, the first mover needs to add resources at this point to build on an initial advantage. Often, these resources will be additional technology to expand the site and keep it robust. There have been a number of problems with e-commerce sites experiencing failures and outages, some of which have temporarily depressed the firm's stock price. A successful e-commerce firm is constantly investing to add more capacity.

Another important resource grows with the move to the Internet and electronic commerce—management skills and competence. According to the business model and the nature of the resources involved, why have hundreds of firms not copied the Dell and Cisco business models? Compaq has tried, so far without much success, to imitate Dell. Each firm has, or can buy, the same resources. What is different about the leaders? I believe the difference is due to the resource that Dell and Cisco have created through their business models: They have developed an organization structure and the skills necessary to make this model of Net-enabled lean production work. Lucent, one of Cisco's major competitors, in comparison, is still struggling with the organization structure and managerial mind set of AT&T, its parent company until a few years ago.

Responding to Competition
Not every firm can be the first mover; most will be followers. How should you respond if you are not the first mover? The first task is to decide on a business model. For Toys "R" Us, the choice was clear; it needed to match eToys and other Web-based toy retailers. (However, Toys "R" Us had significant problems filling its orders, which probably prompted its agreement with Amazon.)

Imitating Resources   The follower may be able to keep pace simply by imitating the resources of the leader. It is fairly easy to imitate a retail toy site. In addition, a bricks-and-mortar toy business has warehouses that can be modified to ship directly to the customer instead of just to retail stores. Toys "R" Us was extremely successful in attracting business during the 1999 Christmas season: It ranked second in the number of customer visits to its Web site with 8.9 million hits versus 11.1 million for top-ranked eToys (*New York Times*, January 2, 2000). However, by early 2001 eToys had failed after a disappointing 2000 Christmas season. EToys lacked capital and did not attract a critical mass of business.

Taking Advantage of Brand and Reputation   Many firms have spent years developing their brand and reputation. Customers frequently respond to a familiar brand and when the branded store becomes a dot.com, it draws business from the Internet start-up. Existing companies have sometimes had the edge in marketing an Internet site to their established customer base.

Merck-Medco, a division of Merck & Co., is a prescription benefits manager (PBM), a type of company that makes agreements with pharmacists and employers; pharmacies sell prescription drugs to those eligible for small fees, and the PBMs pay the balance out of insurance proceeds. PBMs are often invisible to the customer, and they evidently were invisible to the founders of Drugstore.com. This Internet start-up has been struggling whereas Merck-Medco's Web transactions have increased by a factor of ten in 1999 (*Wall Street Journal*, 13 April 2000).

Merck-Medco and other PBMs had a valuable resource in their agreements with pharmacies and insurance companies; they refused to deal with sites like Drugstore.com. Early buyers at these sites found that they could not get reimbursed from insurance companies for their purchases. This policy forced Drugstore.com to sell a 25 percent share to Rite-Aid, which owns a PBM.

The head of Merck-Medco decided to move quickly to the Internet out of fear of the competition. The company had recently invested heavily to improve its mail order service, an important complementary asset, and had built an automated drug warehouse in Las Vegas for eighty-five million dollars. Pharmacists at the warehouse simply punched a button to send pills through a series of tubes to bottles on the level below them. The bottles and literature about the medicine went into bags, which were then addressed and placed in the mail. For 75 percent of the orders, the entire process from dispensing to packing was automated. Machines at the warehouse filled five thousand bottles an hour. This investment in order fulfillment cut cycle times from two weeks to two days; the company now ships three-quarters of its orders on the day of receipt. The company is building a duplicate warehouse in New Jersey, and has started an experiment with two thousand doctors who use Palm Pilots to send electronic prescriptions to Merck-Medco.

Merck-Medco saves money for employers and makes more itself if customers order from it rather than the corner pharmacy. It makes the most money when customers order from the Internet rather than by phone or mail. The company has continuously invested in its site, providing health information and descriptions of each customer's insurance plans. It soon plans to sell products, including over-the-counter products, to the general public via its Web site as well. Now, some 20 percent of its customer transactions come via the Web, and Merck-Medco expects this number to grow to 75 percent. Drugstore.com gets four times the number of visitors as Merck-Medco, but the latter firm gets eight times as many prescription sales.

In this example, an "Old Economy" firm reacted quickly and took advantage of its existing resources, especially its agreements with insurance companies, to start a Web site. The company was successful in marketing to an existing customer base, and achieved a critical mass of users quickly. One of the key success factors for Merck-Medco was its chief executive who became convinced that the company had to compete on the Internet, and then took advantage of the firm's resources to create what appears to be a sustainable advantage.

Obtaining Substitute Resources   Another way of keeping pace with a first mover is to find a substitute for its resources. For Toys "R" Us, the brand and name recognition worked to its advantage; they are a resource that the firm has built up over the years, a resource that eToys and other dot.com companies have tried to create through massive advertising.

Looking for Other Assets   For Toys "R" Us, the presence of a physical store might be considered a liability as the firm moves to electronic commerce. However, the company turned this potential liability into a complementary asset by allowing customers to return any merchandise ordered through the Web to a local store. This feature made returns easier for Toys "R" Us than for the firstmover, eToys, which required that the customer ship items back to them.

Moving Late to the Internet   One way for a firm to catch up when moving late to the Internet is to forge alliances. Staples is a good example of such a firm. The company launched a retail site almost a year after its major competitor, Office Depot, had done so. Staples quickly formed links with dsl.net, Geocities, hotoffice, pint.com, and register.com (*Wall Street Journal*, January 14, 2000). The company integrates retail, catalog, and Web site orders and accepts the return of goods at its 1,125 stores. Staples is installing electronic kiosks in stores so that customers can order out-of-stock goods and place special orders online. Staples has one Web site for small businesses and another for consumers. Midsized companies can aggregate purchases for discounts and set up machine-to-machine links with the office supplier (*E-Week*, November 13, 2000.) Staples.com generated $95.7 million in sales in the second quarter of 2000, and management expects to see annual electronic sales of $350 million.

Staples offers an array of services to small businesses, and is taking an equity stake in a number of small Internet companies in the process. It provides services like payroll management, insurance, and communications. Staples has an agreement with Ariba to include Staples' office catalogs in Ariba's e-commerce software, programs designed to eliminate physical stores like Staples! The small sites and services yield limited amounts of revenue, but up to 50 percent profit margins.

With alliances, the late arrival can add resources to its effort to catch up, which is easier and faster than trying to develop the same resources in-house. In addition, the alliance often does not require capital so that financing is not a constraint on the acquisition of resources and complementary assets.

Embracing the Internet

Grainger

Sometimes, the least likely firms turn out to be leaders when a new technology comes along. W. W. Grainger, located in Lincolnshire, Illinois, for example, is an unglamorous merchant that sells 210,000 industrial supplies. This relatively unknown firm has five hundred stores, 1.5 million customers, and over four billion dollars in annual sales (*Wall Street Journal*, December 13, 1999). Its products are basically boring—electric motors, cleaners, mops, and light bulbs. The firm was founded in 1927 and today puts out a seventeen-pound catalog.

In the last four years, Grainger's online business has become one of the largest business-to-business sites on the Internet, posting $100 million in sales in 1999. The company expects to have $400 million in Internet sales in 2000. Grainger gets about 6 percent of its business through e-commerce, and most of it comes from customers who switched from calling or faxing orders to the Web site. However, customers using the Internet increased their business by about 17 percent from 1998 to 1999, compared to an 8 percent growth rate for other customers. The company is investing $120 million in e-commerce in 2000 with an emphasis on creating a seamless linkage between the warehouses and the Internet ("bricks and clicks") (*New York Times*, September 20, 2000).

The key to Grainger's success is a vision that goes beyond treating the Internet as simply "another 800 number"; instead, management rethought their business model. Their insight: The Internet would reduce search costs for customers, and reduce process costs for Grainger.

Before the Web, Grainger sold products to nearly 10 percent of all U.S. businesses including factories, garages, grocers, schools, and military bases. The business was built around a gigantic inventory of maintenance and repair supplies, all listed in its four thousand-page catalog. The company ships orders directly to customers, or customers pick up their orders at one of five hundred stores around the United States.

In 1995, the company became aware of the Internet when it received calls from telephone and cable companies wanting to form an alliance. The firm decided to proceed on its own and allocated five million dollars to get started. Some 150 people are now dedicated to the operation. The company has added products from six other companies to its site, and added an auction site for discontinued and excess inventory. It also offers use of a search engine for its multicompany product listing of five million items.

The company uses the Net to keep track of special pricing; it will build online customized catalogs for companies that have negotiated special discounts on its products. The search engine looks at four thousand electric motors sold by the company to find the right RPMs and size, and indicates whether the motor is available for shipping or is already in a store. Web customers spend an average of $240 per order compared to $130 for phone or in-person orders, and nearly 25 percent of Web orders come in when stores are closed. To protect its sales force, representatives receive commissions when one of their customers orders over the Web.

Banks and Insurance Firms Move Carefully

Have you ever visited an insurance company? Do you look forward to meeting with an insurance agent? Do you spend hours on the phone getting competitive quotations? Internet brokers are trying to make buying insurance easy, if not pleasant; they seek a piece of the $250 million that Americans spend yearly to insure houses, cars, and health (*Business Week*, November 22, 1999). Sites like Quotesmith, InsWeb, eCoverage, and ebix all compete to sell insurance without an agent.

The response? Allstate has said that it will reduce its workforce by 10 percent and start selling its products over the Net. Insurance is not a commodity product like a book or a CD. These sites sell policies created and underwritten by licensed insurance companies. However, how long will it take for a firm to develop software for configuring and underwriting policies so that it can sell custom insurance products over the Web?

How often do you visit your bank? How often did you visit it before the introduction of ATMs? I used to think that physical branch banks would always be necessary for safe deposit boxes and traveler's checks. Of course, with global ATM networks today, you hardly need traveler's checks anymore; even if you do, at least one bank will send them to your home and let you sign them there. That leaves only safe deposit boxes.

Bank One in Columbus decided to take a different approach to offering online banking; it started a separate Internet-only bank called "Wingspan." This virtual bank is happy to compete with its parent, and offers higher interest rates than a customer can get at any of Bank One's one thousand nine hundred branches in fourteen states (*Wall Street Journal*, August 25, 1999). The idea is to have a bank unencumbered by its physical parent. Wingspan's board includes a college student, a programmer, and a mother who does not work outside the home. The board meets online as well as in person.

Wingspan did not have to figure out how to hook up with Bank One's massive transactions-processing computers; it outsources processing to a company in Pennsylvania that processes transactions in real-time. The Internet bank also offers a broad choice of investment vehicles from a variety of institutions. Bank One customers can choose from forty-nine mutual funds; Wingspan's, from seven thousand. Unlike a conventional bank, Wingspan will steer customers to E-Loan and similar firms. The bank's main drawback? How to handle cash. It is at the mercy of the U.S. mail for taking deposits. The company will reimburse customers up to five dollars a month for ATM fees as one way around the cash problem. (Wingspan's recent growth has been less than expected and its future is in doubt, partially because of Bank One's difficulties.)

Wells Fargo and Bank of America have taken a different approach, effectively adding an Internet branch through their Web sites. If a physical branch or presence is unnecessary, then why cannot anyone be a banker? What scares the banks is a firm like Wal-Mart, which is currently buying a small Oklahoma thrift institution—a purchase that will give the giant retailer the ability to offer car loans, mortgages, credit cards, and other banking services.

Net banks are not a U.S. phenomenon. Prudential Assurance of London established an Internet bank called "Egg" last year. Competitors were unworried, given that the company lacked banking experience; the bets were on failure (*Business Week*, October, 25 1999). A year and a half later, the new bank had thirteen billion dollars in deposits from young, wealthy clients. Balances average a profitable thirty thousand dollars compared to an average of five thousand dollars at a bricks-and-mortar bank. Now, Barclays and National Westminster Banks are setting up online services that range from bill payment to stock trading.

The low cost structure of the Internet favors the start-up over the bricks-and-mortar bank branch. One study estimated that it costs over $1 to handle a transaction in a bank branch, $.55 on the phone, $.25 at an ATM and $.02 on the Internet. Internet banks also can track what interests customers on their Web site and cross sell products using that knowledge. The question yet to be answered is whether the Internet is merely an extension of an existing bank, an electronic branch, or whether the Internet offers the opportunity for a completely new banking business model.

So far, the advantage seems to be with the traditional bank that has adopted the Internet for some aspect of the services it provides. In 2000, Wells Fargo had 14 percent of the Internet banking market share, Bank of America 9.6 percent, Citigroup 4.8 percent, and Bank One 4 percent (*Wall Street Journal*, January 21, 2000). It appears that purely Net banks have not been able to reach critical mass. Some of them have had difficulty providing customer service and convincing people that the Internet is safe for banking. In contrast, it has proven easy for traditional banks to copy some of the features of online banks—for example, making customer account balances and transactions available on the Web. It is reported that Wingspan opened 144,000 accounts in its first year; in comparison, its parent's Web site at Bank One has 500,000.

Abandoning the Traditional Model

The discussion so far suggests how the traditional company can move to take advantage of the Internet and electronic commerce. Change can be viewed as a continuum from minor modifications to radical transformation. This section looks at two firms at the radical extreme of the change continuum. Both firms largely abandoned their existing business models and adopted new models enabled by the Internet.

Egghead Software to Egghead.com

An entrepreneur dissatisfied with his own software shopping experience founded Egghead Software in 1985. The format was very successful, and eventually the chain had 150 retail stores, staffed by sales help who could actually provide customers with help and advice about software. By 1992, the chain had 12,500 employees in more than 180 retail stores in the United States. It had a net income that year of fifteen million dollars on seven hundred million dollars in sales.

The average store was about two thousand square feet and stocked two thousand items. In addition to retail operations, Egghead employed a direct sales force of 350 people who worked with the government, corporations, and educational institutions to sell software. Rapid growth caused a number of problems for the chain; George Orban, a board member who eventually became the CEO, commented that the firm had no vision of a business strategy. It lacked the management systems to support stores, and had developed a very complex business model to manage (Rangan and Bell 1999).

The biggest threat to Egghead was the development of "superstores" like CompUSA, which sell both hardware and software. These stores make most of their margin selling hardware and are inclined to give away software or sell it for a low price. By the end of the 1990s, superstores accounted for 30 percent of software sales. Egghead's performance was not impressive, and stockholders were dissatisfied with the firm.

Orban became CEO in 1997 and moved to close seventy unprofitable stores, reducing the geographic areas in which Egghead had a presence from fifty-four to twenty-six regions. Orban formed an alliance with Surplus Direct, a company that specialized in selling closeout software. The two companies opened a combined superstore selling software and hardware that was very successful, and quickly moved to open three more stores. However, further analysis showed that finding good locations for a series of these stores would be difficult.

In August of 1997, Egghead opened a Web site oriented toward electronic commerce. Surplus Direct also offered sites for direct purchase and for auctioning goods. Eventually, the two firms received approval by the SEC to merge. By December of 1997, Orban saw that the model for selling software and hardware was changing, and that retail stores, even superstores, would have trouble competing in the future. At that point, Egghead's management decided to get away from the bricks-and-mortar business model and become an electronic merchant exclusively. The company closed all of its stores in six weeks and took a $37.6 million, one-time charge against earnings. The number of employees dropped from two thousand people to three hundred, and the company changed its name to Egghead.com.

Egghead.com has forty thousand products for sale including hardware, software, and peripherals. There are about ten thousand software products, and a customer can download a few of them. The company has EDI connections with major suppliers and stocks only its top two hundred items; the rest distributors ship upon notification from Egghead. Surplus Direct continues to maintain separate Web sites, with about 150,000 customers for its auction site and 100,000 for its direct sales site. While the change has had a negative impact on profits, the stock market responded very favorably to the new model.

By 2000, Egghead had merged with OnSale, an Internet auction site. Their combined site sells fixed price goods from Egghead, and runs auctions of Onsale's and Surplus Direct's products. The CEO of the merged companies posted the following letter to the Onsale/Egghead Web site; it illustrates the advantage of being a Web merchant.

I'd like to tell you about some recent changes to our business. Onsale and egghead.com—two of the leading Internet retailers—have joined forces to create a single shopping site for new and surplus computers, electronics, sporting goods, and vacations. We've taken the best of both companies, put them together, and added new features to better serve you.

By combining our efforts and resources, we can offer:

More products—our expanded buying staff can secure a greater selection of new and surplus merchandise to meet your needs.

Better deals—our increased purchasing power, stronger vendor relationships, and efficiency of scale means better prices for you.

Improved information—we've expanded product descriptions and added technical tutorials to help you select the right products.

Convenient and prompt customer service—you can look up the status of your order or visit our online Customer Service Center 24 hours a day to answer a question or to resolve a problem quickly and easily.

Faster service and delivery—by pooling our warehouses and distributor relationships, you will find more items in stock and quicker delivery to your location.

Enhanced web site—with our online tools, such as Bidwatch and Easy Search, we offer one of the most advanced shopping experiences on the web.

If you are a returning Egghead or Onsale customer, you will find the familiar products and services that you have enjoyed in the past, in an updated format.

Egghead customers will notice that the Surplus Auctions site has been combined with Onsale Auctions, while the Surplus Direct® Store now appears as a tab on our home page. Onsale customers will notice that we have merged Onsale atCost into the egghead.com Superstores, with a broader array of products and the same great prices. Existing Egghead and Onsale accounts can be used throughout the combined site.

Table 7.2 presents a resource-based analysis, using our dynamic strategy model of Egghead's dramatic transformation into an Internet company. Initially, the chain had a resource in its retail stores; however, as business conditions and competition changed, these stores became more of a liability than an asset. The superstore venture with Surplus Direct had promise, but Orban felt that the nature of the business was changing to favor the Internet. By purchasing Surplus Direct, Egghead acquired complementary assets in the form of additional products so that it could compete with superstores selling hardware and software.

Egghead's most dramatic redeployment of resources was its move to the Internet and the closing of all its physical stores. This move affected resources in a number of ways; the most important being that it freed them to be applied to a new business model based on exclusive sales through the Internet. These additional resources could be used to create and promote the site, develop an effective supply chain, and expand the range of products offered. Surplus Direct's Internet auctions, are another resource for the company; as with other auctions they illustrate network externalities and the critical mass phenomenon. Surplus Direct and Egghead complement each other nicely; their interaction is a unique resource for the company. The merger with OnSale allows both firms to apply additional resources to their combined businesses. It provides larger group of customers and may help the site reach critical mass.

Although Egghead has undertaken dramatic change, table 7.2 shows that none of its actions has created an advantage based on resources. Its model can easily be imitated, or other resources can be found as a substitute. The company has transformed itself into an Internet business, but this analysis suggests that it will continue to face intense competition from both superstores and other Net merchants.

Table 7.2
Egghead Resource Analysis

Resource	Rare	Valuable	Inimitable	Nonsubstitutable	Other Model Components
Initial Resources					
Egghead stores	Yes	Became less so	No	No	
Superstores with Surplus Direct	No	Yes	No	No	
Additional Resources					
Purchase of Surplus Direct	No	Yes	No	No	Acquire complementary assets/product line
Move to Internet	Yes	Yes	No	No	
Internet auctions	No	Yes	No	No	Network externalities and critical mass of bidders/products
Merge with Onsale	Yes	Yes	No	No	
Interactions					
Surplus Direct ↔ Egghead software↔Onsale	Yes	Yes	No	No	Cospecialized asset of similar products, purchasing; add products and customer base

A Small Promotional Company

Egghead is a large company, and large organizations are very hard to change. The Net and new business models also affect small firms. One such firm is eCompanyStore.com, a distributor of promotional items like T-shirts, logo-imprinted golf shirts, and mugs. At first, the company had a small presence in Atlanta and was one of the nineteen thousand traditional firms in this field (*Wall Street Journal*, January 3, 2000).

Walt Geer and a friend started the business in 1994, accepting orders via phone and fax. After three attempts at a Web site, the company did succeed in setting up a custom site for a new client in Texas that owned eighty-four apartment complexes. The client intended to use the site online to order logo products for its employees. At the real estate company's meeting, Geer made a presentation of the site and found an enthusiastic response from managers. At this point, he realized that the Net provided the opportunity for a new business model.

Over the weekend, the two partners wrote a new business plan for the company to become a totally Internet firm. For small customers, they would maintain a general Web site for ordering. For customers who spent at least two hundred thousand dollars on promotional products per year, the firm would set up a customized Web site and take a percentage of the Web-generated sales.

It took three months with a technology partner to develop Web sites for the firm's three largest customers including the Texas apartment management firm, Miller Brewing, and the Leukemia Society of America. Because of the workload setting up the sites, the company continued to handle its small customers in the conventional way, taking orders that averaged five hundred dollars. A new CFO convinced the company's founders that it was too expensive to serve these small, long-time customers who only generated one million dollars in sales in total each year. The company notified 98 percent of its customers that it was now an "Internet company" focused on providing online stores for its clients.

At first, large company contracts did not come in, and managers were worried that they had made the wrong decision. Within a few months, however, the firm began to get contracts from large customes to create stores for them. The company has a number of competitors, but its site works well, and this feature was the deciding factor for at least one large customer, the Southern Company, a large Atlanta utility that spends two million dollars a year on logo products. By the end of 1999, the company had thirty customers.

ECompanyStore.com is a small firm that has adopted a completely new business model based on the Internet. Egghead.com was converted into a virtual store and, in the process, changed the way in which it interacts with its customers. ECompanyStore.com actually dropped most of its customers to focus a new business model on a different set of customers. It is too early in its development to know if this strategy will be successful, but the example does demonstrate how radically a firm may have to change to adapt to the Internet and electronic commerce.

Recommendations

The traditional firm is handicapped when competing with the dot.com start-up because of its investment in an existing business model. Its resources have been applied to using this model to compete, and it has a hard time changing directions. What can the traditional firm do to adapt its strategy?

Take the Lead

If you can become the first mover, it may be possible to build up critical mass and sustain an advantage, at least for a few years. Many of the firms described in this book responded to competitors, often dot.com companies that came out of nowhere and took market share. Examples include Merrill Lynch versus E*Trade and other e-brokers, and Toys "R" Us versus eToys and other online toy companies.

In contrast, the Detroit auto manufacturers are exploring new ways to conduct their business on the Internet. Ford directs customers to services that provide the invoice price of a car, and lets them put in a bid on a specific model at the Ford site. Ford then directs that bid to a group of dealers in the area to see if one will accept it. Detroit is trying to take the lead, but it is also responding to auto buying services on the Web that make use of individual dealers.

Think Boldly

One of the most difficult challenges for the traditional company is to think about a new business model, to do something bold. Egghead.com and eCompanyStore.com thought boldly and took major risks in adopting new business models. Is your firm capable of this kind of thinking? Is it ready and able to take the risk of doing something radical? What would happen to your firm if it decided only to accept orders via the Internet? What physical facilities could you close and replace with virtual services?

The Dynamic Strategy Model: How Does It Help?

The dynamic strategy model in figure 1.1 can be used to guide the traditional firm as it makes the transition to the Internet. Consider the following steps:

1. Identify your initial resources. What are the characteristics of these resources? Are they rare, valuable, inimitable, and nonsubstitutable?

2. If you have a sustained competitive advantage, what resources are responsible? One of these resources is likely to be a well-known brand that you have built up like Toys "R" Us. Another resource may be management skills at executing a particular business model like Dell and Cisco.

3. In the new digital economy, are any of your resources and assets a liability? Do you have the equivalent of Egghead's outmoded retail stores, or are your retail stores a possible cospecialized asset with an electronic store as with Toys "R" Us?

4. What new resources do you need to combine with existing ones to provide an initial advantage? Some of these resources are likely to be technical such as the ones required to create a robust Web site.

5. Does your business model require a critical mass to succeed? If so, how do you achieve that mass? Egghead initially sponsored a contest in which it gave away a Dodge Viper to draw people to its site. Are there likely to be network externalities? If so, reaching a critical mass is very important.

6. What is the likely interaction among your resources, and how can you take advantage of it?

7. What additional resources do you need as your initiative becomes more successful? Can you create a system of resources through added investment, as the airline CRS vendors did through continual enhancements to their reservations systems?

The analyses to date using the dynamic strategy model have shown that it is very difficult to create a sustainable competitive advantage. However, the guidelines and the model can help you compete successfully while building a system of resources aimed at providing a sustainable advantage. In a hypercompetitive economy, competing successfully is a first step and a prerequisite to not being forced out of business because of an outmoded business model.

Appendix: More on the Internet

The Internet is not a single network. It is a collection of over sixty thousand networks, all of which have at least one server. Networks can be connected directly to one another, but most often are linked through a small number of official network access points in the U.S. Hundreds of service providers exchange traffic at these access points. A large service provider will have its own communications network. This network will include a number of local access points so customers can minimize their long distance charges. The service provider's backbone network connects all of its local access points to the Internet.

Although it is not known with any certainty how many users exist, there are over 80 million host computers on the Internet and over 150 million users in at least 150 countries. Although scientists and engineers were the earliest users, followed by academics, today the Internet is available to commercial firms and to the general public. Figure 7.1 shows the tremendous growth in Internet hosts.

You can connect directly to the Internet through an organization's computers. The domain name identifies the type of organization; for example, our address is first initial followed by hlucas@rhsmith.umd.edu. *Edu* stands for an educational institution; *com*, a commercial firm; *gov*, the government; and *mil*, the military. With this kind of address, your organization has a computer connected directly to the Net. From home, many

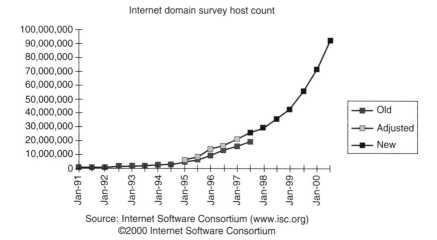

Figure 7.1
The Growth of Internet Hosts

people use access providers to reach the Net. Mass market services like America Online offer access to the Web. Near the end of 2000, additional domain names were added to the Internet to expand the types of names available for Web sites.

There are also Internet service providers that exist only to connect you with the Net and generally charge ten dollars to twenty dollars a month for this service. In November of 1994, the business volume of 800 (toll free) calls exceeded the volume of other business calls for the first time. AT&T wants to see that it captures data as well as voice calls through connections to the Internet on its AT&T Worldnet service. These access providers also have to contend with cable TV companies offering Internet access via cable modems, as well as newly developed satellite broadband providers.

The ArpaNet was originally designed so that scientists and others could conduct research on computer networking itself and gain access to remote computers and files. The government also wanted to tie together diverse networks developed for the military by various low bidders, each providing different equipment. Within months of the opening of the ArpaNet, however, interpersonal communication in the form of electronic mail and computerized bulletin boards became the dominant application. Today, there are approximately eight thousand bulletin boards distributed across the Internet. Online, real-time conferences in which users join a group and chat by passing text messages back and forth are becoming increasingly popular. There are also various multi-user games for recreation.

Government agencies post requests for proposal (RFPs) to Internet servers, and contractors can file their bids electronically. There are a number of job postings available on the network, and companies including AT&T list information about themselves on the Internet. Mead Data Central provides Internet access to its Lexis/Nexis database on a subscription basis.

The Internet is also used extensively to share and distribute software. Dell distributes new versions of its software via the Internet as well as through other channels.

Business Week estimates there are 150 journals published electronically. Some scientists are calling for the elimination of paper journals given that the lead time for publication is so great. A large number of journals are posting their table of contents on the Internet, and some hope to provide information that is not included in the printed version. There are some fifty thousand peer-reviewed technical journals, a four billion dollar industry. The threat of Internet publishing is very real to these businesses.

At first, the Internet was criticized for its difficulty of use; the World Wide Web and graphical browsers represented major breakthroughs because they facilitated its use. Researchers at CERN in Geneva developed the World Wide Web, which connected an estimated thirty thousand network servers using the Hypertext Transfer Protocol (HTTP). The Web uses hypertext links produced with the Hypertext Markup Language (HTML) to link documents and files. Hypertext is created by placing links on words to reference other sections of text or other documents. Clicking on a highlighted piece of text with a computer mouse results in the retrieval of a new file or document, allowing the user to browse through related pieces of information. The retrieved documents may all reside on different computers, but the Web makes all retrieval transparent to the user. Extensible Markup Language, (XML) is applied to electronic commerce applications because it can be used to identify the data on a Web page. A developer using XML tags identifies the meaning of data such as price; the visitor's browser then knows the piece of data is the price of an item for sale on the site.

HTTP is a connectionless protocol, which means that each client-server connection is limited to a single request for information. This way, the network is not tied up in a permanent connection between the client and server. (The disadvantage is that many connections may be made repeatedly to the same server to request information.) The Web is an excellent example of a client-server architecture—your computer is the client, and you visit a variety of Web servers as you search for information. To see an example of hypertext source documents, run your Internet Browser and click on "View" and then "Source."

To use the Web, one needs a net browser. The development of a graphical Web browser is a second breakthrough, one made possible by the connections provided by HTML and the Web. These programs are activated by the user by "pointing and clicking" with a mouse, which is a vast improvement over character-based terminal access to the Internet. A browser connects users to different services, helping them navigate around the confusing and disorganized structure of the Internet. One can also use browsers to create forms and facilitate the publication of data.

Host computers on the Internet generally provide some form of content, information that users access with their browsers. With millions of Web hosts, there is an incredible amount of content available. To help you find information, there are over thirty search engines on the Web. These services, funded by advertising, accept your search queries and look for matching content on the Web.

Search engines do not actually search the Web for each query; rather, they search the web at various times (the middle of the night?) and build an index of terms. When you make a query, the engines search their indexes and give you the Universal Resource Locators (URLs) that look like <http://www.rhsmith.umd.edu>, plus a few lines of text from the page that the URL references.

The interaction with the Web described thus far depends on the initiative of the user who searches for and decides which sites to access. "Push" technology refers to services on the Internet which come automatically to the user, who can sign up with companies that will send news and other information to her client computer on a continuous basis. Wheat First

Union, a financial services firm in, Richmond, Virginia, for example, uses push technology to alert its stockbrokers of important news and stock-selling opportunities from the large blocks of shares that the firm purchases several times a day. Originally, push technology developed on the Internet, but it is spreading to Intranets as well.

Internet technology is having a major impact on companies through Intranets. A firm sets up servers and clients following Internet protocols and distributes a web browser to its users. The network is probably not connected to the Internet, but rather is used to publish information internally within the company. This information is likely to be proprietary; thus, the company does not want other Internet users to have access to it. An Intranet also provides a platform for developing and distributing applications that anyone in the firm with a browser can access.

How can a company benefit from this kind of technology investment? Morgan Stanley is a major investment bank, and since its merger with Dean Witter, a retail broker. Morgan Stanley has developed an extensive Intranet, which contains research information developed by various parts of the firm. Because the information is posted on the Internet, it is available to anyone in the company. Members of the firm do not overlook research because it happens to be in someone's bottom drawer.

At Chrysler, an Intranet has replaced the company telephone directory; it provides a photograph and job descriptions in addition to phone numbers. The automaker uses its Intranet to broadcast information, monitor projects, and reduce the amount of time, employees spend hunting for information. Vehicle program managers post car-design changes to Chrysler's Intranet so that they are instantly available.

The engineering department has invested $750,000 in its part of the Intranet in an effort to link isolated systems. Using the same browser interface, engineers can move from its main software design system, CATIA, to regulatory manuals and home pages that describe how different projects are proceeding. The minivan team home page links to a progress report on the design of a new vehicle's body. Executives can check progress without convening a meeting. The Intranet should help Chrysler achieve its goal of reducing the cycle time for vehicle design to two years from the current four or five years (*Wall Street Journal*, May 13, 1997).

Intranets have the potential to link employees in an organization as well as disparate information systems. As firms create links between Intranet standards and legacy transactions-processing systems, it is possible to envision an environment in which the major desktop application for each user is a browser. Using the browser and Intranet, an employee accesses all types of corporate information along with the data from internal, proprietary information systems in the company.

It is also possible to provide external access to an Intranet, creating an Extranet, so that customers and others can access your internal servers. An Extranet uses Internet technology to provide online access to your internal net servers, generally through a password for each external user. With an Extranet, you can create an online system very quickly since you are taking advantage of the existing, worldwide Internet.

The technology of the Internet makes electronic commerce possible; it is a resource for all firms. Because it is universally available, a firm cannot gain an advantage from merely using the Net. Your business model and strategy incorporate the Internet, but other resources are required for a sustainable competitive advantage.

III

Strategies for Innovation

Although they have recently lost some of their attraction in the investment community, dot.com start-ups are exciting places to work and typically draw new MBAs and veteran managers from large companies, who are attracted not only by their general lack of structure and hierarchy but also by the prospect of wealth. The dynamic resource-based model of strategy applies to the dot.com start-up just as it does to the traditional firm. An analysis of these companies using the model suggests how hard it is to gain a competitive advantage. The start-up's business model is public, and there is little that can be done to protect it. A few entrepreneurs have tried to patent their business processes and software, but it remains to be seen if these patents will be upheld.

Chapter 8 presents examples of new businesses enabled by the Internet, such as Service Providers, portals, hubs, and worldwide auctions. Companies that start on the Web generally need help from a diverse set of partners. Chapter 9 explores some of the resources available to start-ups, and the challenges typically faced by their business partners, the companies to which the start-up outsources aspects of its business. Because these companies are what makes a virtual firm succeed, we will analyze their strategies as well.

8

Strategies for New Businesses on the Internet

There are two kinds of new businesses on the Internet—those that start from scratch in the form of dot.com companies and units of traditional firms that have made a commitment to a new business model implemented through a new division or subsidiary. Both types of ventures face the same environment on the Net, but their resources and history put them in different competitive positions.

The huge initial advantage of the dot.com start-up was the fact that investors did not seem to require an immediate profit. The more that dot.com firms lost, the higher their market valuations rose. The division or subsidiary of an existing firm has to be concerned about the extent of its losses, because the traditional firm has established a set of earnings expectations over the years. This chapter focuses on new kinds of businesses on the Internet, most of which are Net start-ups. Today, the magic is largely gone, and dot.coms are having more difficulty attracting investment funds, and a number have gone out of business. A business model that postpones earnings indefinitely no longer appears sustainable.

Some New Business Models

The Internet has stimulated a torrent of innovative ideas for new businesses as entrepreneurs see new kinds of products and services that can be offered through the Net.

Portals
Before the Internet, there was no such thing as a portal, though mass media services came close. These pre-Internet services provided many

features like chat rooms, e-mail, and access to information. The most advanced service prior to the Internet was the Minitel system in France. This system, based on inexpensive terminals and a character-based rather than graphics interface, still has a major presence in France. However, the Prime Minister said recently that Minitel was a significant impediment to France's technological progress, and he allocated funds to help the country move more toward the Internet. With Minitel, the subscriber generally connects to a service provider directly without going through a portal.

The U.S. mass market information services included Prodigy, AT&T Worldnet, and America Online, among others. At first, these systems consisted of the service providers' computers, and subscribers were restricted to the services offered on those computers. Each service provider created its own private network with access points in a large number of physical locations so that most subscribers would only be a local telephone call away. The Minitel model was different in that the system had open standards and made it easy for any service provider with a computer to connect to the network, much like today's Internet.

On the Internet, one finds a number of portals that grew from search engines, along with several of the old mass-market firms that connected to the Internet. Examples of search engine portals are Yahoo, Lycos, and Google. Users of the Internet need a search engine to find Web sites and to locate content. Suppose that you are interested in learning more about the TCP/IP Internet protocol. You could enter this information into a search engine, and it would retrieve a very large number of references to documents that contain the search term. A good engine will help you refine the conditions of the search to reduce the number of references returned, and will hierarchize the references in terms of what it considers most relevant. Because a large part of using the Web involves searching, it was natural to use a search engine to attract people to a site and to extend services to make it a portal.

What is the advantage of being a portal? The portal provides or directs its users to a large number of services. The more services the portal provides, the more users it attracts. The more users at a portal, the more interested service providers are in being included in that portal. For example, Amazon.com would like to recommend books to you when you search a particular topic. They would like the portal to link to Amazon.com for these recommendations, and to direct the user to Amazon's site to purchase the books. Because the portal charges the linked Web sites for the services that it makes available to users, the more services it provides, the better its revenues. Portals also earn revenue from the considerable advertising they attract.

Of the old mass-market information services, the most successful is America Online. By taking advantage of the Internet, offering access in 1995, and claiming a loyal customer base, AOL has become the world's largest commercial online service with over twenty-five million subscribers. In the year it offered Internet access, subscribers increased by more than 200 percent, revenue tripled, and AOL's stock value quadrupled (Stohr, Viswanathan, and White 1999). AOL bought the subscriber base of Compuserve when MCI Worldcom purchased this service provider, and also bought part of Netscape.

Why has AOL remained so popular, despite problems with its pricing plan several years ago, and one monumental technical problem that took them off the air for twenty hours? Industry experts attribute it to information content instant messaging and buddy lists, and the large AOL chat audience. Successful chat rooms require a critical mass of users, and exhibit network externalities. Generally, the more people participating in a chat, the more interesting the chat becomes. The large number of users, in turn, attracts more content. In particular, AOL is an extremely desirable partner for other Web companies because of its large customer base.

Similarly, AOL's instant messenger feature and its buddy lists have achieved a critical mass and continue to exhibit network externalities. Instant messenger allows a subscriber to exchange messages via the keyboard with other subscribers who are logged on at the time. A user provide a list of buddies, and AOL notifies him if any buddies are logged on when he is using the service. AOL has labored to keep instant messaging proprietary, but there are increasing demands to allow it to interoperate with other ISPs like the Microsoft Network. Interoperability is the spirit of the Internet; it would let subscribers of MSN exchange instant messages with AOL subscribers. Eventually, instant messaging would become available to all ISP subscribers. It is easy to see an extension to this service when more homes are wired for broadband access, which would bring full videoconferencing for simultaneous users of the Internet.

In comparing sites, advertisers are interested in "stickiness," that is, how long does a user stick with the site? AOL's content and chat rooms tend to keep the customer interested and involved in the site. Another portal, Yahoo, allows users to create a "My Yahoo! site that is customized with a particular choice of information when the user logs on. Yahoo has been consistently profitable, but a recent drop in advertising has forced it to post lower earnings and make management changes.

In January 2000, AOL adopted a dramatic new business model as it initiated the purchase of Time Warner. In 1999, AOL had more than four times the net profit of Time Warner, earning $762 million in its fiscal year, ending on June 30. However, Time Warner's revenues of nearly $27 billion dwarf those of AOL at a little under $5 billion.

AOL faced two significant problems that it hoped the merger would solve. First, a number of sites were beginning to offer free Internet access; AOL needed new content to justify its monthly access charges. Second, AT&T had become the largest U.S. cable company, and had not decided whether or not to share cable access with other ISPs. AOL needed high-speed access or it would lose its customers.

AT&T wanted to become independent of the local phone companies and to stop paying for access to each home or business. A cable connection would allow the firm to bypass the local telephone company; it would also position AT&T to become a provider of high-speed Internet access. AOL had been arguing that AT&T (and others) should open up their cable systems to allow competitors to use them. (The impact of AT&T's recent move to split into independent companies is not clear as of this writing. It is possible that the cable unit will become even more competitive under the new structure.)

The lack of high-speed access for AOL could have had a very negative impact on the firm, dramatically reducing its subscriber base and eventually forcing it into a merger in which it would not come out on top. Cable systems are a specialized asset for high-speed Internet access; if they are dedicated exclusively to one portal, they become a cospecialized asset. The portal that gains control of this asset has a resource that provides a significant competitive advantage.

Through its purchase of Time Warner, AOL gained access to new content in a variety of formats, and Time Warner became a major Internet player. AOL faces competitors that offer free Internet access in return for demographic information from users, or users who are willing to subject themselves to extra advertising. There are also Web services that contract with large corporations, like Delta Airlines and Ford, to provide services to hundreds of thousands of employees. Time Warner's content is an important resource for competing with free and contractual service provider. With the merger, AOL also acquired control of a specialized and possibly cospecialized asset—Time Warner's cable properties. (AOL has indicated that it will open cable access to competing Internet Service Providers.)

In addition to cable, America Online is becoming a force in the telephone business through the purchase of bits and pieces of technology for handling calls over the Internet. In addition, AOL is looking at ways to provide access to its portal through wireless devices. Steve Case has spoken of a future in which people use "AOL phones." The voice market was first dominated by traditional carriers using land lines. The explosion in cellular phones is the first threat to the traditional phone company. Cheap calls on the Internet represent another major threat. AOL, to succeed, will have to leverage its resources, including its customer base, instant messaging services, and the one hundred million customers who are registered for text chatting (*Wall Street Journal*, March 13, 2000). To add to a formidable base of resources, AOL has made investments in a number of technology firms.

AOL's latest plan includes expanding access beyond personal computers; the firm's new theme is "AOL Anywhere." A new set of services includes a toll free number members can call and use voice commands to read e-mail, get stock quotes, and hear the news and weather. A member's address book is stored centrally so that one can access it anyplace. AOL is developing a subscription music download service as well. Additional plans call for a Gateway-AOL Net computer and an AOL set top box for cable television sets allowing members to surf the Web and participate in instant messaging from their TV sets. Instant messaging is also available on Sprint PCS cellular phones (*Wall Street Journal*, October 25, 2000).

Table 8.1 is a resource-based analysis of AOL. In the pre-Internet days, the company created a significant asset in the combination of a subscriber base and content, including popular chat rooms and, later, instant messaging and buddy lists. However, other sites could imitate these offerings

Table 8.1
America Online Resource Analysis

Resource	Rare	Valuable	Inimitable	Nonsubstitutable	Other Model Components
Initial Resources					
Subscriber base	No	Yes	No	No	
Content/chat rooms	Yes	Yes	No	No	Use to develop critical mass; demonstrates network externalities
Additional Resources					
Acquire other companies	Yes	Yes	No	No	
Provide Internet access, add instant messaging buddy lists	No	Yes	No	No	
Add capacity	No	Yes	No	No	
Buy Time Warner	Yes	Yes	Yes	Partially	Gain control of complementary assets (content) and cospecialized asset (cable TV operations)
Offer voice and phone service	Yes	Yes	No	No	May have subscriber base for critical mass and to provide network externalities
Interactions					
Internet access as portal ↔ content/loyal subscriber base, Time Warner content	Yes	Yes	Yes, given Time Warner's unique content	Possibly, but difficult to substitute, given Time Warner's unique content	Combination of resources becomes a resource for competitive advantage

and did. Upon opening a portal for the Internet, AOL had to expand capacity to keep up with the demand. However, the Internet service it provides is not significantly different from other ISPs. It is important to note that each of AOL's resources alone is subject to substitution by using another ISP. However, through its merger with Time Warner, AOL gained both content that is hard to imitate or substitute for, and access to important cable franchises that provide high-speed Internet access. With its large number of users, AOL is well positioned to move into voice communications; the users provide a critical mass, and there will be network externalities. This set of resources—the twenty-five million loyal subscribers, Time Warner's content and cable access—provides an interacting system of resources for a sustainable competitive advantage.

The portal business is competitive today. Experts predict that there will only be enough advertising to support three or four portals by 2005, suggesting a need for changes in existing business models for the survivors.

Intermediaries

When the Internet opened for commercial use, there were a number of predictions of the demise of different kinds of intermediaries, from stock brokers to real estate agents. An intermediary is one who stands between two parties in a transaction, usually with the intention of facilitating that transaction. Although there will undoubtedly be groups that suffer "disintermediation," a number of intermediaries have been very clever in finding a role for themselves on the Internet. In addition, the Net has created the opportunity for new intermediaries.

The classic intermediary is the real estate agent. Through multiple listings for a geographic area, real estate agents have close to a monopoly on selling homes. There are a few sites that list homes for sale by owner, but the largest real estate site is run by the professionals, realestate.com. Buying and selling homes seems like a natural application for a worldwide communications network and one that, in the future, may reduce the role and compensation of the agent. Today's agents have taken advantage of the resource provided by being a part of an industry that is able to capture the majority of listings while maintaining fixed commission prices.

The Internet has affected auto sales; dealers report that customers come to the showroom armed with extensive information about each vehicle and the dealer's invoice price from the manufacturer. Long before the Internet, Edmunds published its guides to new and used automobiles. It has placed the most important contents of these guides on the Internet at no charge. Edmunds refers visitors to Auto-by-tel, which also has moved to the Internet. Auto-by-tel is a new intermediary; it takes information about the model car and accessories that a customer wants, and forwards it to subscribing dealers within a certain distance of the customer. The dealers put in a bid price on the car, a price that is generally lower than the showroom price due to the lower overhead of selling via the Web.

Auto-by-tel is also moving to a business model where it will sell cars directly over the Internet. A potential buyer looks at the Auto-by-tel site and finds prices for different cars posted there. The customer selects a car and arranges financing online if needed, and Auto-by-tel arranges to have the car delivered to the customer's home; you never have to visit a dealer! Of course, if you want to see a car or take a test drive, there is no alternative at present but to visit a dealer. Auto-by-tel will charge a closing fee to the dealer of $150 to $300. (I have twice found dealers who will beat the Auto-by-tel price, but the Auto-by-tel price is useful in bargaining.) Edmunds receives a fee for referring a customer to Auto-by-tel, and the latter firm receives subscription fees from participating dealers.

Both of these companies moved to the Web quickly when it became available for commercial use. Edmunds built on the resource of its brand name, while Auto-by-tel's resource was both its brand and the roster of dealers who had signed up to be a part of its service. Auto-by-tel needs a critical mass of customers to interest dealers, and a critical mass of dealers to encourage customers to use the service. These characteristics apply to other intermediaries as well: Their most important resources are the various groups for whom they intermediate. If they can capture a substantial proportion of each group, then they have a resource that is rare, valuable, inimitable, and nonsubstitutable.

Auctions

Prior to the Internet, the customer had limited access to auctions. Auctions exist for expensive goods like high-quality art and jewelry, and for lost and found or confiscated goods. However, for most retail transactions, customers accept the price offered by the vendor, or they do not make a purchase. The Internet auction has changed the standard economic model of the seller setting the price; in a typical auction, it is the consumer who chooses the price.

The most successful of the auction sites is eBay, an amazing Web site that became profitable its first month in operation. What the Internet does is to make available a worldwide critical mass of buyers and sellers, which is just what an auction needs to succeed. EBay has over seven million registered users and $4.5 billion in sales of some three million items (*Time*, December 27, 1999). The company has succeeded in making the auction experience positive for both buyers and sellers; the site has extensive feedback opportunities built into it. Network externalities again come into play here as well. The more people who visit eBay, the more attractive it is to offer goods for sale there. The more goods for sale, the more attractive it is for buyers to visit, and the more valuable is the auction site.

Hubs and Auctions

Dell Computer and one hundred other companies are linking their Web sites and forty-six million users into an auction consortium to be run by FairMarket. What about business-to-business e-commerce via auction? Ford, GM, Daimler-Chrysler, Nissan, and Renault are planning auctions for many of the goods and services they buy. By the end of 2001, GM expects all of its purchases to go through the Covisint exchange hub, and the company is inviting its suppliers to use the site for their purchases (*Wall Street Journal*, December 3, 1999). Even with EDI, the automakers figure it costs them one hundred dollars to generate a purchase order; the Web auction site should reduce that cost significantly.

To put this effort into perspective, GM spends eighty-seven billion dollars a year among thirty thousand suppliers; Ford's numbers are only slightly smaller. (Only the U.S. government buys more each year.) GM expects that, within a few years, the shared site could be handling five hundred billion dollars in business, with its suppliers doing business not only with GM but with each other as well. An auction site changes the economic model of the purchase transaction to one of bidding instead of accepting posted prices, and it reduces transactions costs at the same time.

The major resources that Ford, Daimler-Chrysler, GM, Nissan, and Renault bring to this business are their size and purchasing power.

Suppliers will have little choice but to participate if they want to do business with the automakers; whether they will choose to do business with each other on the same site remains to be seen.

In general, hubs bring together parties with special needs. For example, a good hub application first appeared on the French Minitel system. Companies with goods to be hauled from one location to another posted that information on a Minitel electronic bulletin board. Truck drivers returning from a trip who would otherwise have an empty truck, consult the site and arrange to haul goods on their return trip. This model generalizes to many other kinds of business; for example, a shipping company with empty containers can use a hub to contact firms with goods to move between different locations.

You can start a hub to promote any existing business. A company that sells and installs supply chain management software, for example, is i2. Its software analyzes orders and forecasts demand to produce a manufacturing schedule. It attempts to satisfy customer delivery dates and maximize profits on the product mix selected for manufacture, and is capable of scheduling multiple plants that manufacture the same product. It can even find substitutes that meet the customer's requirements when a requested part is not available.

The company has developed a Web site to encourage its customers to trade with each other. If the customer has implemented most of i2's software, then companies that place orders with it can inquire directly about work in progress and monitor their orders. This hub will link i2's customers more closely to each other; they will be integrated by the hub and the fact that they are using common supply-chain management software.

Hubs are successful if they attain a critical mass of participants; the more firms involved, the more valuable the hub becomes because there is more chance that a buyer will find what she is looking for. Buyers and sellers become cospecialized assets; the hub that captures most of them should have an advantage.

Demand Aggregators

Jay Walker, the chairman of Priceline.com, claims that his firm is a "demand aggregator" rather than a "reverse auction." A customer on Priceline enters a bid on an item like an airline ticket, and the Priceline Web site tries to find a supplier who will accept that price. Of course, the customer does not get exactly what she might like; you have to be flexible on time of day and the need to make intermediate stops. Priceline has a patent on this business process.

This kind of demand aggregation returns price setting to the consumer; you do not pay the airline's advertised price, but submit a price that you are willing to pay. The vendor makes a decision on whether or not it is willing to sell at this price. For airline tickets, the model works very well. Airlines are very adept at price discrimination; they charge high prices to business travelers who tend to make reservations at the last minute and are most sensitive to convenient flight times. The airlines sell discounted seats to leisure customers who are willing to plan ahead and stay over a Saturday night. An airplane seat is perishable; once the plane takes off, an empty seat is spoiled and cannot be sold on that flight. It is to the airline's advantage to fill every plane because almost any amount of revenue is better than an empty seat, as discussed with yield management systems earlier in the book. The business traveler provides the airline with most of its profits, and yield management and businesses like Priceline provide additional revenue.

Priceline sells more than airline tickets, and its model is applicable to a variety of products. What is needed, as with other new Internet markets, is a critical mass of buyers and sellers. Although Priceline's business model is innovative, it remains to be seen if it can protect the model with a patent. If it cannot, then its primary resource, its demand aggregation business process, is imitable.

Even if Priceline's patent is upheld, the company faces stiff competition from the airlines, the source of the seats it sells. The airlines want to sell these seats themselves. There are a number of new sites, backed by the airlines, that are offering discounted seats on the Web without requiring a bid. Hotwire.com accepts a customer's itinerary, compares it with a database of "distressed tickets" from the airlines, and then it presents the best price to the traveler who has thirty minutes to decide whether to accept the offer (*Wall Street Journal*, September 23, 2000).

Priceline has recently been suffering from declining bookings as the economy has softened and its future is now in doubt.

Information Providers

As long as the U.S. and other developed economies have been in a "post industrial" stage, sellers of information have flourished. In fact, before the United States became the Internet Economy, or the Digital Economy, futurists saw it as the Information Economy. Why is information so valuable? First, it is used to make decisions; the better the information, usually the less the uncertainty in decision-making. Information is the lifeblood of business processes. The last section mentioned supply chain management, which covers a process beginning with order entry and ending with the delivery of goods to a customer. Think of the information that is involved in this process: You need to know what has been ordered, develop a production forecast, order the raw materials needed to manufacture the product, follow the status of an order as it moves through production, where and how to ship the product, how much it costs to build, and how much you should sell it for.

Why are customers willing to pay for information? They must value it at more than its cost, and it must be cheaper than their cost to collect it in some other way. The Internet is a natural mechanism for the information seller because it makes access so easy. Millions of potential users around the world can access the information you sell, using their existing connection to the Internet; this business is an excellent example of the benefits of having a worldwide network infrastructure in place. (The original Web was motivated by physicists around the world seeking access to each other's work—in other words, by the need to find information.)

An example of a company that is a pure information provider on the Web is Internet Securities (Applegate and Goldman, 1998). The company, founded in 1994, provides its subscribers with difficult-to-locate financial, business, and political information about twenty-five emerging market countries, including China, Russia, India, Brazil, Turkey, and others.

The "business intelligence" market is highly competitive; the Internet made it possible for small start-ups to challenge the large providers like Reuters, Dow Jones, Dun and Bradstreet, and Bloomberg. Internet Securities grew quickly by signing up content providers and creating technology infrastructure in various countries. The company pays about 15 percent of subscriber revenues to the content providers, based on the amount of use of their information. It first worked to line up subscribers; Internet Securities priced its services to be at the middle to low end of the market.

It is interesting to note that one of the company's major problems was developing an organization structure to manage rapid growth. The company finds that many of its customers also subscribe to services from its competitors, yet customers are increasing the amount of information they buy from Internet Securities. It would appear that the price and quality of Internet Securities' information is attractive to its customers, otherwise, it would not be successful. Its major resource is its information and collection of information providers, which, unfortunately for the company, can be imitated or substituted for by other providers.

One of the traditional providers that has moved to the Net is an example of competition among information producers. Reuters has a 150-year history as a provider of information, beginning with carrier pigeons distributing financial news in 1849. The company has five billion dollars a year in revenues. Reuters has treated the Internet as another channel, selling news to over two hundred Internet sites including portals like Yahoo!. Reuters says that 55 percent of its U.S. media revenue comes from the Web (*Wall Street Journal*, August 4, 1999). Rather than develop its own Web page, the company decided to "flood the Internet" with news through other sites. (The company does have a free site for some of its news stories.) Reuters receives revenue from ads running near its stories, and whenever a user clicks to read any of its content.

Unless one has a monopoly on a rare type of information, it is difficult to gain a sustainable advantage by being an information provider on the Net. It is very easy for a competitor to imitate your offerings and the Internet provides a low cost delivery mechanism for information.

Competing with Free Goods

The Web defies the rules of classical economics. One example is the number of free services provided on the Internet. One could argue that this trend is simply a continuation of the spirit of the early days of the Internet when users contributed both labor and content to the community without any thought of personal gain. The Internet benefited everyone, and it grew from the largely uncompensated efforts of many individuals.

However, for most companies, there is a need to at least break even eventually if not make a profit. How can you make a profit by giving away your product for free? How can you compete with someone who gives away his product?

The answer to the first question is a little easier than the second. As an example, take Egreetings Network, which used to sell e-mail birthday cards for $.50 to $2.50 each. It had a hard time finding customers until it made its online cards free of charge; it now has seven million registered users, up from three hundred thousand when it charged for its products (*Wall Street Journal*, 28 July 1999). The company expects to make a profit by selling advertising and setting up online shopping for flowers, candy, and other gifts.

There is a strategy, then, behind giving things away for free on the Internet. The idea is to build up a huge pool of users—a critical mass—and then sell advertising and other products online. The portals follow this model: Yahoo does not charge users for its directory services or search engine, but it has enough users and advertising to command a multi-billion dollar stock valuation. Microsoft offers Hotmail as a free service and has attracted one hundred million e-mail users who view its ads every time they check their mail.

Competing with firms that give away a similar product to the one you are trying to sell is difficult. You must find a reason such as better service or more attractive features to justify a higher price. Net companies are just beginning to develop creative revenue models to accompany their new business models.

The Chance for a Sustainable Advantage

There are a myriad of new businesses on the Internet; this chapter has been able to review only a few of them. Table 8.2 summarizes the key resources for each industry and business discussed in the chapter. A review of the table suggests that the most important resources for these new businesses on the Net are generally imitable and substitutable. Is there anything that the start-up Internet business can do to increase its chances for a sustainable advantage?

The dynamic resource-based model of figure 1.1 may be able to help in the case of a specific firm. It suggests that a business enhance its original resources in a number of ways. First, most of the firms discussed in the book that are starting businesses on the Web need to reach a critical mass of customers or suppliers. Often, these businesses exhibit network externalities, that is, their sites become more attractive as more people use them, thus adding importance to achieving a critical mass of users.

The model also suggests that the firm look for other assets to supplement its resources. The hub gains by signing up customers and suppliers who want to interact in one market; the electronic space of each participant becomes a cospecialized asset.

Given an initial advantage, the firm cannot stop investing; all Internet start-ups seem to concentrate on growth and market share. The start-up has to invest in new products and services, and in creating appealing Web sites to capture users. It also has to invest in new technology to keep Web sites running, and a company like Internet Securities has to place servers with local language content in different countries.

Amazon.com continually expands the number of products it sells over the Internet. The company builds warehouses to be sure that order ful-

Table 8.2
Summary of New Business and Key Resources

Business/*Company*	Key Resources
Portals	Critical mass of users, providing services to retain and attract users, robust technology
America Online	*Content and customer base interacting with Internet access*
Auctions	Critical mass of buyers and sellers
eBay	*Critical mass of buyers and sellers, positive experience for both parties*
Priceline.com	*Critical mass of buyers and sellers*
Hub (and auction)	Critical mass, control of cospecialized assets (capture majority of both sides of a transaction)
Covisint Exchange (Ford/GM/ Daimler-Chrysler/Nissan/ Renault)	*Brand name, size of purchases, power over suppliers*
Information providers	The information, itself
Internet securities	*Information and information providers*

fillment is successful. All of its resources interact as a system in the attempt to build a brand that customers think of first when they want to order something. In fact, Amazon has set up a service that includes vendors for products it does not sell simply to entice users to visit its site.

If an Internet firm can accomplish what the CRS vendors did, that is, create a site that would be almost impossible for a competitor to imitate and for which there are no substitutes, it has a chance for a sustainable advantage for some period of time. At no time, however, can it become complacent about its success; there is always a new business model out there. Sears was the leading retailer at one point in time, then along came Wal-Mart and various category stores that featured low prices on one kind of merchandise, like computers or consumer electronics.

A resource-based view of competitive advantage forces you to identify your most important resources and encourages you to protect, enhance, and strengthen them. Your objective should be to create a system of resources that reinforce each other in such a way that the emergent system is rare, valuable, inimitable, and nonsubstitutable.

9

Providing Resources for New Business Models

Electronic commerce is more than just ordering on the Internet. Many of the business models described thus far involve an e-commerce firm that sells a good or service that must be delivered to the customer. A service company providing only information, for example, Internet Securities, has all of the information its customers want on its Web servers; they access it themselves using a browser. Online firms providing a physical product have to see that it is available and that it reaches a customer. A manufacturing firm has to see that needed products are in inventory, or it must build them as Dell and Cisco do. This chapter looks at some of the complementary assets that Internet firms employ to serve their customers.

Many of the models in this chapter rely on alliances, partnerships, and outsourcing. There are three reasons for choosing another company to help your Internet business. The first is the core competence argument from the first chapter: A firm should adhere to what it knows best, executing its business model. For example, it does not make sense for Amazon to become a book publisher; it is an online distributor and knows that business well. The second reason for turning to others is to take advantage of an existing infrastructure. Amazon ships its products in a number of ways including through the U.S. mail and UPS. These two organizations have a huge infrastructure for moving packages from point A to B; no one would think of setting up a delivery service when these alternatives are available. Finally, time is of the essence. When you are competing with others, working with a partner can save tremendous amounts of time. A start-up Internet company might very will go to a Net service provider for Web site development and hosting, as did eCompanyStore.com.

External Resources for New Business Models

Many businesses on the Internet are "virtual," that is, they provide one appearance to the customer while behind the scenes, they look entirely different. Cisco looks like a design and manufacturing firm to the customer; however, when you are inside the company, you find that much of its production is outsourced to contract electronics manufacturers, thus making Cisco a virtual firm. The companies discussed in this chapter provide special services to other firms; many of them are the virtual components of companies like Cisco.

Fulfillment and Delivery

When a customer buys something on the Internet, he expects to receive it without delay. Many customers would be surprised to learn that the company selling them merchandise actually neither has the merchandise in stock nor handles it in any way. When Amazon started business, it located in Seattle partly to be near one of the large book distributors, Ingram, so that this company could provide order fulfillment. Amazon was quite happy at first to avoid handling most of the items in its catalog, particularly those that did not have very high sales volumes. Egghead.com stocks its top two hundred or so products, relying on the manufacturer to ship less frequently ordered goods.

There are a number of advantages to this approach. It is hard to find a product that gets better as it is handled more. The more one touches something, the more costly are the logistics. Dell Computer is obsessed with reducing the number of times someone has to touch a personal computer during its construction. By working with a fulfillment partner, an Internet company can concentrate on merchandising and on order processing. As business expands, the Internet firm may decide to take over some of its own processing in order to have better control, handle high volume periods, and possibly reduce costs. Amazon has built a series of highly automated warehouses in low-wage parts of the country to handle fulfillment.

Part of the reason that e-commerce works so well in the United States is the infrastructure provided by the U.S. Post Office, UPS, and FedEx. Amazon ships a large number of packages via parcel post. Many Web sites use UPS as the default shipper, while others rely on the post office. UPS has worked at providing a range of services for e-commerce; the company carries 55 percent of all e-commerce shipments, compared to 10 percent for FedEx. Customers return some 10 percent of online purchases and UPS has an online return service that allows the customer to use a browser to arrange a return. The system ties in with the vendor's order entry system to generate credits and route the return to the right location. UPS also offers integrated supply management services for new e-commerce businesses.

When a product must be delivered in a specific time frame or is perishable, or when it weighs more than the 150 pounds that UPS will handle, then the e-commerce company must arrange shipping. Webvan, an electronic commerce firm that sells and delivers groceries, has its own fleet of vans and drivers. It must deliver during a promised window of time, and some of its products are perishable.

FedEx is more than a delivery company; it also handles fulfillment. If you have an e-commerce or catalog business, FedEx will maintain your inventory in its own warehouses, and its employees will pick and deliver products to your customers when you forward an order to them. Other companies provide similar services, and their charges run about 10 percent of the price of the goods. Fingerhut, a mail-order catalog company, provides order fulfillment services for e-commerce firms. It is a natural extension of the fulfillment process already in place for its own business. It can cost up to eighty million dollars to build a one-million square-foot warehouse, and then you must operate it efficiently. For this reason, many e-commerce firms are happy to outsource fulfillment. Some of the fulfillment and delivery firms had an infrastructure in place when e-commerce began. They had to add minimal resources in order to attract business from e-commerce companies. The resources they bring to electronic commerce are valuable, but they are not all that rare, inimitable, or nonsubstitutable. When UPS had a strike several years ago, its customers found alternatives for delivery.

When Fulfillment Is Not Enough
FedEx has benefited from online commerce. However, it is concerned that businesses are becoming more efficient through their use of the Internet

and systems that improve supply chain management. Much of FedEx's business comes from companies trying to operate lean or just-in-time manufacturing plants that have to express parts at the last minute. As companies become more efficient, they have fewer emergencies that require FedEx shipment.

FedEx is responding by becoming a provider of a different kind of service (*Wall Street Journal*, November 4, 1999). FedEx wants to build a network that will carry a company's information about demand, factory schedules, and the availability of materials. The system would use software to select the most economical transport for materials, air, land, or sea. It would also coordinate customs clearance around the world and minimize the time that goods spend sitting in warehouses. A company could conceivably eliminate all warehouses and rely solely on FedEx.

The delivery firm's first client is Cisco Systems, a company with a long history of outsourcing. FedEx is coordinating all of Cisco' shipping over two years, and during the next three years, Cisco will gradually eliminate all of its warehouses. FedEx will work out a system to merge orders in transit; hundreds of boxes for a customer will be shipped independently as soon as they are manufactured, and they will all arrive within hours of each other to be assembled, never having spent any time in a warehouse. FedEx will redesign its delivery system to control shipping and pick the most economical shipping method, even UPS!

FedEx's vision is to become a partner with its customers, to become more than a delivery company. With this kind of service available, a start-up can build a virtual manufacturing firm quickly and with little capital. Your biggest competitor in the future may be a couple of people with just an idea today!

Archrival UPS has started a new unit called "eVentures" to expand the company's logistics division to small-and medium-size companies. UPS Logistics runs warehouses and fills orders for clients that do not want to handle their own fulfillment. UPS has several resources that give it an edge in this business. First, it has the management knowledge and skills to run a global logistics operation. Second, it has an infrastructure in place throughout the U.S. and much of the world including a huge fleet of well-known brown delivery trucks. Third UPS has a great brand name. Logistics operations like those at FedEx and UPS will handle the entire back end processing for an e-business. In addition to warehouse management, the delivery firms will handle phone calls and customer returns.

There are also start-up companies whose business plan is to provide warehouse and fulfillment services for e-commerce companies. Submitorder.com for instance, handles electronic fulfillment which it advertises on its Web site:

If it involves e-fulfillment we do it.

By bringing together core competencies in information technology, small package distribution, customer service and marketing, we provide the e-fulfillment services your business needs to get an e-tail site up and running quickly, while keeping your customers happy and sales growing steadily.

We'll work with your site designers, or ours, to ensure your site is shopper-friendly and seamlessly integrated with our flexible distribution management system.

We'll work with you to streamline the supply chain, determine inventory levels, train our service specialists on your products, and use the information collected on your site to help you grow sales.

And, we'll make sure your customers get the products they ordered and the world-class service they demand.

Manufacturing

Why would a manufacturing company not want to make its own products? One reason is that the company prefers to be a design and sales company, leaving manufacturing to someone else; it does not want to develop a competence in manufacturing. By designing a product and turning its manufacture over to another firm, the new company does not have to wait for a manufacturing facility to be set up and staffed; it also does not have to raise the capital needed for such a facility. Finally, some electronics firms have discovered that specialty outsourcers can build products of comparable quality at a lower cost!

One of the most successful of these outsourcers is a contract electronics manufacturer named Solectron. This company began business in 1977 and claims to be the world's largest electronics manufacturing service. The company has changed its stated mission of being a contract manufacturer to becoming an "integrated supply chain partner" for its customers. The company claims that it can provide advanced manufacturing technologies (manufacturing is its core competence), shortened time-to-market, reduced total costs and more effective asset utilization.

Solectron received the Baldrige National Quality Award in 1991 and, again, in 1997, becoming the first company to win the award twice for manufacturing. The company has sixty-five thousand employees and eleven million square feet of capacity. In November 2000, it announced that it would acquire NatSteel Electronics of Singapore; with the latter's eleven factories, Solectron will have a total of seventy plants around the world. The use of outsourcers is not a rare strategy; it is estimated that 26 percent of electronics manufacturing goes to companies like Solectron. Companies such as Solectron manufacture for a variety of industries, making products like computers, peripherals, communications, networking, and consumer electronics devices.

Solectron offers the following reasons for outsourcing:

1. Time-to-market. There is only a small window of opportunity for new products, and there can be significant first-mover advantages. Since Solectron has a large manufacturing capability already in place, it can ramp up production for a new product very quickly, helping its customer capture a leadership position in the market.

2. Lower costs. Solectron claims to have low manufacturing costs, which it passes on to customers. Some companies have sold their plants to Solectron with the understanding that the outsourcer will continue to produce their products at that plant.

3. Technology. Because manufacturing is Solectron's core competence, it buys and installs the latest manufacturing equipment and technology.

4. Supply chain partnership. Solectron has built a major Electronic Data Interchange infrastructure so that it can communicate electronically with customers. It can accept electronic customer forecasts, purchase orders, invoices, payments, computer-aided design files, bills of material, and engineering data.

Solectron's overall mission is to reduce costs and increase efficiencies through the entire product life cycle, while facilitating its customers supply chains. Solectron is a complementary asset for e-commerce manufacturing firms.

What is Solectron's competitive strategy? Table 9.1 analyzes the firm's strategy according to the dynamic, resource-based model of strategy from figure 1.1. Solectron's biggest resource is the scale and scope of its manufacturing; plants in twenty-eight countries, many with low wages, provide it with a low-cost, high-quality production capability. With its EDI infrastructure, the firm is capable of integrating itself with customers' supply chains; it can be a very effective partner for an Internet or electronic commerce firm.

Although each of its resources alone can be imitated, and there are other firms a customer could substitute for Solectron, this contract electronics manufacturing offers a system of resources that interact. It would be hard for a competitor to create a network of seventy plants and an equivalent information technology infrastructure from scratch. Similarly, potential substitutes may not be able to offer the breadth and range of manufacturing and technology services of Solectron. Given the interaction among its resources, Solectron may be able to sustain its current advantage for some time.

High Labor E-Commerce: FreeMarkets.com

The Internet and electronic commerce are associated with high levels of efficiency, following the low or no touch model for handling merchandise. Dell Computer concentrates on reducing handling during production. Information Securities does not have to physically handle any of the information that it provides to customers; everything is electronic. However, there is at least one successful firm on the Internet that has a relatively high labor content in its business model. It is also not clear that this firm can ever outsource the labor requirements to another firm. It is useful to contrast this company's business model with others that are able to take advantage of complementary assets.

The company in question is FreeMarkets.com. This firm's business model is aimed at industrial markets, and it seeks to help companies making purchases from their suppliers (Rangan 1999). The idea is to use the Internet to run auctions for the buying company. Suppliers bid for the buyer's business during the auction. The company doing the buying can see the identity of all bidders, and the bidders can see other bids, but do not know what company has entered them. The U.S. market alone for industrial goods is estimated at six hundred dollars billion annually.

Although the model seems simple in theory, there are some requirements for it to work. First, the suppliers need accurate and complete product specifications. They also have to understand what the buyer requires in the way of delivery services and inventory management. The products and industries have to be selected carefully as well. For example, it would not make much sense to have a bidding auction on sophisticated aerospace parts in a situation where the buyer and supplier have to work closely to design and build the part. Commodities are also not a good candidate because market prices are easy to discover. FreeMarkets competes in the middle; the products are not commodities, nor are they sophisticated, custom-designed parts. According to the company's founder, "The technique is most successful when the product is specifiable, when competition among suppliers is sufficient, and when the buyers' purchase is large enough to stimulate that competition" (Rangan 1999).

Labor is involved at several stages of the FreeMarkets model. First, there is a sales staff to find clients for the company. The process leading up to a Competitive Bidding Event (CBE) involves four steps, all requiring human labor:

Table 9.1
Solectron Resource Analysis

Resource	Rare	Valuable	Inimitable	Nonsubsti-tutable	Other Model Components
Initial Resources					
Highly efficient, high quality, global manufac-turing in twenty-eight plants	Yes	Yes	No	No	
EDI infrastructure	No	Yes	No	No	
Additional Resources					
Supply chain facilitation for e-commerce	Yes	Yes	No	No	
Interactions					
All resources	Yes	Yes	Partially	Partially	

1. FreeMarkets works with buyers to identify potential savings; what products look the best for a CBE?

2. The next step is to prepare an RFQ (Request for Quotation) for potential bidders. This document has to contain drawings, volume forecasts, logistics, quality levels, and all other elements of total cost. This step involves a FreeMarkets team working with client buyers and engineers.

3. The third step is to identify and contact suppliers. FreeMarkets works with client buyers to screen potential bidders, and also provides information to potential bidders.

4. The CBE follows involving both the FreeMarkets team and company buyers.

5. FreeMarkets works with the buyer to analyze the bidding process and validate quotations.

FreeMarkets claims that, on average, it saves its customers about 15 percent and helps to change the balance of power between suppliers and buyers. It has conducted auctions for over thirty clients. FreeMarkets itself generates revenues from a combination of service fees and sales commissions from buyers. Free Markets essentially has replaced or disintermediated manufacturer's representatives who have historically charged a 4–7 percent commission on the products they represent.

Table 9.2 is an analysis of FreeMarkets' strategy; the company, however, is very new and all of its resources may not yet be apparent. FreeMarkets has an appealing business model, but it can be imitated by others, and there are competitors offering the same kinds of services. The company has developed valuable software to run the CBEs, software that is easy to use and that requires little or no training. Its major resource is its staff's knowledge and the skills it has developed to work with clients—the high labor content part of its business model. The company hopes that the interaction among its resources will give it a competitive advantage; however, it appears that competitors can imitate Freemarkets and substitute for it.

GM, a company that accounted for 17 percent of FreeMarkets' revenue in the first nine months of 1999, has taken its business to Commerce One and is buying a stake in this company. This decision is part of its plan to move all procurement to the Web (*Wall Street Journal,* January 5, 2000).

GM has been able to substitute for the services provided by FreeMarkets, suggesting that Freemarkets has not developed a system of resources that gives it a sustainable competitive advantage. FreeMarkets maintains that giant companies like GM are likely to set up their own supplier auctions like Couisint; FreeMarkets is targeting smaller firms that want to outsource procurement bidding events.

Net Service Providers

Should a firm trying to move business to the Internet do so with an internal IT staff, or should it outsource? There are arguments in favor of either option. A number of firms have chosen the outsourcing route for different reasons. One of these is speed; if you do not have a lot of Internet experience and are unlikely to be able to hire IT staff to develop a Net-based application, an outsourcer should be faster than an in-house team. The outsourcer also has the expertise needed to develop the application. Web providers offer a range of services, from design to Web site hosting.

US Internetworking is one of a number of companies that provide these types of services. USi develops applications for its customers, and then

Table 9.2
FreeMarkets Resource Analysis

Resource	Rare	Valuable	Inimitable	Nonsubsti-tutable	Other Model Components
Initial Resources					
Appealing business model	Yes	Yes	No	No	
Software	Yes	Yes	No	No	
Additional Resources					
Staff knowledge of clients, suppliers and products	Yes	Yes	Difficult to imitate	No competitors can hire and learn these skills	
Interactions					
All resources	Yes	Yes	No	No	

hosts them at its data centers. It is one of a group of companies known as "applications service providers," or ASPs. These firms use a combination of proprietary, custom and other vendors' software to create applications for customers.

USi has a global network with multiple data centers—one on the East Coast, one on the West Coast, and centers in Japan and Europe. The sites are mirrored so that all applications can be run from another site in case of a massive failure. The company connects the data centers to a number of backbone service providers to reduce communications latencies.

USi sees an increasing amount of its business coming from electronic commerce. It offers to build digital stores and supply chains for its customers so that they can focus on their core business. This ASP has an agreement with Broadvision to offer its products; Broadvision sells software for setting up a sophisticated retail operation on the Internet.

One client has used USi to expand and take over the hosting of its Web site. This manufacturing company had a Web site developed by a local company; when its needs grew beyond the local firm's capabilities, it turned to USi. It is also possible that the manufacturer will involve USi in making its order entry system available on the Internet. An outsourcer provides a valuable resource for companies trying to move to the Internet and begin electronic commerce.

Conclusions

Many of the organizations described in this chapter are complementary assets for other firms. Complementary assets supplement your resources and facilitate business processes. Firms outsource fulfillment, contract manufacturing, and technology development to these providers. It should be noted that none of these complementary assets confers a competitive advantage. They are easily available to competitors, and are nonexclusive. UPS and FedEx work for thousands of customers as do ASPs and other network service providers.

The benefits of using a partner as a complementary asset come from the ability to take advantage of existing infrastructure and skills. The use of partnerships and complementary assets is consistent with the core competence strategy: A firm concentrates on what it does best, and leaves other activities to partners. Outsourcing can drastically reduce capital requirements, especially for a manufacturing business. Outsourcing to a network service provider is a way to "rent" scarce expertise, and to develop an application faster than most organizations can in-house.

How do you make the decision to outsource? This question is one of the most significant ones facing senior management. Cisco outsourced because it had to; the company had no factories and probably could not have built them fast enough to keep up with the demand for its products. How does a company that has an existing asset decide to outsource it? Why have companies like HP decided to sell a manufacturing facility to Solectron to run for them? There are a few questions managers should ask when facing an outsourcing decision.

1. Is the business activity that we are considering outsourcing part of our core competence?

2. What is the difference in costs between outsourcing and continuing to do the activity ourselves?

3. Are there competent, dependable outsourcers?

4. Can we manage the relationship with the outsourcer?

5. If we decide to outsource, what happens to our employees, to their positions, career paths, and benefits?

The answers to these questions should help the firm in making its decision on whether or not to outsource an activity. If the activity is a core competence, and the cost differentials between doing it in-house versus outsourcing are small, then management will in most instances continue to perform the activity. If the candidate for outsourcing is not a core competence, and the answers to questions three through five are satisfactory, outsourcing is very attractive.

This chapter has described a number of complementary assets available to the firm. Although not providing the basis for a sustainable competitive advantage alone, these assets can become part of a system of resources, a system the firm creates to sustain its competitive advantage.

IV

Change and Transformation

Strategies for the Internet, electronic commerce, and new business models entail massive change. Change is perilous in the best of times; how do you redirect an organization in a hypercompetitive economy and do so in Internet time? Chapter 10 reviews different approaches to change, and suggests which are the most likely to succeed for a firm trying to implement a new business model and strategy simultaneously. Senior managers will have to take the lead in bringing about the conditions for such change.

Earlier, we argued that to succeed in the Internet economy, a firm needs an appropriate business model, strategy, and an organization structured to execute the model and strategy. Chapter 11 discusses organization structures, especially those enabled by technology, that facilitate new business models and strategies. The conclusion is that networked organizations have the most flexibility, as well as other advantages, in a hypercompetitive economy. The chapter also discusses some of the challenges of managing networked organizations.

10

The Dynamics of Change

Whenever a firm adapts a new business model, it undertakes a change effort. The difficulty of the change depends on the nature of the new model and the degree to which it differs from the status quo. The problem of change is greater for the traditional firm that is trying to move to a new business model than it is for the Internet start-up. The latter expects to be doing something different, to have an organization culture and norms different from the traditional firm. All the descriptions of Internet firms highlight this difference. However, even for Internet entrepreneurs, there is need for change. Successful Internet start-ups change as they grow; one of Internet Securities' biggest problems, recall, was designing an organization to grow along with its growth in business. This chapter, then, concerns both the traditional organization and the start-up.

There are several levels of change that are likely to be confronted:

• Business model
• Intraorganizational relations
• Organization structure
• Interorganizational relations
• Partnerships and alliances

This chapter discusses changes that occur within the organization. The topics of new organization structures, interorganizational relations, and partnerships and alliances are discussed in chapter 11.

In the past, there were many motivators for change. Today, competition from e-commerce and the Internet seems to provide the primary reason to change. Start-up companies, as well as existing competitors, are creating new business models, models that force change on traditional organizations. Firms that are successful in planning make changes before they are forced to by the competition, whereas other organizations undertake change as a reaction to competition. Some firms fail to change at all, and these companies are not likely to continue in business for long.

Before the Internet and the radical new business models discussed in this book, most change involving IT took place one technological application at a time. Changes in organization structure, interorganizational relations, and the economy all occurred as the result of the implementation of many individual technology initiatives. In today's hypercompetitive economy, change can happen much more quickly as entire organizations restructure themselves to take advantage of the Internet.

Types of Change

There are many different views of change in the organization; no one of which all change agents embrace. Orlikowski (1996) has reviewed a number of change models, and we will combine characteristics from several of these models to develop a change strategy.

Planned Change

The kind of change that most managers would embrace is planned. Managers see themselves as deliberately making changes in the organization; they initiate and implement change. The model assumes that senior managers know what changes they want to bring about, and are capable of influencing the organization to make them. It also takes for granted that senior managers are leaders and have a vision for the firm. This model works well in a situation where there needs to be a single, heroic change, and requires strong senior management to implement, as was the case, for example, for when Merrill Lynch adopted a new business model that includes electronic trading.

Planned change is important because so many firms are changing their business models, and such changes have major implications for the organization and the way it operates. When contemplating major change, it is helpful to think of change in terms of an equilibrium with forces aligned on either side (see figure 10.1). Some of the forces are restraining forces working to maintain the status quo whereas others are driving forces pushing for change. To bring about change, the manager can reduce the restraining forces, increase the driving forces, or both. Increasing the driving forces alone creates more tension and strain in the organization. Reducing the restraining forces is unlikely to be enough in and of itself to bring about change.

It is helpful to analyze a change situation with a simple force field model like the one in figure 10.1; which can identify places where there is major resistance to change, and places where there may be natural forces encouraging change. You can also think of figure 10.1 as a way to itemize the costs and benefits of a change. Often, the group of people who pays the costs is not the same group that obtains the benefits! This kind of analysis can help you determine what kind of incentives might be appropriate to encourage change. In today's economy, maintaining the status quo is not an option for the competitive firm.

The manager or change agent has to sell the benefits of change to others in the organization. The idea is to help those resistant to change to see the reason for the change, and to agree to help. The leader has to present her vision for the organization, and convince people to go along with it. It is very hard to implement change without the enthusiastic support of everyone in the organization. In the Internet economy, there is not much time to waste, and the task of leading change has become much more difficult than it was in the past.

Technologically Inspired Change
According to one view, technology is the autonomous driver of change. Technology leads to logical changes in the organization, that affect the structure of the organization, work routines, information flows, and interorganizational relations. This model has gained a great deal of prominence with the adoption of new business models. Although some experts prefer the view that technology enables change, many practitioners of new Net technologies assume that organizations change in order to be consistent with the technology.

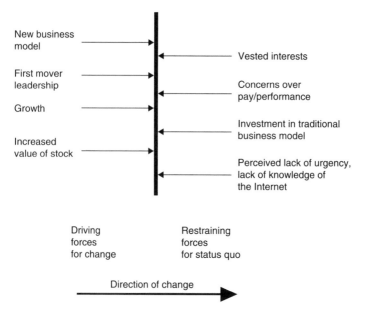

Figure 10.1
Planned Change as an Equilibrium among Forces

Emergent Change

A different approach suggests that individuals adapt technology in a number of diverse and interesting ways, and this kind of emergent change (Orlikowski 1996) occurs in the absence of explicit intentions and objectives. In fact, such changes cannot be anticipated in advance because people adapt to the technology as they use it. Emergent change can be a positive, unintended consequence of a new application, for example.

Zeta Corporation, a leading software vendor, installed Lotus Notes to support its customer services department (CSD). This group provides customer service; the fifty representatives in the department answer phone inquiries from customers and try to solve their problems. Notes is a groupware product that promotes sharing and coordination. Management encouraged CSD representatives to enter all of their calls, the nature of the problem, and information about the solution into the Notes database. CSD members can access this database in a number of ways and can search it for past incidents that are similar to the one they currently face.

Within a year, the database contained thirty-five thousand entries of problems and their resolution.

How did change emerge from this technology investment? First, CSD representatives found a similar problem in the database for 50 percent of their calls; past solutions let them respond quickly with the correct answer to these customers. With this level of access, the representatives quickly became highly dependent on the database and technology. Management noted the change in the way representatives solved problems and reorganized the department accordingly, dividing representatives into two groups based on their experience and expertise. The idea was that junior staff members would field all calls and pass the difficult ones on to the senior staff. Junior representatives, however, were not comfortable assigning problems to senior colleagues, so management created the role of an intermediary who would review problems and decide when they needed referral to a senior representative.

CSD employees noticed a decline in face-to-face contact, and began to find reasons for meeting each other. Some of the representatives became proactive, looking for open problems in the database when they were not too busy. The company then expanded use of the system to two overseas offices, which initially created some problems when the foreign representatives did not completely understand the process for creating and using the database. As the groups adopted shared norms for the system, the problems disappeared.

When others in the company requested access to the data, the CSD staff was concerned, given that the database contained so many details. To solve this problem, non-CSD employees were given access to "sanitized" reports. The CSD staff also began to publish technical notes for the company based on the database. Finally, Zeta used Notes to create a "bug" database to facilitate identifying and fixing problems with their products.

This example of emergent change is very positive; CSD staff members found ways to integrate the Notes database with their jobs and to improve the quality of customer service. They expanded their use of technology to have a broader impact on Zeta than originally planned. In this case, information technology facilitated changes that emerged spontaneously from employees using the technology. You cannot plan for emergent change, but you can support and encourage it as changes become evident.

Punctuated Equilibrium

The punctuated equilibrium model of change concerns a much longer period of time than the views thus far discussed. Adherents of this model suggest that periods of dramatic change are followed by longer periods of equilibrium. Until the Internet combined with hypercompetition in the economy, the business cycle in different industries provided evidence for the validity of the punctuated equilibrium view. If one looks at the computer industry, for example, there are several discontinuities followed by periods of equilibrium. Major changes in this industry include:

• The invention and adoption of the vacuum tube and the first computer
• The invention and adoption of the transistor
• The invention and adoption of integrated circuits
• The unbundling of hardware and software
• The development of the minicomputer
• The development of the personal computer
• The creation and distribution of database software and high capacity storage devices
• The advent of networking
• The Internet

Others might choose a different list of major events that changed the industry. However, the point is that in a fifty-five-year history of computing, here are nine major changes, or one every six years.

It is also important to note that the pace of change has increased; the punctuating events occur more frequently, and build upon each other. For example, the power of modern technology comes from the combination of several innovations—computers, databases, and networks. Technologists talk of "Internet Time," by which they mean an extremely short period of time. Internet start-ups are associated with long hours and all-nighters as companies race to be the first-mover with a new idea.

Although the punctuated equilibrium model appears to have some empirical support, the time periods in which to enjoy the respite of equilibrium are getting fewer and farther between. Today, there seems to be more punctuation than equilibrium!

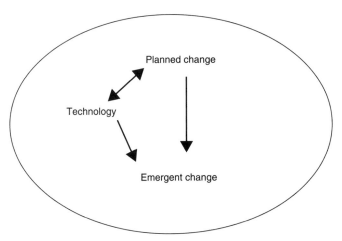

Punctuated equilibrium
(shorter periods of equilibrium,
more frequent and intense periods
of change)

Figure 10.2
An Integrated Model

An Integrated Model

Figure 10.2 presents an integrated model of the views of change discussed so far in this chapter. The model retains the longer-term perspective of punctuated equilibrium, recognizing that periods of equilibrium are getting shorter and shorter. Changes are depicted in the oval; these changes may occur in an industry, a group of firms, or an individual firm. There is interaction between change stimulated by the technology and planned change initiated by management. In today's business environment, it is almost impossible to separate the impact of management and the impact of technology. The technology enables new business models. The manager, wishing to take advantage of these new models, adopts Internet and electronic commerce technology. He then has to plan changes in the organization to implement the new business model and the new technology. The manager has to sell a vision to employees and convince them to support the change effort. The technology and any planned changes in the organization may also lead to emergent change, especially as the organization gains experience with the new technology.

The discussion of change thus far has been general in nature; what exactly is being changed?

• The most obvious change is in the firm's business model.
• This change may lead to changes in an individual's tasks.
• It is possible that an individual's work group may change.
• The structure of the organization is a candidate for change.
• The organization may work with new partners and form new alliances.
• The technology will change for different users.
• Some individuals may have to find new jobs.

All of these changes can be traumatic for individuals and the organization; management needs to find a way to maintain morale and enthusiasm for its change program.

Examples of Change

OptiMark: A Failed Alternative Securites Market
OptiMark is an interesting company not because of the massive changes it has undertaken, but because it represents a group of organizations that is trying to force significant changes on traditional securities markets. OptiMark also presents an opportunity to use the dynamic, resource-based model to examine a company that was unable to execute its original business model successfully. Although Optimark did not succeed as a separate securities market, other Electronic Communications Networks are forcing changes on the traditional exchanges. The New York Stock Exchange is planning to go public and is creating its own small ECN within the traditional exchange.

William Lupien and Terry Rickard founded OptiMark; Lupien is a thirty-year veteran of the securities markets. His fundamental belief is that the New York Stock Exchange, the world's major securities market, is outdated and does not meet the needs of institutional investors. OptiMark's original goal was to provide more liquidity to the market by creating a trading system that goes beyond trading based on price and size of an order. *Liquidity* refers to the ability of a market to absorb trades. A market that can trade a fifty-thousand share order without the trade affecting the stock's price is very liquid. These large trades, known as "block trades," are very important to institutional investors. The typical retail investor trades less than twenty-five-hundred shares whereas institutions trade typical block sizes of fifty to one-hundred-thousand shares. With the increase in stock prices in the 1990s, there are more than ten mutual funds with over twenty billion dollars in assets. Organizations like this demand liquidity for trading large blocks of stocks. Institutions account for 75 percent or more of the NYSE volume.

The block trading industry exists to assist institutions in the placement of large blocks of shares. A block trading desk uses contact with major investors to match buyers and sellers, and then sends the block to the stock exchange floor where specialists execute the trade. The problem is that information often leaks in the process, and this information has the ability to affect prices. Traders are aware of the impact that large orders exert on the market, and they will often break a large trade up into smaller pieces.

Rickard, a Ph.D. in engineering physics, found an analogy in the process of matching large blocks of stocks and his prior work in signal processing for submarine detection. The problem in the securities markets is to search out and find who should do what for whom and at what price and trade size (Dailey 1998). Rickard worked out the algorithm for OptiMark over a weekend when he was sick in bed.

The two partners raised nearly $130 million in start-up capital, and created OptiMark. This market is an example of the many technology-enabled markets that have grown with the Internet. The ECNs are in the process of becoming additional securities markets that supplement traditional exchanges.

OptiMark received a transactions fee from each share traded; it attempted to be broker-neutral. The key to being successful as a market, as one might guess, is critical mass and network externalities. OptiMark needed a critical mass of users; it must have both buyers and sellers for its market to work. The market exhibits positive externalities because the more users, the more valuable the system is to each user. As we shall see, OptiMark was unable to attain this critical mass.

What distinguished OptiMark from some other electronic networks is the fact that a trader entered not just a price and volume, but also an investment profile for a trade. A profile is a graphical representation of a trader's strategy; a trader can indicate his interest in trading at each price and order size. OptiMark claimed that a trader could enter a trading strategy easily, a strategy that went beyond one price and size. The system held profiles until the next periodic call, which is the time during which a supercomputer attempts to match buyers and sellers. (OptiMark was not a continuous market like the NYSE; rather, it had period calls or times when it executed trades.) Rickard's patented algorithms matched the buy-and-sell profiles to maximize mutual satisfaction for both parties.

The Pacific Stock Exchange was the first exchange to make OptiMark available to investors of U.S. listed equities. In November 1999, Knight Securities formed a strategic alliance with OptiMark. Knight Securities is the largest wholesale market maker in U.S. equities. Knight makes markets in over seventy-three-hundred equity securities listed on Nasdaq, Amex, and the NYSE. It is the largest destination for online trade executions; the firm can handle 1.2 million trades a day. Knight aggregated some of its order flow into blocks and traded them with OptiMark, providing the company with more liquidity and helping it develop trading volume.

However, OptiMark was unable to survive as a separate electronic market. On September 20, 2000, it announced a strategic refocus of business to become a consulting service and designer of electronic markets. As a part of this strategic change, OptiMark suspended operations of its existing equity trading operations on the Pacific Exchange and the Nasdaq. In addition to changing the existing management team, the company had to eliminate 110 positions. It has announced agreements with several electronic marketplaces to provide customized trading platforms. These platforms will incorporate OptiMark's patented "matching engine," which matches buyers and sellers.

Table 10.1 is an analysis of OptiMark based on the dynamic resource-based strategy model presented in the first chapter. The company began with a large amount of venture capital, which helped it begin operations. The firm's patented software for matching trades based on trader profiles and maximizing mutual satisfaction is a key asset; a competitor cannot

The Dynamics of Change   221

Table 10.1
OptiMark Resource Analysis

Resource	Rare	Valuable	Inimitable	Nonsubstitutable	Other Model Components
Initial Resources					
Start-up capital	Yes	Yes	No	No	
Patented software	Yes	Yes	Possibly	Possibly	Is this resource enough for a competitive advantage?
Additional Resources					
Pacific stock exchange agreement	No	Yes	No	No	Need to achieve critical mass; presence of externalities
Knight Securities alliance	Yes	Yes	Possibly	Possibly	Entry barriers for others?
Interactions					
All resources	Yes	Not enough	No, but not easily	No	OptiMark offered a unique trading service, but it could not reach critical mass and had to be abandoned

copy this resource and would have to develop its own algorithms. The agreement with the Pacific Exchange was valuable, but offered little in the way of competitive advantage. The agreement with Knight might have helped Optimark reach critical mass, but it did not do so. It is possible that OptiMark's unique approach to block trading was ahead of its time. In addition, users criticized the system for the amount of input required for the trader to enter a profile. OptiMark will now concentrate on helping other ECNs make use of its most valuable resource—the patented matching software. It remains to be seen if this resource will provide the refocused firm with a strategic advantage.

Although OptiMark was not successful as a separate market, it is likely to have a continued impact on the financial markets. ECNs and alternative markets are exerting great pressure for change on traditional markets like the NYSE and regional, physical stock exchanges.

Responding to ECNs: The NYSE Strikes Back

The OptiMark story is interesting in its own right, but part of its significance lies in the impact that electronic markets are having on traditional securities exchanges. These exchanges must be concerned about Internet securities markets and even auction sites like eBay, where one can envision trading stocks as easily as collectibles.

The NYSE produces thirty-five billion dollars of commerce each day, trading three thousand one hundred different stocks. The Exchange has steadily been losing market share to other exchanges. The NYSE, as mentioned above, is a specialist market. The specialists, who are unique for each stock, make a market by posting bid and ask spreads. The specialist receives a commission for executing a trade. The specialist is charged with maintaining an orderly market; often he will buy or sell from an inventory of securities. The specialist also has to maintain a limit-order book and see that limit orders are executed properly.

The specialists represent a strong restraining force for major change on the NYSE. They are very well compensated and are not eager to see changes that might let trades bypass them. The NYSE chairman, Richard Grasso, is proposing to create an ECN within the Exchange. This new system will feature an electronic limit-order book that will be fully visible to investors over the Internet. Investors "sponsored by a member" will be able to execute orders for one thousand shares or less automatically. This same platform will allow after-hours trading. By seeing the limit-order book, investors will be able to estimate liquidity; the book will show buy and sell orders at different prices, indicating the depth of the market.

The NYSE has also announced a plan to become a public corporation and to sell stock. With the governance structure of a corporation with a board of directors representing shareholders, it should be easier to reduce the influence of vested interests at the Exchange.

Unfortunately, the NYSE does not publish the details of its deliberations. If you think about the change models presented at the beginning of this chapter, it appears that Mr. Grasso and his staff are trying to execute planned change. There are strong restraining forces, and it does not appear possible to reduce them. As a result, the strategy is to increase the driving forces by overlaying an ECN on the Exchange and changing its ownership structure to give management a greater ability to create driving forces.

Merrill Lynch Revisited

How has Merrill Lynch engineered the changes we described in an earlier chapter? Like the NYSE, it, too, has followed the planned change route with strong leadership from several managers. The only question is why it took it so long to see what was happening. As mentioned, Merrill finally took notice on December 28, 1998 when Schwab's market value topped its own. By any other comparison, Merrill was the stronger firm, even if investors felt they did not understand new business models on the Internet. The company has $11.4 billion in equity compared to Schwab's $1.9 billion, $1.5 trillion in assets under management compared to $600 billion at Schwab, and 66,000 employees to Schwab's 17,400. However, Schwab's assets were growing twice as fast.

One thing that Merrill has that Schwab does not is brokers paid on commission. Schwab pays its brokers a salary—a crucial difference. The first task at Merrill was to get everyone's attention. Interestingly enough, it was John Steffens who had said that electronic brokerage was bad for the investor and bad for America, and then energized Merrill to consider a change (*Business Week*, November 15, 1999). In March 1998,

Steffens, the Merrill vice-chairman who oversaw seventeen thousand brokers, made an eight-hour presentation to the management committee, arguing that Merrill had to offer an online account or risk losing much of its assets, and also losing the next generation of investors.

Steffens's message to brokers was that they would have to work online or wither away. Steffens had to convince David Komansky, Merrill's chairman, that online trading and a new business model were appropriate. He was aided by a new chief information officer, John McKinley, who had to divert some of Merrill's $3.2 billion IT budget to moving online.

Looking at this change effort as a force field, the forces arrayed against change were great. There were seventeen thousand brokers whose jobs would change dramatically. The other forty-nine-thousand Merrill employees would also fear the new business model, which changes the retail business to a fee-base rather than commission base for revenues. The most publicized changes were to retail, but Merrill was also setting up an Internet presence for institutional business. The driving forces for change were people like Steffens and McKinley, and the forces from events in the marketplace were equally strong. Merrill's franchise was threatened, and it had ample evidence that it needed a new business model.

Making Changes at Avon

Avon Cosmetics has a business model that seems to defy the Internet and electronic commerce. The company still has a quaint sales force of "Avon Ladies," who ring door bells and sell direct. What operation could be less oriented toward the Web? Every electronic move Avon makes requires it to reassure its existing sales channel, the army of women who call door-to-door. A few years ago, Avon carefully began to sell its cosmetics at certain retail outlets. Its new president, Andrea Jung, wants to use the Web as another distribution channel, but she must first gain the cooperation of Avon's expensive direct sales force. Avon saves one to three dollars for every U.S. order processed over the Web instead of in person (*Wall Street Journal*, December 28, 1999). The company has about 2.8 million sales representatives worldwide.

How is Avon changing its business model and gaining the acceptance of its sales representatives? The company is using a combination of planned and technologically induced change. The idea is to encourage representatives to establish their own Web pages that link to the Avon corporate site. Customers will enter orders through their sales rep's site. Avon will get the orders, but will not be seen as taking them away from their sales force. The company also wants to preserve the tremendous brand loyalty that customers have for Avon.

Avon plans to invest sixty million dollars over three years to develop the site and has chosen IBM as a partner. Avon is encouraging its reps to get their homes ready for the Internet and has arranged discounted deals on computers and Internet service. The company will help its sales force set up Web pages. Avon is using a combination of change strategies to take advantage of the opportunities provided by electronic commerce. At Avon, technology-based change and planned change initiated by top management combine to protect a large sales force as the company moves to a new business model.

Conclusions

This chapter has presented different views of change and used them to analyze changes resulting from new business models and the Internet in several companies. It appears that in these companies, there is interaction between planned change and technology; the technology stimulates new business models, and firms adopt some variation of the new models.

Because the magnitude of the change is so great, management, particularly top management, must carefully plan the move to a new model. In the process, managers may find the force field model helpful in identifying driving and restraining forces. When implementing new model, the manager will have to allay the concerns of employees as well as to avoid angering customers and suppliers. Major questions that should be asked include: What the costs and benefits for each person and organization involved? What incentives are there for them to participate in the change?

Hypercompetition and Internet time should create a sense of urgency in making the change. Merrill converted its business model and developed an online trading product between the March staff meeting where Steffens made his presentation and December 1 of the same year. For a large organization, that is a significant change effort with impressive results. Could your organization successfully orchestrate a similar change?

11
Organization Structure and New Business Models

This book is about strategy; however, a company cannot succeed with strategy alone. The first step for the competitive firm is to develop an appropriate business model; the second step involves developing a strategy that enables it to achieve a sustainable competitive advantage with this model. The third ingredient is a suitable organization structure. In a number of instances, firms have been unable to execute their business strategy, I believe, because their organizations got in the way. The purpose of this chapter is to discuss the network organization, which is a popular structure for companies that have adopted the Internet as a way of doing business.

Networks include alliances and partnerships, which are a natural part of the new business models discussed in this book. Two or more firms form an alliance when they agree to work together in some way.

• In December 1999, Kmart announced an agreement with Yahoo to create a new company to provide free Internet access and a cobranded shopping site.

• Ford, GM, Daimler-Chrysler, Nissan, and Renault have agreed to develop a bidding site for automakers and suppliers.

• Oracle and Boeing are exploring the possibility of creating an electronic marketplace for airplane parts.

• Wal-Mart and AOL have formed an alliance to offer Wal-Mart customers easy access to a joint Web site; the two companies plan to work together to bring access to underserved rural customers.

• Amazon.com has set up a shopping mall on its site that allows customers to search and purchase goods from vendors other than Amazon.

• Microsoft announced in December 1999 that it was investing two hundred million in Best Buy; one part of this alliance involves Best Buy selling and promoting Microsoft's MSN Internet service.

• EDS formed an alliance in January 2000 with Ariba to establish and operate electronic procurement and online auctions for corporations. EDS is a major computer services firm, and Ariba develops software for electronic commerce.

• EBay and E-stamp began a three-year alliance to sell electronic postage to eBay's auction customers.

Almost every day, the news brings another story of an alliance between different firms, an alliance related to the Internet and electronic commerce.

One of the most closely watched alliances is that between Toys "R" Us online and Amazon.com. Toys "R" Us opened a Web site to compete with eToys; it has the advantage of a large number of physical stores where customers can return products ordered on the Web. However, Toys "R" Us had a difficult time fulfilling orders and running its Web site, especially during the 1999 Christmas season. At the time, Amazon.com was expanding into toy sales. In August 2000, the two companies announced an alliance in which Toysrus.com would choose and buy toys while Amazon would operate the Internet toy store on its site. This alliance capitalizes on the strength of Toys "R" Us in product selection and purchasing and Amazon's capabilities as an online merchant.

An alliance adds a resource to a company's bundle of resources. This added resource may be a proven technology as in several of the examples above, or it may be access to products or services as in Amazon's mall. An alliance binds the partners together into a network structure. The ultimate form of an alliance is a merger or outright purchase. In January 2000, America Online offered to buy Time Warner for $156 billion. This purchase (eventually at a lower stock price) brought many new resources to AOL including content and cable networks to provide high-speed connections to the Internet for its subscribers.

Previous chapters have suggested that speed and access to expertise often motivate alliances (Powell 1990). It is much faster to partner with an organization that already has the necessary technology than it is to develop it oneself. Another reason for alliances is flexibility; companies need the ability to change rapidly as they face new competitors, particularly in the age of the Internet. How should newspapers, for instance, prepare for the day when the Internet takes over all classified advertising? Or what should banks do to be ready for the eventuality of the Internet eliminating the need for branches? If they have a series of alliances, they can add or delete parts of their business at will.

Another motivation for making alliances is the belief held by some organizations that it is difficult to be a pure Internet-only store, or a bricks-and-mortar store without an Internet presence. As a result, pure e-commerce companies are making alliances with physical stores in an attempt to have the best of both worlds. It is too early to tell if this strategy will be successful, if the Barnes and Noble model will work better than that of Amazon, or if the two will coexist in the future.

The Social Network of an Alliance

An alliance requires careful management, and for many organizations accustomed to doing everything themselves, alliance management can be intimidating. Several researchers examined the alliance of two Fortune 500 firms and reached a number of important conclusions (Hutt et al. 2000).

1. Interpersonal relationships matter a great deal in an alliance.

2. Boundary-spanning efforts are needed at many different organizational levels; boundary spanning involves coordination between alliance partners, through mechanisms like joint committees.

3. Negotiating the original agreement for an alliance is difficult; if parties are too legalistic they learn to mistrust each other. Contracts must be balanced with interpersonal relationships.

4. Personal relationships are needed because you cannot write a contract that covers every eventuality; members of both organizations have to work together to solve problems.

5. It is important to place committed, well-qualified employees on the alliance teams.

6. Executive leadership is needed to communicate the strategic reasons for an alliance.

7. Communications across the firms in the alliance are very important.

8. The alliance has to carefully manage information flows. The information needed to make the alliance work has to be available to all parties whereas information that might compromise competition and is unnecessary needs to be kept within each firm.

The Network Organization

An organization that interacts with many different partners through alliances is one type of network organization. The relationships among various firms forms a network structure.

Calyx and Corolla

A good example of a network organization is Calyx and Corolla. The entrepreneur Ruth Owades founded Calyx and Corolla. Before starting C&C, she was successful at introducing a new distribution channel for gardening products. Owades founded a company called "Gardener's Eden," a mail-order business for gardening tools and accessories. After a few years, she sold the business to Williams Sonoma and operated Gardener's Eden for over four years as a division of Sonoma.

Four years later, Owades decided to launch Calyx and Corolla after careful research. Her first observation was the inefficiency of the flower and plant market in the United States. Second, she was aware that flower and plant sales in the United States run to ten billion dollars annually, with a substantial proportion of the flowers imported from Columbia the Netherlands, and other countries.

The distribution channel to retail florists, Owades also noted, is lengthy and involves a number of parties. Typically, a grower sends flowers to distributors in a growing region. From there, the flowers go to various wholesalers that distribute the product to florists, supermarkets, and other retailers.

Owades's insight was that she could dramatically "reengineer" this distribution process if she could negotiate agreements with growers and a carrier to deliver flowers directly to the consumer. She wanted to eliminate all of the steps and organizations between the grower and the consumer.

Although this idea was appealing, there were many in the industry who thought it impossible.

Owades, a master saleswoman, worked with growers, encouraging them to experiment with her. One acquaintance, Peter Barr at Sunbay Growers, cooperated in a test with Owades. They tried shipping flowers via retail carriers in different kinds of packages. The experiment showed that it was feasible to package flowers for this kind of shipment.

Owades knew that she needed two things to be credible with parties that might provide financing. The first was a group of growers willing to make arrangements and package flowers for delivery to the end customer, a new role for the grower. A number of growers responded positively to her approach because they were looking for additional distribution channels and were sensitive to growing foreign competition. Second, Owades knew that she needed a first-class overnight delivery firm to lend credibility to her new business. She campaigned to interest management at FedEx in the concept. At the time, FedEx was seeking more mail-order delivery business, and eventually it agreed to deliver flowers for Calyx and Corolla. Owades had to guarantee that she would cover damage from packages left without a signature to finalize the deal.

Owades and her management team decided that the best way to interest the consumer was with an upscale catalog that contained appealing photos of arrangements and plants along with information about the plants. The catalog had to be interesting reading. By 1991, Calyx and Corolla was mailing over twelve million catalogs annually.

The final component needed to make Calyx and Corolla work was information technology. Indeed, the entire concept of the company depends on electronic linking and communications between it, its customers, growers, and FedEx. A staff in a San Francisco suburb answers calls on an 800 number and charges merchandise to the caller's credit card. Several times a day, C&C transmits orders via modem or fax to growers. Each grower appoints a Calyx and Corolla account manager to supervise order printing, the selection and packing of flowers, the writing of gift messages, and preparation of FedEx shipping papers.

Federal Express picks up the orders at the end of the day and delivers the flowers the next morning anyplace in the Continental U.S. Calyx and Corolla must maintain a computer system to process orders and select orders for transmission to growers based on the customer's desired delivery date. C&C must also handle accounting; it has to remit to the growers and to Federal Express. Finally, it submits its credit card receipts to the appropriate card-processing company.

Calyx and Corolla is an example of a "negotiated agreement" organization. Calyx and Corolla itself is relatively small. It has a number of virtual components, including a production and inventory facility (the grower), a highly computerized logistics and delivery system (FedEx), an accounts receivable operation (credit card companies), and a large sales force (the catalog). Ruth Owades started Calyx and Corolla by "snapping together" various virtual components coordinated by information technology.

What are the characteristics of C&C that make it a network organization? First, it consists of a series of different organizational entities—C&C's own offices, growers, FedEx, and credit card companies. (See figure 11.1). The components of the network are all linked together by formal and informal ties. For example, C&C has a formal contract with its growers, and it is also in touch with grower personnel on a regular basis. The relationship with FedEx is more formal; C&C established certain policies with the carrier and from that point on, had only to handle the operational details of shipping the product. The growers, themselves, form another, informal network of suppliers to C&C.

Are Networks Different?

The network is characterized by relational ties. Although there may be contracts, the most important aspect of the network is the fact that organizations in it are committed to a relation. Organization theorists call this kind of arrangement a "relational contract." What is so radical about arrangements based on relations? What are the alternatives?

A framework provided by Transactions Cost Economics (TCE) highlights the differences between networks and their relational contracts and other forms of organization (Williamson 1985). Williamson argues that firms organize themselves to minimize transactions costs. TCE explores the reasons why a firm exists, at least from an economic standpoint. A firm that relies entirely on the market to supply the goods and services it needs remains relatively small and tightly focused. When firms can no

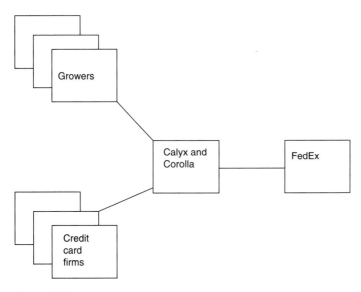

Figure 11.1
The Calyx and Corolla Network

longer rely solely on the market, they become more hierarchical, forming divisions and subsidiaries, and sometimes merging with other firms.

The market offers minimum transactions costs for commodity items; it is easy to discover and compare prices, and to complete a purchase. Under these conditions, buying in the marketplace minimizes transactions costs. What happens when the product a firm needs to acquire is more complex, or when it is so specialized that there are only a few vendors? What is the best alternative when a product has an extremely complex description, or when a firm must work with a supplier to develop the product? Under these conditions, one might argue that the market has failed; there are not enough sellers to constitute a market, and the firm must find some alternative. A good example would be a complex machine to manufacture an electronic component; the firm in question has to purchase equipment designed for another purpose and modify the equipment for its production needs.

Under these conditions, the firm is likely to operate via hierarchy, to bypass the marketplace and deal directly with potential vendors. Years ago, it might have considered buying its vendors to assure a steady supply.

General Motors bought Fisher Body to be sure that there would be a supply of coaches (bodies) for the chassis that GM built at the time. Today, the trend is more toward establishing a long-term relation with a supplier, and forming a network of manufacturer and suppliers.

With this kind of network, the firm ends up someplace between the market and the hierarchy. In the extreme form of hierarchy, buying or merging with a supplier, the firm loses contact with the marketplace. For example it is widely acknowledged that GM is the high cost producer in the auto industry. One reason for this is that the automaker only buys about 30 percent of the components in its cars and makes the rest. Toyota has just the opposite ratio: It buys 70 percent of what goes into a car. GM with its large hierarchy allowed costs to rise as in-house manufacturing removed it too far from the market.

The kind of relational contracting that one finds in a network is partway between a hierarchy and the market. The network partners have a long-term relationship that resembles a hierarchy, but the relationship can be ended if a partner's prices deviate significantly from the market. The idea is to combine the benefits of a long-term commitment with the competitive pressure that a market puts on suppliers of goods and services. A relationship that is based on a contract of fixed duration is far easier to change than the results of a merger or acquisition, so the network organization has a lot of flexibility. In an economy working on Internet time, this kind of flexibility is very important. For all of these reasons—economic and transactions costs, long-term relations and flexibility—the Internet economy is characterized by network organizations.

Network Dependencies

The firms in a network are interdependent in various ways. There are three major types of dependencies, all of which may be found in a network of firms—sequential, pooled, and reciprocal (Thompson 1967). In sequential interdependence, organization B depends on organization A, but not vice versa; there is a one-way flow from A to B. A good example of a sequential dependency is an auto manufacturer and the firm that produces seats for its cars. From an operational view, the automaker depends on the seat manufacturer to deliver, or its production line will stop working.

Two organizations exhibit a pooled dependence if they both depend on some third organization. Organizations A and B both need resources or services from organization C. Organization C could be an Internet service provider, and firms A and B both depend on its resources to run their electronic commerce sites.

Reciprocal dependence exists when organizations A and B both depend on each other. The example discussed at the beginning of the chapter shows reciprocal dependence: EDS depends on Ariba for electronic commerce software, and Ariba depends on EDS to provide computing and network services to its customers.

One of the major tasks in a network organization, or in making an alliance work, is managing interdependence. The easiest kind of interdependence to manage is sequential, and the most difficult is reciprocal. In many of the examples in the book, organizations depend on each other. Procedures, coordinating committees, automatic software routines, and task forces can all be used to overcome problems caused by interdependence. There is nothing surprising about these issues; interdependence is a natural part of a networked organization or an alliance among firms.

The T-Form Organization

In 1996, I published a book that proposed a new form of networked organization based on information technology design variables (Lucas 1996). This model is very appropriate for organizations in an Internet economy, given the objective held by most firms today of high efficiency and minimial overhead (see figure 11.2).

The T-form organization has a flat structure, with a minimum number of layers of management. The classical approach to organization design stresses concepts like span of control. How many subordinates can a supervisor manage? Numbers like seven or eight are popular answers to this question. Other designers say, "When a person has too much work to do, we provide her with subordinates to help out."

Having a rigid span of control and providing subordinates whenever needed is a very expensive way to design organizations. Over the years, firms have built up huge bureaucracies that are very costly to support. The T-form organization substitutes technology for layers of management. First, communications technology demolishes old ideas of spans of

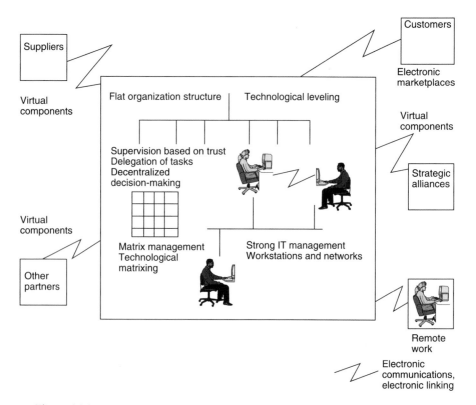

Figure 11.2
The T-Form Organization
Source: From H. Lucas, *The T-Form Organization: Using Technology to Design Organizations for the 21st Century.* © 1995 Jossey-Bass. Reprinted by permission of Jossey-Bass, Inc., a subsidiary of John Wiley and Sons, Inc.

control; a manager can stay in contact with and supervise a large number of subordinates electronically. Of course, this supervision will be more remote and will require much more trust than the close supervision made possible by sitting near one's subordinates.

Second, technology will be used to help the manager perform his tasks rather than hiring a subordinate. The kinds of support available through a personal computer workstation connected to a network makes a manager far more productive today than in the past.

Another objective for the T-form corporation is flexibility. Market needs and business conditions change rapidly. The firm will have to respond quickly to these changes, a characteristic not associated with large bureaucracies. The T-form organization uses matrix management and temporary work groups to create this flexibility. Matrix management involves multiple assignments for staff members. The information technology function has used this structure for many years; systems analysts and programmers typically work on more than one project at a time. They report to a project manager for each project, and to an overall manager of systems and programming.

Matrix management was popular twenty years ago, but seems to have fallen out of favor, except in naturally team-oriented activities like systems development. One reason may be that matrix management is more complex than the typical hierarchical form of organization; it also can be unsettling to employees who have multiple reporting relationships. Electronic communications, however, make it easier to form task forces of employees who cut across a number of functional areas of the business. In fact, it is likely that these task forces will include individuals from external organizations. The engineer designing a new automobile, for example, will include personnel from outside parts suppliers on the design team.

Technology alone is not enough to produce the T-form organization; to take advantage of IT, the culture and climate of the organization have to change. In addition to introducing matrices and temporary task forces, management has to decentralize decision making. In order to provide flexibility, firms have found that managers closest to a problem are in the best position to solve it. Technology makes it possible to provide managers at any level in the firm with information; management has to be willing to delegate decision making to individuals who are close to the problem.

What does delegating decision making mean? You have the ability to make a decision if you can commit the organization and its resources *without prior approval.* You may have to report on your actions, but you will only rarely be overruled, and you are free to act without checking with someone else first.

Decentralized decision making implies that there is a high level of trust in the organization. Management must have faith in managers at all levels in the firm, and they must believe that the information systems in place provide the appropriate information for managers to take action. Trust, then, is an essential part of the culture in a T-form organization.

The T-form organization is much less concerned with the physical structure of the firm; instead, it is interested in a "logical view." What you see may not be exactly what is there! We are accustomed to organizations that are housed in an identifiable location; these firms have well-defined organization charts that show where everyone reports. The T-form organization uses communications technology like electronic mail, groupware, and distributed offices to provide itself and its employees with more flexibility. Reporting relationships can and will change as the firm faces new demands.

One of the major business and technology trends in the last part of the twentieth century has been the development of interorganizational systems (IOS). Companies have established electronic links with their customers and suppliers. Beginning in the late 1960s with the American Hospital Supply order entry system, firms have been forging links with the organizations with which they do business. At first, these links focused on routine, well-specified transactions.

Electronic data interchange has proven very effective in a variety of industries, including trucking, auto manufacturing, and retailing, among others. In addition to routine transactions, firms can easily establish electronic mail and groupware connectivity with external organizations. Manufacturing firms are working more closely with suppliers; electronic communications facilitate this kind of relationship.

Business process redesign focuses attention on processes regardless of the department or functions that might have partial responsibility for a task. An order entry system cuts across a number of departments from order taking to inventory control to the warehouse. Instead of looking at each of these functions, process engineering concentrates on the order cycle process itself. In the T-form organization, functional organization is less important than it is today; this kind of firm identifies its processes and has process "owners" who are responsible for seeing that the process works.

The T-form organization has a number of virtual components. A virtual component is a part of a company that exists physically in a traditional organization, but that has been replaced by an electronic version. Where did the inventory at Chrysler go when the company implemented EDI and JIT manufacturing? It exists in a different form through information systems that let Chrysler's suppliers know exactly what to produce and when to deliver it to a Chrysler plant. Calyx and Corolla has a virtual accounts receivable department in the form of credit card processing companies.

Allegiance offers a stockless service to hospitals; it delivers medical supplies to the department that needs them on a just-in-time basis. The hospital has a virtual inventory that is kept and supplied by Allegiance. Virtual components are an important part of the T-form organization; they are responsible for much of its efficiency and flexibility.

A virtual organization can be created through a negotiated agreement with another firm. You could say that the Allegiance stockless inventory service involves a negotiated agreement with each customer. Earlier in this chapter, we discussed Calyx and Corolla, a direct-sales flower company that has negotiated agreements with growers to supply flower arrangements and with Federal Express to provide delivery services.

These types of agreements produce a network of cooperating organizations, which have intertwined their production, logistics, and even their marketing functions to create what looks like a traditional organization to the customer. Note that an alliance implies more than just a "make or buy" decision; the firm is purchasing more than a component to plug into some part of the organization. An alliance involves a pooling of interests, not a one-time purchase or sale. The firms in an alliance become interdependent and form a partnership; each is interested in the success of the other.

A network allows each firm to do what it does best; that is, each firm operates where it has a comparative advantage. A trend in today's business is to return to one's "core competence" following attempts at diversification or buyouts of other firms. Xerox has sold its financial services divisions to concentrate on being a document processing company. It would not make much sense for FedEx to acquire firms in order to ship its products; FedEx's core competence is in running a first-class delivery and transportation system. It can be a strategic partner with a number of businesses.

Investments in information technology enable the T-form organization. Each of these investments may show a return, but it is their combined effect that is most significant. All of the technology taken together creates a firm whose structure and operations differ from the traditionally organized enterprise. The T-form organization is more flexible, responsive, and efficient than the comparable hierarchical firm.

Managing in a Network Environment

Managing the kinds of organizations described in this chapter is not easy, especially for the manager who has worked primarily in conventional, hierarchical firms. Looking first at the overall network, the manager is in a position of trying to influence individuals who have no reporting responsibility to her and who do not work for the same organization. Growers work for people other than the managers at Calyx and Corolla; C&C can fire a grower, but it must replace that grower with someone else who can provide the same flowers. C&C managers try to influence the grower, but the grower does not report to them, and probably does not work exclusively for Calyx and Corolla.

The manager in a network environment will be a member of a number of coordinating committees. These committees have the responsibility to work out problems caused by mutual dependence, but no traditional hierarchical reporting relationships. Managers do not have the traditional incentives to motivate subordinates. The manager cannot fire a person in another firm in the network, nor does the manager determine that person's raise or bonus. The network manager has to instill a spirit of cooperation and trust without resorting to the use of orders and threats.

The issues above apply to the entire network. What happens if the manager's firm adopts a T-form of organization or becomes the kind of virtual firm discussed in chapter 3? Under these conditions, the manager also has to trust employees, and delegate decision making to them. The idea behind both forms of organization is for employees on the scene to respond quickly to customers; there is no time, nor is there any need, to contact a superior at some remote location for approval. In an economy running on Internet time, one of the keys to success is fast response. The manager will be unable to supervise subordinates closely, and will have to get used to working with people who are located remotely. The manager works through influence, expertise, and by providing leadership and vision in the organization.

Conclusions

A new business model is valuable only if the firm (1) adopts the model and (2) executes it successfully. It can be difficult for an existing organization, given its history and structure, to execute some of the new models. The firm may have to make significant changes, not just in its operations, but in how it is structured to do business. If one looks at successful companies today, those that have integrated the Internet into their activities or companies that are Net start-ups, usually one sees some kind of network structure.

Network organizations, in particular, the T-form organization and the virtual firm, are well suited to the Internet economy. They provide fast response and flexibility, but they also require the manager to adopt a different philosophy. Workers will be more decentralized; traditional managers may not be comfortable supervising remote workers. Superiors will have to trust subordinates, and some workers will find the lack of structure difficult.

The rigid, bureaucratic hierarchical organization is on the way out. Managers need to become familiar with structures that can replace it; the network organization is one structure that is working for a number of firms. Internet-based businesses like Dell and Cisco attempt to be efficient and lean; they substitute electronics for physical processes and labor wherever possible. Their business models are inconsistent with a large, hierarchical organization, but fit very well with a network structure.

The organization that offers the best chance of success with the kind of business models discussed in this book is a combination of a T-form and a team-based virtual structure. Like its traditional predecessor, this organization has managers, subordinates, and reporting relationships; however, it actively incorporates technology into its design and uses technology to coordinate activities internally as well as with other firms in its network. The organization moves quickly to establish relational contracts with network partners. Teams work on various projects, with team members taking on varied tasks. Individuals work on a number of different teams. Information is widely available and shared, and decision making is decentralized. The objective is to take advantage of expertise where it exists in the network, and to remain flexible to respond to opportunities and the competition.

With the kind of organization structure described in this chapter, a strategy, and a business model, you are ready to compete in the Internet economy.

V

Sustaining an Advantage

This section consists of one chapter in which we review the evidence presented in the rest of the book to assess the dynamic resource-based model of strategy. The chapter stresses the threats that confront traditional businesses, and the opportunities offered by the Internet and electronic commerce. The book suggests four important steps for the manager in creating a new business model and strategy, and in structuring an organization to execute new models. The resource-based model is one way to look at strategy. It reminds the manager that one starts with an initial set of resources, and then looks for other assets that strengthen these resources. If they provide an initial competitive advantage, then one adds resources to enhance them. All of these resources form an interacting system, and from the interaction emerge other resources that contribute to a competitive advantage. One of the most important resources that emerges from the system is the managerial skills needed to execute one's business model.

12
Opportunities and Threats

The Internet and electronic commerce provide both opportunities and threats. The book has presented a number of firms that have been very successful, either as start-ups or as traditional firms moving to embrace the Internet. Other firms have lagged behind and face declining market share and investor confidence. What distinguishes the two? This chapter reviews key examples in the book and assesses the contribution of the dynamic resource-based model of strategy in chapter 1. It closes with recommendations for management on how to compete in the Internet economy.

The Threats

The threats from the Internet come in two kinds—a direct assault on your business model and missed opportunities. In the case of Amazon and eToys, the threat was direct and immediate. Amazon was initially aimed at Barnes and Noble and similar booksellers, although, as it turns out, books were merely the first product in a strategy to become the largest retailer on the Net. EToys threatened Toys "R" Us. Both of the traditional companies have fought back, and have had some success, to the point that eToys failed. Compaq and other PC manufacturers, on the other hand, are examples of missed opportunities; they have tried, so far without success, to imitate Dell's model.

Who else is threatened by the Internet and electronic commerce? At first, attention was paid only to intermediaries—people like stockbrokers and real estate agents. Now, however, managers need to realize that there

are a variety of new business models out there, and more than intermediaries are likely to be affected. A partial list of those in endangered pro-
fessions includes:

• Intermediaries like stockbrokers, realtors, and auto sales persons who
potentially can be replaced by electronic brokers in electronic markets, or
eliminated through direct sales through the Internet.

• Traditional academic faculty who face replacement by distance-learning
faculty and courses on the Internet

• Print journalists and others working with print media, due to the ease
of access and distribution on the Internet as well as the lower cost structure of Internet publishing

• Music publishers who increasingly find that recordings are downloaded
from the Net rather than purchased on CDs; some new performing groups
actually "publish" their own recordings on the Web, completely bypass-
ing the record label

• Integrated manufacturers whose high costs do not let them compete
with lean production and outsourcing

• Employees of Banks and insurance companies who may be entirely replaced by virtual analogues

The list continues, and it is unlikely that anyone is completely safe. The
good news is that a number of firms have adapted and are flourishing in
the Internet economy. You need a business model and a strategy, and the
ability to execute the strategy.

New Economics and New Organizations?

As can be seen from the examples in this book, the Internet and electronic
commerce have brought many changes in their wake. Although it is difficult to draw conclusions at this relatively early stage of the phenomenon,
the Net appears to have made some fundamental changes in the way that
companies relate to their customers. The most significant change is the
shift in power from the vendor to the consumer. As Web sites compete
for customers and try to reach a critical mass, they provide enticements,
including free services, to visitors. Auctions let the customer rather than
the seller determine price. Online trading results in lower brokerage com-

missions for investors, and gives them more control over trading. Although the United States has long had a consumer-oriented economy, electronic commerce and the Internet seem to be transferring even more power to the buyer, away from the seller.

The long-term impact on organizations is the subject of much controversy. Some experts believe that traditional firms that adapt to the Internet will be more successful than start-ups. Another view is that the economy will move to a series of small, microenterprises. Microcompanies with two or three employees will generate huge sales through outsourcing. The Internet is driving communications costs to zero, making the completely outsourced, virtual firm an attractive model.

The examples in the book support both of these views; there are start-ups that fit the microfirm model, and there are existing firms that are revising their business models to adapt to the Internet and electronic commerce. It is likely that both kinds of firms will exist in a global economy. Large firms have been around for a long time, and many of them will to adapt to the Internet economy. On the other hand, the Internet has leveled the playing field, and offers tremendous benefits for the small firm. The small company does not have to invent a worldwide technology infrastructure; it already exists and is available for a reasonable cost.

There does seem to be a consensus, regardless of whether you favor the view of the large firm or the microenterprise, that successful organizations will be decentralized, virtual, and structured into networks. The extremely low cost of communications, the push toward global business, and an emphasis on customers favor these kinds of organizations.

Why Is Everyone Not Successful?

The strategy model and analysis in this book suggest that it is difficult to build and execute a successful business model for the Internet and electronic commerce. The recent history of many Internet firms confirms the predictions from the model in figure 1.1. CDNow, for example, generated a great deal of excitement when it started selling CDs on the Web. A CD is a natural product for B2C electronic commerce; the product is easy to describe, warehouse, and ship. A customer can listen to a section online and click to buy. However, if we look at CDNow's strategy using the dynamic strategy model, it is easy to see that its business model offered no sustainable advantage.

CDNow was a first mover and had a well-publicized brand—resources that are valuable, but not rare, inimitable, or nonsubstitutable. CDNow never developed a system of resources for advantage. As a result, it was easy for Amazon.com to apply its resources—including brand, shopping site, critical mass of customers, and a associates program—to selling CDs. Bertelsmann, a large German music company and publisher, bought CDNow when the company faltered.

CDNow is not alone; a number of e-commerce vendors have closed their businesses including boo.com, furniture.com, and pets.com. Priceline also closed its subsidiary that sold groceries and gasoline, among other products. I believe these dot.coms lacked resources capable of providing a competitive advantage, and they failed to attract a critical mass of customers.

The dynamic strategy model in this book can help explain what is happening to many firms. The dot.com start-up has a great idea for a business, and obtains capital to get started. However, the start-up cannot protect its innovation; it is easy for established companies to imitate the start-up's business model. A traditional company uses a strong resource base like brand, reputation, and technology skills to create a highly competitive business. The bricks-and-mortar firm has an established brand, and is able to turn its physical presence in the marketplace and its logistics skills into an advantage.

Resources like brand, reputation, and innovative ways to take advantage of physical location give some traditional firms an edge over the dot.com start-up in selling consumer goods. The start-up is unlikely to be able to protect its innovation, and may not be able to find additional resources to provide it with an advantage. When Priceline closed its subsidiary that allowed customers to name their price for groceries and gasoline, it said that it could not attract enough capital to finance a firm that showed little promise of achieving a critical mass of customers and merchants any time soon.

The B2B dot.com faces much the same situation; it cannot protect its business model from imitators. The resources it possesses may meet two or three of the criteria from the dynamic strategy model, but they do not satisfy all four. If the B2B firm cannot create a system of resources that is rare, valuable, inimitable, and nonsubstitutable, then it has little chance of building a sustained competitive advantage.

The model and the analysis above may explain part of the reason that investors have cooled on dot.com stocks. As a result, easily available capital is no longer a resource for the start-up company, and it appears that investors are no longer willing to wait many years for profits. At the same time, we are seeing traditional companies with a strong resource base adapting to electronic commerce and the Internet. These traditional firms have resources like abundant capital, brand names, and a physical presence that is a complementary asset for their Web businesses.

A Review of Examples

Table 12.1 presents highlights from the dozen companies whose strategy we analyzed in past chapters using the dynamic resource-based model of strategy in figure 1.1. The table contains the most significant and interesting resources taken from the more detailed tables in the chapters for each organization. In table 12.1, which companies have been the most successful in building a sustainable advantage? The airline computerized reservations systems vendors maintained an advantage for over ten years, though that advantage is now being challenged by new services on the Internet. The most important aspects of the CRS vendors' advantage came from efforts to automate travel agencies and tie agents to a particular CRS. In the process, the CRS vendors took advantage of critical mass and continued investments to create a formidable asset—the CRS as a travel supermarket. The airlines were also successful in working out exclusive contracts with agents so that they gained control of a cospecialized asset, the agency itself, denying its business to competing CRS vendors. Now, the action has moved to the Internet, and the CRS vendors are trying to establish themselves as travel portals.

The airlines that did not develop a strong CRS business are trying to reduce the fees they pay to the CRS vendors. More than two dozen carriers are involved in the creation of a one hundred million dollars reservations site originally called "T2" (possibly standing for "Travelocity

Table 12.1
Summary of Selected Resources from Strategy Model Analyses

Resource	Rare	Valuable	Inimitable	Nonsubstitutable	Other Model Components
Airline CRS					
CRS ↔agencies	No	Yes	Gradual	Gradual	Cospecialized assets grew in value
CRS ↔ revenue, investment	Yes	Yes	Gradual	Gradual	
Decision Support → Revenue	Yes	Yes	Possibly	Possibly	
Amazon.com					
Capital → virtual store and expanded range of products	Yes	Yes	Moving toward Yes	No	
Port of Singapore					
Infrastructure ↔ IT, operations and port equipment	Yes	Yes	Difficult	Difficult	
IT and operations capabilities for a port	Yes, due to size and scale of port operations	Yes	No, in principle, but few ports have this scale	No, if another port is to provide acceptable service	Create many specialized assets; software and equipment
IT management skills ↔ port technology and operations	Yes	Yes	No, in general, Yes, for running a large port	Yes, given that outsourcers do not have experience with this scale	

Resource/Capability					
Dell Computer					
Original skills at direct ordering and lean production	Yes	Yes	Yes	Yes	Dell became skilled in managing its model creating a cospecialized asset
Web site ordering in 1996	Yes	Yes	No, originally, hard to catch up now → yes	No, could substitute a similar resource, premier programs and customer lock-in → yes	Web ordering quickly reached critical mass, provides network externalities within premier companies
Skills at managing direct, Web ordering, and lean manufacturing	Yes	Yes	Yes	Yes	Dell executes its model well; others have had trouble trying to adopt it; management a cospecialized asset
Lean production model ↔ direct and Web ordering, a new business model	Yes	Yes	No, but few have demonstrated skills → yes	Yes, can substitute model, but can a competitor execute it?	Interaction has created new business model that is based on technology investment, Internet infrastructure, some customer lock-in
Cisco					
Web IT management skills	Yes	Yes	Yes, hard to imitate currently, less so in the future	Yes (difficult to find substitutes)	
Web ↔ business model	Yes	Yes	Yes, but not easily imitated; Cisco encourages others to adopt its model	Yes, there are no viable substitutes for the Internet	Lock-in from dominant product position?

Table 12.1 (continued)

Resource	Rare	Valuable	Inimitable	Nonsubstitutable	Other Model Components
Schwab					
Advisors and OneSource	Yes	Yes	Maybe, but very difficult	Possibly substitute another product or group of advisors	May have created lock-in for advisors; threatened by competitors with lower fees
Online trading, physical presence (new business model), brand ↔One-source, advisor network	Yes	Yes	Possibly	Possibly	Investment in technology and infrastructure; expanded scale and scope of products all interact, coming close to creating sustainable advantage
Merrill Lynch					
Internet brokerage services —retail and institutional	No	Yes	No	No	
New business model of online and physical presence	No	Yes	No, Merrill is imitating Schwab	No	
Internet brokerage services and Merrill Lynch name	Yes	Yes	Possibly	Possibly	Merrill's leadership combined with the Internet could turn out to be sustainable; switching costs for current customers
Egghead.com					
Move to Internet	Yes	Yes	No	No	
Internet auctions	No	Yes	No	No	Network externalities and critical mass of bidders/products
Surplus Direct ↔ Egghead software	Yes	Yes	No	No	Cospecialized asset of similar products, purchasing

America Online					
Buy Time Warner	Yes	Yes	Yes	Partially	Gain control of complementary assets (content) and cospecialized asset (cable TV operations)
Internet access as portal ↔ content/loyal subscriber base, Time Warner content	Yes	Yes	Yes, given Time Warner's unique content	Possibly, but difficult, given Time Warner's unique content	Combination of resources becomes a resource for competitive advantage
Solectron					
All resources (including, high quality global manufacturing, EDI and supply chain facilitation)	Yes	Yes	Partially	Partially	
FreeMarkets					
All resources	Yes	Yes	No	No	
OptiMark					
Knight Securities alliance	Yes	Yes	Possibly	Possibly	
All resources	Yes	Yes	No, but not easily	Yes, currently	OptiMark offered a unique trading service, but it could not reach critical mass and had to be abandoned

Terminator"). Continental, United, Delta, and Northwest started the site, and twenty-three other carriers have since joined them, including American. In a separate venture, Continental and other unnamed carriers are investigating a site to offer unsold seats at deeply discounted prices through the Web. The obvious model and target is Priceline.com. Travel is now the largest Internet commerce category, and it is clear that customers like making their own reservations (*Wall Street Journal*, April 11, 2000). Will the resources of the combined group of airlines allow them to obtain an advantage over the existing Net vendors like Travelocity?

The Port of Singapore Authority, in conjunction with Singapore's government, created an impressive system of resources that has contributed to the competitive advantage of the port. The port and government used their resources to create specialized assets, especially Operations and Information Technology, for running a large port. The port also developed information technology management skills to develop and maintain specialized systems for shipping. The government contributed housing, open policies on foreign investment, and a transportation infrastructure. Given the massive investment required to duplicate Singapore's port, it appears that PSA has a sustainable advantage for at least five years or more.

The analysis of Dell and Cisco is similar. Both of these firms developed new business models that feature lean production and degrees of outsourcing through alliance partners. Both companies have at least a short-term advantage from the management skills they developed to execute their respective business models.

Schwab is a good example of a company that adopted a new business model; managers there understood the Internet and its potential for the brokerage business. Schwab's existing approach to business adapted easily to the Net. Brokers are paid on salary so that trading commissions are not an issue. In addition, Schwab had two rare and valuable resources before the Internet—One Source and its network of independent financial advisors. The Internet became an additional channel for customers, and Schwab committed itself to becoming a Net broker. Schwab leveraged its system of resources by adding Internet access to them, and in doing so challenged the historical leader in the brokerage business, Merrill Lynch. In the third quarter of 2000, 82 percent of Schwab's trades took place online.

America Online presents an example of a bold strategic initiative—the purchase of Time Warner. This large merger demonstrates the power of the Internet economy. Who would have predicted that a mass market online information service that began business in 1985 and only became AOL four years later would offer $156 billion for one of the largest media and entertainment companies in the United States? With this move, AOL added a huge amount of content to its existing content resource, and gained access to a specialized and possibly cospecialized asset—high-speed access to the Internet for its subscribers through Time Warner's cable TV networks. The very size of AOL's resource base when combined with that of Time Warner may make it impossible for a competitor to imitate it, and, at least for now, there do not appear to be any substitutes on the horizon.

The Dynamic Resource-Based Model

The model in figure 1.1 that is the basis for the analysis in this book is one approach to formulating corporate strategy in the age of the Internet and electronic commerce. It helps you identify the key resources that lead to an advantage, and emphasizes that a resource has to be rare, valuable, inimitable, and nonsubstitutable if it is to provide a sustainable advantage. Many firms have found to their dismay that a resource, did not meet these criteria, and that competitors quickly offered similar products and services.

The model points out that one is likely to encounter substantial network externalities with business models based on the Internet. If you are starting an exchange for companies in your industry to use in purchasing supplies, the value of the hub increases as more companies and suppliers join the network. The model also suggests that there is a critical mass that a new business must achieve to be viable. At some point, the number of companies in your industry and the number of suppliers becomes sufficiently large that the exchange functions smoothly; you have to do very little to attract new participants.

Other assets contribute to the basic resources responsible for a competitive advantage. Complementary assets add to resources; if you are establishing an industry purchasing hub and you are the leading manufacturer in the industry, then your name is a complementary asset. A specialized asset is one that applies only to a given resource. Airline reservation systems turned into specialized assets for a large number of travel-related services. Similarly, cospecialized assets depend on each other. The travel agency is a cospecialized asset for the CRS vendor.

A major contribution of the model in figure 1.1 is the feedback loop and the concept of an emergent system of resources. The model is dynamic as it stresses the need to develop and protect resources continually; a firm has to add to the resources and assets that give it an initial advantage. Especially in the hypercompetitive economy associated with the Internet and electronic commerce, it is unlikely that a set of resources that confers a competitive advantage can be put in place and left alone. It is necessary to invest continually in strategic resources. Companies on the Internet are constantly revising their Web sites to add new features, products, and services.

You create a system by building an interrelated set of resources such as Schwab's online brokerage operation combined with its One Source product and its relationship with independent financial advisors. This emergent system may be thought of as a resource in its own right; the individual resources may not be rare, valuable, inimitable, and nonsubstitutable, but their combination is. Different competitors might be able to develop one of Schwab's resources, but imagine how difficult it would be for a competitor to develop a system of these three key resources.

Recommended Actions

Based on the analysis in the book, what action steps should senior management take?

1. Choose a business model. The models presented in chapter 2 are broad; they illustrate how some firms have chosen to compete, and they highlight some of the new models for Internet start-up firms. They are a place to start, but they are not detailed enough for planning a business.

In thinking about an appropriate model, start with the details of the models for the companies in table 12.1.

As an example of a new business model, consider Merrill Lynch with an existing model based on a research staff communicating results to brokers, who, in turn, communicate the research to customers. Clients were supposed to trade with Merrill through its seventeen thousand brokers, generating commissions. Merrill's new business model is radically different, and will have a dramatic impact on its brokers as well as other employees. Now, a client can open an account for a set fee based on assets in the account, and trade as much as she likes without paying a commission on each trade. It remains to be seen how this business model will impact brokers, but it will certainly have an interesting impact on Merrill's revenues.

Start by developing a detailed business model, which needs to be widely reviewed in the firm. Then, as discussed in chapter 10, senior management must plan and execute the changes required to adopt the business plan. You cannot wait for change to emerge; strong leadership is necessary to sell change and implement it.

2. Develop a strategy. Most of this book is about strategy; the analysis employs a resource-based view of strategic advantage. There are other views but the most important thing is to have a conscious strategy. If you follow the model of figure 1.1, it suggests the following:

• Identify the firm's existing resources. Every organization has resources, or it would not exist. These resources may be tangible like a computerized reservations system, or they may be intangible like the set of management skills that makes you proficient at executing a lean production business model.

A. As a part of a review of resources, be aware of the role of critical mass and network externalities, in Internet-related businesses; your resources may not become strategic until business has reached a critical mass.

B. Look for assets that enhance resources; assets may be complementary, specialized, or cospecialized and they contribute to a resource-based advantage.

• Add more resources to your existing stock. Added resources should help implement your strategy and create a sustainable advantage. Typically, these added resources will involve technology and investments in IT infrastructure, especially as you become more involved with the Internet and electronic commerce.

• Stir all resources together to promote interactions; the objective is to create a system of interacting resources from which new resources for competitive advantage will emerge. Remember that one of the most valuable, intangible resources to emerge will be management's skill at executing a new business model. This resource is likely to be the basis for a sustainable competitive advantage, at least for several years.

3. Design an appropriate organization. This task involves determining partners and forming alliances; once established, you will have to coordinate and manage the business processes of the network. You will also have to design the internal structure of your firm. What kind of organization is likely to help you execute your business plan and strategy? It is probably not a hierarchical one! Consider the advantages of the T-form and virtual organizations as you develop an internal structure for the firm.

4. Be prepared for change as it is probably the only constant in the Internet economy. Schwab, Dell, and Cisco moved quickly to adopt new business models; Merrill Lynch lagged behind. Business models change, strategy is dynamic, and competitors will enter and leave your industry rapidly. The Internet has helped level the playing field; an entrepreneur can start a company in a short time frame. You must review your business model and strategy more frequently than in pre-Internet days when the pace of business was more relaxed.

In Conclusion

The model and analytical framework in this book are intended to help managers adopt new business models and develop resources to provide a sustainable advantage in an Internet economy. It is a truly exciting time to be in business, to participate in the breathtaking changes enabled by information technology. Managers work in a hypercompetitive environment and must live with constant change. To succeed under these conditions as the world moves to the Internet and electronic commerce, you need a business model and a strategy; a strategy that focuses on your firm's resources as a dynamic system. One path for obtaining a sustainable competitive advantage is through an interacting system of resources, at least some of which emerge as rare, valuable, inimitable, and nonsubstitutable. The challenge is clear: You must create an appropriate business model, articulate a strategy, and develop the management skills and organization structure to implement both the model and strategy. Meeting this challenge is the essence of management in the Internet economy.

References

Applegate, L., and K. Goldman. 1998. *Internet Securities, Inc.: Building an Organization in Internet Time*. Boston: Harvard Business School.

Bakos, Y., Henry C. Lucas, Jr., Wonseok Oh, Sivakumar Viswanathan, Gary Simon, and Bruce Weber. 1999. *Electronic Commerce In The Retail Brokerage Industry: Trading Costs Of Internet Versus Full Service Firms*. New York: Stern School Working Paper.

Barney, J. 1991. Firm Resources and Sustained Competitive Advantage. *Journal of Management* 17 (1): 99–120.

Conner, K., and C. K. Prahalad. 1996. A Resource-based Theory of the Firm: Knowledge Versus Opportunism. *Organization Science* 7 (5): 477–501.

Copeland, D., and J. McKenney. 1988. Airline Reservations Systems: Lessons from History. *MIS Quarterly* 12 (3): 353–70.

Cotteleer, M, 1999. *Cisco Systems, Inc.: Implementing ERP*. Boston: Harvard Business School Press.

Daily, M. 1998. Optimark: Launching a Virtual Securities Market. Boston: Harvard Business School Press, 1998.

Duliba, K., R. Kauffman, and H. C. Lucas, Jr. Forthcoming. Appropriating Value From CRS Ownership in the Airline Industry. *Organization Science*.

Eisenhardt, K. 1989. Making Fast Strategic Decisions in High-Velocity Environments. *Academy of Management Journal* 32(3): 543–73.

Galal, H., D. Stoddard, R. Nolan, and J. Kao. 1995. *VeriFone: The Transaction Automation Company (A)*. Boston: Harvard Business School.

Garud, R., and H. C. Lucas, Jr. 1999. Virtual Organizations: Distributed in Time and Space. New York: Stern School Working Paper.

Ghemawat, P., and B. Baird. 1998. Leadership Online: Barnes & Noble vs. Amazon.com (A). Boston: Harvard Business School Press.

Gordon, J., P. Lee, and H. C. Lucas, Jr. 1999. *A System of Resources for Competitive Advantage*. New York: Stern School Working Paper.

Hutt, M., E. Stafford, B. Walker, and P. Reingen. 2000. Defining the Social Network of a Strategic Alliance. *Sloan Management Review* 41(2): 51–62.

Kraemer, K., J. Dedrick, and S. Yamashiro. Forthcoming. Refining and Extending the Business Model with Information Technology: Dell Computer Corporation.

Litan, R., and A. Rivlin. 2001. *The Economic Impact of the Internet*. Washington, D.C.: Brookings Institution.

Lucas, H. C., Jr. 1996. *The T-Form Organization: Using Technology to Design Organizations for the 21st Century*. San Francisco: Jossey-Bass.

Maggioncalda, J. 1996. The Charles Schwab Corporation in 1996. Stanford Ca: Stanford Business School.

Mata, F., W. Fuerst, and J. Barney. 1995. Information Technology and Sustained Competitive Advantage: A Resource-Based View. *MIS Quarterly* 9(4) 487–505.

Orlikowski, W. 1996. Improvising Organizational Transformation Over Time: A Situated Change Perspective. *Information Systems Research* 7 (1): 63–92.

Peteraf, M. 1993. The Cornerstones of Competitive Advantage: A Resource-Based View. *Strategic Management Journal* 14: 179–91.

Porter, M. 1985. *Competitive Advantage*. New York: The Free Press.

Powell. 1990. "Neither Market nor Hierarchy: Network Forms of Organizations. *Research in Organizational Behavior* 12: 295–336.

Prahalad, C. K., and G. Hamel. 1990. The Core Competence of the Corporation. *Harvard Business Review* (May–June): 79–91.

Quinn, J. B., and F. G. Hilmer. 1994. Strategic Outsourcing. *Sloan Management Review* (Summer): 43–55.

Rangan, V. K. 1999. *FreeMarkets Online*. Boston: Harvard Business School Press.

Rangan, V. K., and M. Bell. 1998. *Dell Online*. Boston: Harvard Business School Press.

Rangan, V. K., and M. Bell. 1999. Egghead to Egghead.com. Boston: Harvard Business School Press.

Stohr, T, S. Viswanathan, and L. White. 1999. *America Online Inc.: The Portal Era*. New York: Stern School of Business.

Teece, D. 1987. "Profiting from Technological Innovation: Implications for Integration, Collaboration, Licensing, and Public Policy." In D. Teece (Ed.), *The Competitive Challenge* (pp. 185–219). New York: Harper & Row.

Teece, D., G. Pisano, and A. Shuen. 1997. Dynamic Capabilities and Strategic Management. *Strategic Management Journal* 18: 7:509–33.

Thompson, J. 1967. *Organizations in Action*. New York: McGraw-Hill.

Williamson, O. 1985. *The Economic Institutions of Capitalism*. New York: The Free Press.

Index